Best Rail Trails
NORTHERN CALIFORNIA

Best Rail Trails
NORTHERN
CALIFORNIA

ACCESSIBLE AND CAR-FREE ROUTES FOR WALKING,
RUNNING, AND BIKING

TRACY SALCEDO

FALCONGUIDES

ESSEX, CONNECTICUT

FALCONGUIDES®

An imprint of The Rowman & Littlefield Publishing Group, Inc.
4501 Forbes Blvd., Ste. 200
Lanham, MD 20706
www.rowman.com
Falcon and FalconGuides are registered trademarks and Make Adventure Your Story is a
trademark of The Rowman & Littlefield Publishing Group, Inc.

Distributed by NATIONAL BOOK NETWORK

Copyright © 2024 The Rowman & Littlefield Publishing Group, Inc.

Photos by Tracy Salcedo.
Maps by The Rowman & Littlefield Publishing Group, Inc.

British Library Cataloguing-in-Publication Information available

Library of Congress Cataloging in Publication Data
ISBN 978-1-4930-7415-0 (paper: alk. paper)
ISBN 978-1-4930-7416-7 (electronic)

♾️™ The paper used in this publication meets the minimum requirements of American
National Standard for Information Sciences—Permanence of Paper for Printed Library Materials, ANSI/NISO Z39.48-1992.

The author and The Rowman & Littlefield Publishing Group, Inc., assume no liability for
accidents happening to, or injuries sustained by, readers who engage in the activities
described in this book.

THIS ONE'S FOR YOU, MOM AND DAD.
KEEP ON TRUCKIN'.

CONTENTS

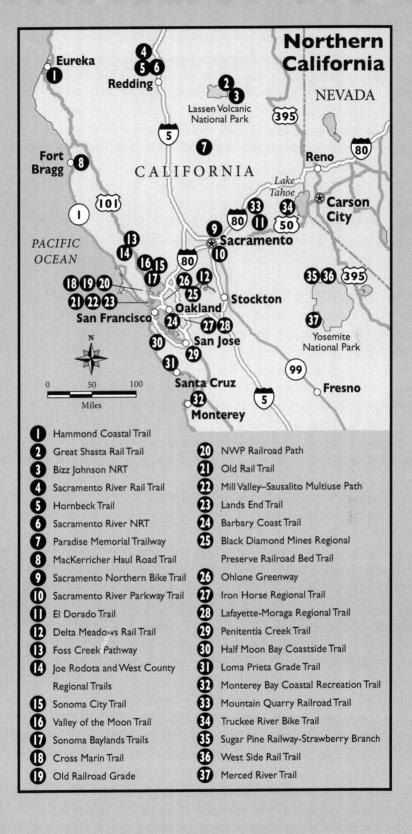

Northern California

NEVADA

Eureka

Redding

Lassen Volcanic
National Park

CALIFORNIA

Fort Bragg

Reno

Lake Tahoe

Carson City

PACIFIC OCEAN

Sacramento

San Francisco

Oakland

Stockton

San Jose

Yosemite
National Park

Santa Cruz

Fresno

Monterey

N

0   50   100
Miles

① Hammond Coastal Trail
② Great Shasta Rail Trail
③ Bizz Johnson NRT
④ Sacramento River Rail Trail
⑤ Hornbeck Trail
⑥ Sacramento River NRT
⑦ Paradise Memorial Trailway
⑧ MacKerricher Haul Road Trail
⑨ Sacramento Northern Bike Trail
⑩ Sacramento River Parkway Trail
⑪ El Dorado Trail
⑫ Delta Meadows Rail Trail
⑬ Foss Creek Pathway
⑭ Joe Rodota and West County Regional Trails
⑮ Sonoma City Trail
⑯ Valley of the Moon Trail
⑰ Sonoma Baylands Trails
⑱ Cross Marin Trail
⑲ Old Railroad Grade

⑳ NWP Railroad Path
㉑ Old Rail Trail
㉒ Mill Valley–Sausalito Multiuse Path
㉓ Lands End Trail
㉔ Barbary Coast Trail
㉕ Black Diamond Mines Regional Preserve Railroad Bed Trail
㉖ Ohlone Greenway
㉗ Iron Horse Regional Trail
㉘ Lafayette-Moraga Regional Trail
㉙ Penitentia Creek Trail
㉚ Half Moon Bay Coastside Trail
㉛ Loma Prieta Grade Trail
㉜ Monterey Bay Coastal Recreation Trail
㉝ Mountain Quarry Railroad Trail
㉞ Truckee River Bike Trail
㉟ Sugar Pine Railway-Strawberry Branch
㊱ West Side Rail Trail
㊲ Merced River Trail

ACKNOWLEDGMENTS

Let's start with the agencies, both public and private, that create these incredible trails and the land managers who maintain them. In the years since I wrote the first edition of this guide, they have diligently continued the work of transforming abandoned railroad rights-of-way, or rights-of-way adjacent to existing railroads, into premier multiuse trails. They are too numerous to name here, but they were critical to the compilation of this guide, and my heartfelt thanks go out to each and every one of them.

The Rails-to-Trails Conservancy is foundational to the rail-trail movement and has a long, storied history of providing walkers, hikers, cyclists, equestrians, and others with spectacular recreational opportunities, not just here in Northern California, but across the country. I am grateful for all the organization has accomplished and could not have written this guide without it.

I am also thankful to the railroad historians, naturalists, park rangers, and previous readers who have taken the time to correct or augment trail descriptions and historical information for each edition of this guide.

Finally, I would like to thank my sons, Jesse, Cruz, and Penn, who were real troupers as we crisscrossed California hiking and cycling these trails back in the day, and have been steadfast supporters of my writing career since the get-go. My love for them infuses this guide and every book, article, and story I've ever written. Thanks, guys.

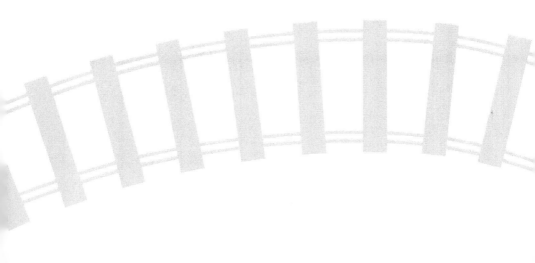

INTRODUCTION

In researching trails for guidebooks over the years, I've had my share of "oh hell no" moments. Sleet storms. A mama bear and her curious cub. Blowdowns that obscured the route forward. Widow-makers creaking overhead.

Don't get me wrong: I love a good challenge. Whether on foot, on a bike, or on skis, I'm up for it. But I took on the task of revising this guide to rail trails with a sigh of relief.

Ah, rail trails. Rail trails, blissfully, do all the things more challenging trails do but also provide a reprieve. They wander through mountains, along beaches, into the boondocks, and through cities and suburbs. They stretch for miles or for little more than a block. But even when they climb, they aren't steep. Trains don't like steep grades. This means you can breathe on a rail trail, chat with a companion (or not), take it easy.

Trains also have straightforward destinations. Even if the rail trail doesn't take you to the end of the line, getting from point A to point B doesn't typically involve complicated route-finding. It's usually a straight shot.

Add in the mythology of railroads, romantic and steeped in a complex and sometimes unsettling Americana, and you've got just about the perfect combination for a day hike or bike ride anywhere in the state—or the country, for that matter.

This guide focuses on the best rail trails in Northern California, from the high country of the Sierra Nevada to the coastline, and from Eureka and the country surrounding Lassen Volcanic National Park south to Monterey and Lake Tahoe. Much of the landscape was considered timberland back in the heyday of the railroad barons, who built their roads primarily to accommodate logging. Many of the trails in this guide, particularly in the North State and mountains, still thread through thick woodlands and snake through spectacular river canyons.

In the San Francisco Bay Area, city and country struggle to find balance. The beauty of the landscape is integral to the region's appeal, and Bay Area residents grapple daily with the conundrum of preservation versus development. The conflict finds some resolution in the number and quality of the rail trails that have been established here. From the relative seclusion of the Cross Marin and Loma Prieta Grade Trails to the more urban, utilitarian Ohlone Greenway and Old Rail Trail in Tiburon Linear Park, the routes in the area are superlative.

Eastward, in the Sierra Nevada, the terrain folds sharply upward from the flats of the Central Valley toward snowy summits. Most of the rail trails in this region lie in the foothills—Gold Country—again following the grades of railroads that served either logging or mining interests. These are perhaps the most challenging of all California's rail trails, for they often stretch for long runs in remote locales. Some, like the Truckee River Bike Trail, are extremely popular and often crowded; on others, like the West Side Rails from Hull Creek to Clavey River, you'll be lucky to see another soul.

Since publishing my first guide to rail trails, the quantity of routes has expanded exponentially. This guide covers the best, with an emphasis on spectacular scenery and interesting stories. I also include honorable mentions for nearby trails that may not be as scenic but connect to other greenways or services. So strap on your boots, climb on your bike, or clip into your skis. It's time to take the easy way—it's time to wander a rail trail.

A Short Take on California's Railroad History

The Golden State's railroads have served a number of industries over the decades, but those that have been converted to rail trails came primarily from two classes: railroads that moved timber and railroads that moved people.

As you might expect, the California gold rush was a major impetus for building railroads in the state. The gold that drew settlers westward by the thousands played out relatively quickly, but the forests held another, seemingly limitless source of wealth: timber. Vast forests carpeted the Sierra Nevada, the Coast Ranges, and much of Northern California, and the American philosophy of manifest destiny demanded, for better or worse, that these resources be utilized. A number of railroads in the state were established to serve logging industries, including the Hammond/Little River Railroad in Eureka, the Fernley and Lassen Branch of the Southern Pacific, and the Loma Prieta Lumber Company Railroad, all of which are now spectacular rail trails.

One of the most rugged in Northern California, the Merced River rail trail follows its namesake through a canyon downstream from Yosemite National Park.

The Depot Historical Museum on the Sonoma Bike Path preserves a snapshot of Sonoma's railroading past.

Transporting passengers from region to region, and from place to place within large urban areas, also proved a lucrative endeavor. Californians fostered a love affair with railways around the turn of the twentieth century, when rail lines exploded in number and reached into the remotest communities. Some of the rail lines established for this purpose blossomed into mini empires, like the Pacific Electric Railway system, which ran its famous Red Cars throughout the Los Angeles area during the early 1900s.

The lines of smaller, interurban railroads, many of which were electric, also have made significant contributions to California's rail-trail system. Two of these systems—the Sacramento Northern Railway system, which ran from Sacramento north to Chico and east into the San Francisco Bay Area, and the Northwestern Pacific Railroad complex, which served the North Bay—enjoyed great success and popularity in the early part of the twentieth century. They both suffered increasing losses beginning in the 1930s, when the automobile began its ascendance, and were gradually abandoned and dismantled, with lengths of track scrapped during World War II. But the rights-of-way remained, and as development encroached, the abandoned lines were transformed into wonderful trails like the Sonoma City Trail and the Lafayette-Moraga Regional Trail in the Bay Area, and the Sacramento Northern Bike Trail in Sacramento.

The History of the Rails-to-Trails Conservancy

As road construction and increased reliance on cars forced railroads to the sidelines, the question arose: What would be done with all the abandoned tracks crisscrossing the state?

Enter the Rails-to-Trails Conservancy, an environmental group that, since 1986, has campaigned to convert the railroad tracks to nature paths.

The beauty of the Rails-to-Trails Conservancy (RTC) is that by converting the railroad rights-of-way to public use, it has not only preserved a part of our nation's history but also has provided a variety of outdoor enthusiasts with thousands of miles of trail to enjoy. Walkers, cyclists, skaters, nature lovers, hikers, equestrians, railroad history buffs, and cross-country skiers enjoy California's rail trails, many of which are wheelchair accessible.

In California about 150 rail trails are in place, stretching more than 1,000 miles, with another 60 or so (and nearly another 1,000 miles) in the works. The concept of preserving these valuable corridors and converting them into multiuse public trails began in the Midwest, where railroad abandonments were most widespread. Once the tracks came out, people started using the corridors for hiking, riding, and exploring the relics left along the railbeds, including train stations, mills, trestles, bridges, and tunnels.

Although it was easy to convince people that the rails-to-trails concept was worthwhile, the reality of converting abandoned railroad corridors into public trails proved a challenge. From the late 1960s until the early 1980s, many rail-trail efforts failed as corridors were lost to development, sold to the highest bidder, or broken into pieces.

In 1983 Congress enacted an amendment to the National Trails System Act directing the Interstate Commerce Commission to allow rail lines to be "railbanked," essentially preserving unused railroad rights-of-way for possible future transportation uses and, in the meantime, allowing interim use as natural/recreational trails. This powerful piece of legislation made it easier for public and private agencies and organizations to acquire rail

A walker and her dog enjoy the shade on the Cross Marin Trail.

corridors for trails, but many projects still failed because of short deadlines, lack of information, and local opposition.

The Rails-to-Trails Conservancy was formed in 1986 to provide a national voice for the creation of rail trails. The RTC quickly developed a strategy to preserve the largest amount of rail corridor in the shortest period of time. A national advocacy program was formed to defend the new railbanking law in the courts and in Congress; this was coupled with a direct project-assistance program to help public agencies and local advocacy groups overcome the challenges of converting a rail into a trail.

The strategy works well. In 1986 the Rails-to-Trails Conservancy knew of only seventy-five rail trails in the United States, and there were ninety projects in the works. As of summer 2007, according to the RTC website, more than 1,400 trails were on the ground, spanning over 13,500 miles. As of summer 2023, the conservancy has fostered nearly 2,500 rail trails spanning more than 25,000 miles nationwide. The RTC vision of creating an interconnected network of trails across the country has become a reality.

Benefits of Rail Trails

What makes rail trails stand out as valuable recreational assets? First and foremost, their flat or gentle grades make them perfect for all kinds of users of all ages, including walkers, cyclists, skaters, and skiers. They are almost universally accessible and usually wide enough for people to share with companions and others, regardless whether on foot or on wheels, self-propelled or along for the ride. They are a comfortable friend that users turn to again and again when they need to stretch their limbs, or when they seek solace, silence, or stress relief.

Rails trails have other benefits as well. Consider:

- In urban areas rail trails act as linear greenways through developed areas, efficiently providing recreational space while also serving as transportation corridors. They link neighborhoods and workplaces and connect congested areas to open spaces. In many cities and suburbs, rail trails are used as commuter routes and provide students with safe routes to school.

Father and son stop to check out the sights on the Old Rail Trail in Tiburon.

- Rail trails also support the health of local businesses. Trail users spend money on food, beverages, camping, lodging, bicycle rentals, souvenirs, and other local products and services. The financial benefits bolster town coffers and even boost property values.

- Rail trails allow for the preservation of historic structures associated with railroads, such as train stations, bridges and trestles, tunnels, haul roads, canals, mills, factories, and other industrial enterprises.

- Rail trails enhance and help protect habitats for birds, plants, wetland species, and a variety of small and large mammals. Many rail trails serve as plant and animal conservation corridors; in some cases, endangered species can be found in habitats located along the routes.

Recreation, transportation, historic preservation, economic revitalization, open space conservation, wildlife preservation—these are just some of the reasons people love and support rail trails. But the strongest argument for the rails-to-trails movement is ultimately about the human spirit. It's about the dedication of the individuals who support the movement with their expertise, advocacy, and dollars, so that folks they will never know have a way to connect.

How to Get Involved

If you really enjoy rail trails, join the movement to save abandoned rail corridors and create more routes. Donating even a small amount of your time can help get more trails on the ground. Here are some ways you can help the effort:

- Write a letter to your city, county, or state elected official in favor of pro-trail legislation. You can also write a letter to the editor of your local newspaper highlighting a trail or trail project.

- Attend a public hearing to voice support for a local trail.

- Volunteer to plant flowers or trees along an existing trail or spend time helping a cleanup crew on a rail-trail project.

- Lead a hike along an abandoned corridor with your friends or a community group.

- Become an active member of a trail effort in your area. Many groups host trail events, undertake fundraising campaigns, and carry out other activities to promote a trail or open space conservation project. Virtually all of these efforts are organized and staffed by volunteers, and there is always room for another helping hand.

California is part of the Rails-to-Trails Conservancy's Western Region; the regional office is located at 304 12th St., Suite 2A, Oakland, CA 94607; (510) 992-4662.

The RTC website, railstotrails.org, is a gold mine of information on everything to do with rail trails. If rail trails are your passion, this is the site to visit and the organization to join. Initiatives include TrailNation, focused on growing trail networks and equitable access nationwide; TrailLink, where you can find and learn more about specific trails; and the Great American Rail-Trail, an effort to build a cross-country multiuse trail for all adventurers. The address is 2445 M St. NW, Suite 650, Washington, D.C. 20037; (202) 331-9696.

When available, contact information for each of the rail trails in this guide has been included with the trail listing. You can support rail-trail development—and other kinds of trail and open space development—by contacting these organizations as well.

Whatever your time and pocketbook allow, get involved. The success of a community's trail system, including its rail trails, depends on the dedication and energy of its citizens. It's time and money well spent.

Some Notes on Rail Trails in This Guide

Given the rapid and ongoing evolution of California's rail-trail system, this guide is not—and can't be—comprehensive. I've selected the best rail trails with several priorities in mind—geographic location, scenic qualities, utilitarian qualities, and historical significance among them. But it's more complicated than that: In addition to trails that will come online after this guide's publication, there may be rail trails on the ground that utilize former railroad rights-of-way but are so obscure that even local governing agencies aren't aware of them. In addition to the RTC, regional cycling coalitions are excellent resources for identifying trails on railroad grades.

A final observation: Some of the trails in this guide are rail trails by virtue of the fact that they are built on abandoned railroad grades; others are technically rails-with-trails, running alongside or in the rights-of-way of active railroad lines. Some are a combination of the two. Trail descriptions make clear the category into which each route falls.

A Note on Electric Bikes

The emergence of electric bicycles makes it all the more important to be aware and courteous on the trails. E-bikes are also so new that agencies are still coming to terms with whether their use is a good fit on their trails. Check with rangers or other land managers for the latest on whether e-bikes are permitted and what kind. Pedal-assisted e-bikes are different from full-throttle e-bikes, and different rules may apply.

How to Use Rail Trails

By design, rail trails accommodate a variety of trail users. While this is generally one of the many benefits of rail trails, it also can lead to occasional conflicts. Everyone should take responsibility for trail safety by following a few simple trail etiquette guidelines.

One of the most basic etiquette rules is "Wheels yield to heels." Bicyclists and skaters yield to other users; pedestrians yield to equestrians.

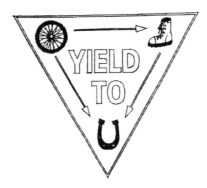

Warn other users of your presence, particularly if you're attempting to pass a slower trail user. This is especially important for cyclists and other users on wheels: If you fail to warn a walker that you are about to pass, the walker could step in front of you, causing an accident that easily could have been prevented. Similarly, those on wheels should alert equestrians: A horse can be startled by a bicycle, so make verbal contact with the rider and be sure it is safe to pass.

Here are some other guidelines you should follow to promote trail safety:

- Obey all trail rules posted at trailheads.

- Stay to the right except when passing.

- Pass slower traffic on the left; yield to oncoming traffic when passing.

- Give a clear signal when passing.

- Always look ahead and behind when passing.

- Travel at a responsible speed.

- Keep pets on a leash.

- Do not trespass on private property.

- Move off the trail surface when stopped to allow other users to pass.

- Yield to other trail users when entering and crossing the trail.

- Do not disturb wildlife.

- Do not swim in areas not designated for swimming.

- Watch out for traffic when crossing the street.

- Obey all traffic signals.

How to Use This Book

The main rail trails featured in this book include basic maps for your convenience. Street maps, topographic maps such as USGS quads, or maps downloaded from agency websites may be used to supplement the maps in this guide. The text description of every trail begins with the following information:

- Trail name and a brief overview of the route's highlights.

- Activities: Icons tell you what kinds of activities are appropriate for each trail.

- Start: The guide points to the trailhead where your adventure begins—but keep in mind that options are usually available, including starting at the other end.

- Distance: The length of the trail, including how many miles are currently open and planned extensions that may not yet be accessible.

- Difficulty: The rail trails range from very easy to hard, depending on the grade of the trail and the general condition of the trail. The difficulty ratings assigned—easy, moderate, and hard—have been derived with all possible users in mind. Some may think a perfectly flat path makes for an easy bike ride, but for a hiker or skater, the length of the route alone may move it out of the "easy" category. Additionally, trails are rated relative to other rail trails, with length and surface being key determinants of a route's difficulty.

- Seasons/schedule: Most of these trails are open year-round, but special circumstances, such as severe winter rains or localized flooding, may preclude the use of certain routes during some seasons.

- Fees and permits: Most of the trails in this guide are free, but if a fee is levied, it's noted here.

- Trail surface and conditions: The materials making up a rail trail range from asphalt and crushed stone to the significantly more rugged original railroad ballast. Trail composition is noted, as is the overall condition of the trail and any special circumstances that might affect use, such as closures due to weather or fire damage.

- Accessibility: Some rail trails are accessible to people with disabilities.

- Canine compatibility: Whether pooches are allowed and applicable leash laws are listed here.

- Amenities: Facilities available at trailheads or stops along the rail trail are noted.

- Trail contact: The contact information for the rail trail's management agency is listed, as are resources available for downloading on agency websites.

- Nearest towns: Locales where you might be able to grab a bite to eat, access rental equipment, shop, visit historic sites, or find lodging are listed.

- Maps: Additional map resources available online or from agencies can be used to augment the information in this guide.

- Cell service: Most of these trails are relatively urban, with good cell phone coverage at the trailhead. That said, don't bank on good coverage along more remote sections. Download additional maps or carry paper copies, and make sure your phone battery is charged.

- Transportation: Contact information for public transit in each area is provided, in the event you decide to travel point to point rather than out and back.

- Finding the trailhead: This book provides you with directions to the rail trails and describes parking availability.

- Trailhead GPS: I've provided GPS coordinates for trailheads solely as a way to confirm you're at the right trailhead. They should not be used for navigating to trailheads. This is especially important when navigating to remote trailheads: Your nav system make take you the long way, the wrong way, the gnarly way, or the way that simply doesn't exist any longer.

Following these categories is a narrative trail description that provides an overview and historical facts and traces the trail, giving mile-by-mile highlights.

Following the "Best" rail trail descriptions, as "Bonus Tracks," I've included brief descriptions of nearby rail trails worth exploring. I tend to prefer trails that traverse wilder terrain, but rail trails also serve a necessary and welcome purpose as urban connectors. That's not always the case, however: A rail trail may also get an honorable mention because it's short, or it's a segment in a larger trail not yet connected. Regardless, bonus tracks are worth checking out.

Legend

Local Roads	⸺ 4N01 ⸺
State Roads	⸺ (151) ⸺
US Highway	⸺ (101) ⸺
Interstate	⸺ (5) ⸺
Main Route	▬ ▬ ▬ ▬ ▬ ▬
Other Trail	‑ ‑ ‑ ‑ ‑ ‑ ‑ ‑
Railroad	⊢+⊣+⊢+⊣+⊢
Creeks/Rivers	⸺ ‑ ⸺ ‑ ⸺
Park/Open Space	▭
Tunnel/Bridge	)(
Picnic	🛆
Rentals	Ⓡ
Parking	Ⓟ
Camping	⛺
Restrooms	🚻
Information Center	Ⓘ
Mountain/Peak	▲
Point of Interest	■
Start/End	START END

Key to Activities Icons

 Backpacking

 Horseback Riding

 Running

 Bird Watching

 In-line Skating

 Swimming

 Camping

 Mountain Biking

 Walking/Day Hiking

 Cross-Country Skiing

 Paddle Sports

 Wildlife Viewing

 Fishing

 Biking

 Snowshoeing

 Historic Sites

NORTH STATE

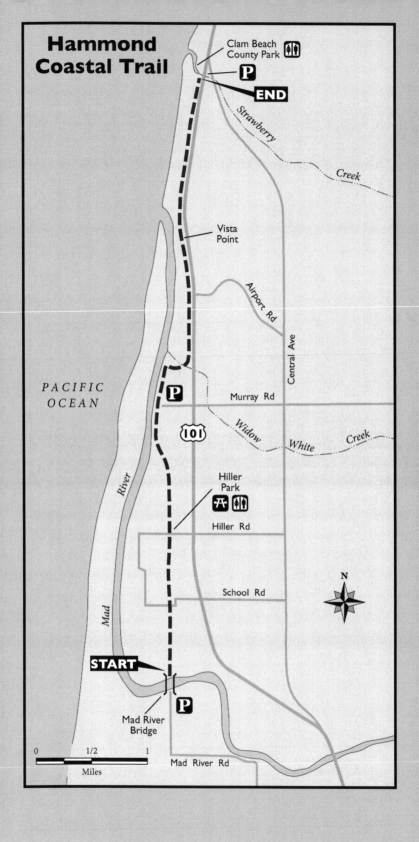

Hammond Coastal Trail

Clam Beach County Park

P

END

Strawberry

Creek

Vista Point

Airport Rd

Central Ave

PACIFIC OCEAN

P

Murray Rd

101

Widow White Creek

River

Hiller Park

Hiller Rd

Mad

School Rd

N

START

Mad River Bridge

P

0   1/2   1

Miles

Mad River Rd

1   HAMMOND COASTAL TRAIL

Although the north coast of California usually brings to mind towering old-growth redwood forests, the Hammond Coastal Trail showcases the spectacular beaches that stretch along the coastline.

Activities:

Start: Mad River Bridge Trailhead

Distance: 5.5 miles one way. Three miles of the trail extend from the Mad River Bridge north to Widow White Creek; an additional 2.5 miles stretch north from Widow White Creek to Clam Beach County Park.

Difficulty: Moderate. The path is exposed and includes some short, steep hills.

Seasons/schedule: Year-round, sunrise to sunset

Fees and permits: None

Trail surface and conditions: Asphalt and crushed stone; well maintained

Accessibility: The 3 miles of trail between the Mad River Bridge and Widow White Creek are accessible for people living with disabilities, including people using wheelchairs, as is the section from Clam Beach south to the vista point. Beach wheelchairs are available at Clam Beach County Park.

Canine compatibility: Leashed dogs allowed

Amenities: Parking, picnic areas, restrooms at Hiller Park and Clam Beach County Park

Trail contact: Humboldt County Parks & Trails, 1106 2nd St., Eureka; (707) 445-7651

Nearest towns: McKinleyville, Arcata, Eureka; Humboldt County

Maps: Humboldt County Parks & Trails map at https://humboldtgov org/2761/Hammond-Trail; Redwood Community Action Agency/Natural Resources Services map at www.naturalresourcesservices.org.

Cell service: Mostly good

Transportation: Humboldt Transit Authority's Redwood Transit System serves McKinleyville. Call (707) 443-0826 or visit https://hta.org/agencies/redwood-transit-system.

Finding the trailhead: To reach the southern end point at Mad River Bridge from US 101 in McKinleyville, take the Janes Road/Giuntoli Lane exit. Go west on Janes Road for 1.4 miles to Upper Bay Road and turn right (west). Follow Upper Bay Road for 0.7 mile to Mad River Road and turn right (north). The trailhead is at the bridge 2.4 miles north on Mad River Road. Parking is available at this trailhead.

To reach the midpoint in McKinleyville at Widow White Creek, take the Murray Road exit off US 101 and go 0.3 mile west to where Murray Road ends. The trailhead is west of the end of the road; ample streetside parking is available.

To reach the northern end point at Clam Beach County Park, continue north on US 101 to the Clam Beach County Park exit. The trailhead is adjacent to the west side of the freeway; a large parking lot serves the park.

Trailhead GPS: N40 55.375 / W124 07.097

The Main Line

The Mad River Bridge, an old railroad trestle that spans part of the Arcata bottoms, is a dramatic launching pad for the Hammond Trail, a section of the California Coastal Trail. From there, the trail leads through McKinleyville neighborhoods and under arbors formed by gnarled shore pines to the spectacular estuary at the mouth of the Mad River. After a quick hop through the riparian zone hugging the shores of Widow White Creek, once the site of a gap in the route called the "Hole in the Hammond," the trail arcs west around a vista point to skirt the beach fronting the Pacific Ocean, passing through rolling dunes to Clam Beach County Park.

Beginning at the turn of the twentieth century, the Hammond/Little River Railroad used the oceanside route to link logging operations in Crannell, east of Clam Beach County Park, with the Hammond Lumber Mill of Eureka. The railroad system was badly damaged in a forest fire in 1945 and, rather than rebuilding, many tracks were converted to roadways. The line

A picnic bench offers views of surf and sea from the Hammond Trail.

was abandoned in the late 1950s, and development of the trail, which has been built in segments, began in 1979.

There's more to the trail than just its railroad history, of course. Those diverse natural and cultural stories, including the story of the Indigenous Wiyot people, who thrived in the Humboldt Bay region until the 1850s when disease and massacres by invading settlers led to their near extinction, can be found on interpretive signs along the route and on a pedestrian side trail at Widow White Creek.

The trail is described here from the Mad River trestle to Clam Beach County Park. Climb a relatively steep hill from the trailhead onto the trestle, which affords a wonderful overlook of the tidal river and the verdant bottomlands that surround it. Beyond the bridge the trail merges with a narrow county road and traverses pastureland to a steep hill at 0.5 mile. Once atop the hill the trail merges with a country lane and runs north through a neighborhood to the intersection of the lane (Fischer Avenue) with School Road at 0.8 mile.

Continue north on Fischer Avenue to the end of the road at 1.1 miles, where the Hammond Trail enters a tree- and blackberry-lined greenbelt that runs between homes. At 1.4 miles cross Hiller Road and enter Hiller Park, which boasts a playground, ballfields, and restrooms. The trail skirts the east side of the park, then passes a gate and again is contained within a lush greenbelt lined with ferns and overhung with evergreens.

At about the 2.4-mile mark, the rail trail crosses Kelly Street/Knox Cove Drive amid a cluster of elaborate homes. Pass a picnic bench, which offers wonderful views of the Pacific and the narrow line of dunes that separate the ocean from the placid Mad River. The paved path is etched into the bluff overlooking the sea until it arcs sharply east at 2.7 miles and ends on Murray Road.

Now unpaved, follow the obvious railroad grade for another third of a mile north to Widow White Creek. An interpretive pedestrian trail explores the creek and links to the rail trail, which continues north along Letz Avenue to a lovely vista point.

Beyond the vista point, the unpaved rail trail parallels US 101, buffered by a greenbelt and the scenic beachfront. As you approach Clam Beach, the pavement resumes, and the route rolls on to the trailhead at Clam Beach County Park at the 5.5-mile mark.

BONUS TRACK: HUMBOLDT BAY TRAIL

It's not yet complete, but the Humboldt Bay Trail traces the shoreline of its namesake bay through the neighboring cities of Eureka and Arcata and, for much of its length, parallels functioning rail lines or rides on railroad right-of-way. When the final 4 miles are finished, expected in 2024, both local commuters and recreationalists will be able to travel between both towns via a designated shoreline path. The route parallels busy US 101, but it also affords users vistas across the tidelands, sloughs, and brackish intertidal zones where freshwater creeks empty into the bay—as well as access to restaurants, parks, and businesses in town.

In addition to being an outstanding multiuse route on its own, the path is part of the California Coastal Trail and the Great Redwood Trail. The trail is accessible at both end points, but it also can be joined along the waterfront in Eureka or in the heart of neighboring Arcata.

Activities:

Start: Trailheads in Arcata or Eureka alongside Humboldt Bay

Distance: 13 miles one way when complete

Difficulty: Moderate due to length

Seasons/schedule: Year-round, sunrise to sunset

Fees and permits: None

Trail surface and conditions: Pavement, rail bridges

Accessibility: The trail is mostly accessible for people living with disabilities, including people using wheelchairs.

Canine compatibility: Dogs permitted on leash

Amenities: All amenities are available in the cities of Eureka and Arcata, with parking available at trailheads along the route.

Trail contact: Humboldt County Public Works/Environmental Services, 825 5th St., Eureka; https://humboldtgov.org/1923/Humboldt-Bay-Trail

Nearest towns: Eureka, Arcata

Maps: A map showing the various trail segments is available via a link on the Humboldt Bay Trail page on the Humboldt County website at https://humboldtgov.org/1923/Humboldt-Bay-Trail.

Cell service: Good

Transportation: Humboldt Transit Authority maintains a website that offers links to schedules for the Redwood Transit System (707-443-0826), Eureka Transit (707-443-0826), and Arcata/Mad River Transit (707-822-3775); https://hta.org.

Finding the trailhead: There are multiple trailheads for this route. The southernmost is the Hikshari' Trail/Eureka Waterfront Trailhead. Take the Herrick Avenue exit off US 101 and head west to Pound Road. Go left on Pound Road to the parking area; parking is also available in the park-'n-ride lots. The northernmost trailhead is in Arcata near the California Polytechnic State University, Humboldt, but a more formal trailhead with parking is at the south end of town. Take the Samoa Boulevard/CA 255 exit off US 101 and head west on Samoa/CA 255 4 blocks to South 1st Street. Turn left (south) on South 1st Street and continue 0.5 mile to Arcata and the Eureka trail parking area.

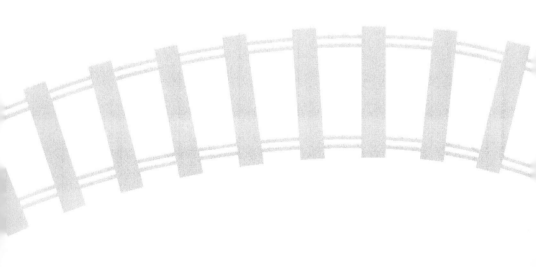

2   GREAT SHASTA RAIL TRAIL

This segment of what will one day be an epic rail trail connecting the volcano country towns of Burney and McCloud ends at a famous bridge spanning Lake Britton.

Activities:

Start: Burney Depot parking area

Distance: 19.5 miles out and back from Burney to Lake Britton; 7.5 miles out and back from junction with CA 89

Difficulty: Strenuous due to length and loose cinder surface

Seasons/schedule: Year-round, sunrise to sunset (and more, if you're camping)

Fees and permits: None

Trail surface and conditions: Red cinder ballast

Accessibility: The route is not accessible to people using wheelchairs.

Canine compatibility: Leashed dogs permitted

Amenities: None along the route itself. All amenities including water, restrooms, and food are available in Burney.

Trail contact: Great Shasta Rail Trail Association, PO Box 221, McCloud, CA 96057; (530) 925-6362; www.greatshastarailtrail.org

Nearest town: Burney

Maps: A detailed trail map is available on the Great Shasta Rail Trail Association website at www.greatshastarailtrail.org/trail-map.

Cell service: Good at the trailhead; none on the trail

Transportation: None along the trail. The Redding Area Bus Authority offers an express bus between Burney and Redding.

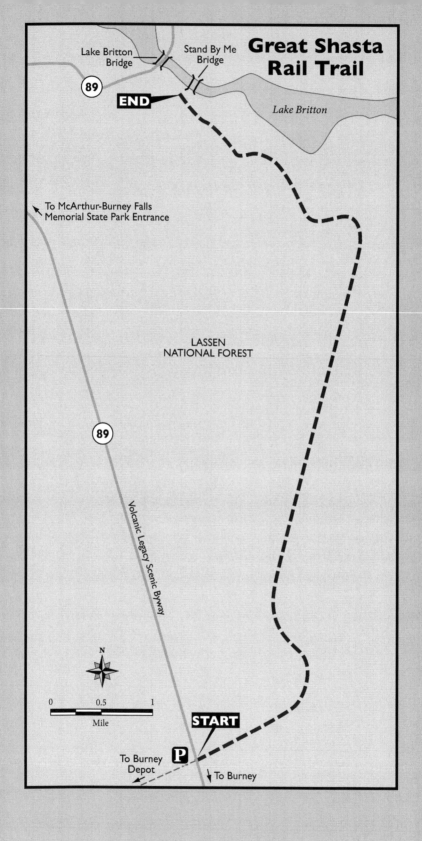

Finding the trailhead: The Burney Depot parking area is an unimproved open patch of ground about 0.2 mile down Black Ranch Road from its junction with Main Street/CA 299 in Burney. There is ample, informal parking in the former railyard. Limited parking is also available along the Volcanic Legacy Scenic Byway at the point where the rail trail crosses the road, about 2.3 miles northwest of the junction of CA 89 and CA 299 (Four Corners).

Trailhead GPS: Burney Depot: N40 53.948 / W121 30.821; Great Shasta Rail Trail crossing at CA 89: N40 58.197 / W121 37.153

The Main Line

The former McCloud Railway corridor, which connects Mount Shasta City to Burney, incorporates the straight shots and mild grades you'd expect along a rail line. It also negotiates remote volcanic terrain, threads through thick, profitable forests, affords endless views, and is steeped in quiet—all of which makes for a stellar rail trail.

The Great Shasta Rail Trail was a work in progress when this guide went to press, with about 40 miles open to recreationalists in two separate segments hitched to mountain towns near towering volcanoes and spectacular waterfalls. The longer, northernmost segment connects a number of trailheads stretching from Pilgrim Creek Road, east of the town of McCloud, to the northeastern-most end point at Hambone, as well as a stretch that heads south to the Bartle Gap Trailhead. The southern section of open trail, described here, stretches from Burney to Lake Britton in McArthur–Burney Falls Memorial State Park and ends at the now-closed bridge featured in the film classic *Stand by Me*.

The former railyard in Burney was completely devoid of facilities of any kind, other than a trailhead sign, in the summer of 2023, but the obvious raised bed of red cinder stretched north from the yard into open woodland. The trail roughly parallels Black Ranch Road—and is accessible at points along the road—for about 4.5 miles, skirting several businesses and subject to road noise from CA 299 at the outset before traversing into sparsely populated ranchland and farmland.

The Stand by Me *bridge is a significant landmark along the Great Shasta Rail Trail.*

At about the 6-mile mark, the rail trail intersects CA 89 at a signed railroad crossing. This is a fine place to start a shorter, arguably more scenic and accessible jaunt along the route, especially for families and hikers. From the highway, the cinder path is a straight shot through scrub and open woodland, rolling gently up and down before beginning a steady but gradual descent toward Lake Britton. Look north from the high points to catch glimpses of the summit of Mount Shasta on sunny days. Forest roads occasionally intersect the trail, but there's no confusing the red cinder way.

Round a bend at about the 8.5-mile mark, just beyond a jumbled lava wall hemming in a broad meadow, and the descent steepens, the curves tighten, and the forest encroaches, providing welcome shade. The Arkright Spring is off the trail to the north, and the shoreline of Lake Britton is out of sight below. Continue the descent to a clearing at the barricaded *Stand by Me* bridge, the turnaround point. Take in views of the ramshackle bridge and the long, green arm of the lake before returning as you came, bearing in mind that though the grade isn't steep, it's all uphill from the bridge to the junction with CA 89, and a long way back to the Burney trailhead.

The McCloud River Railroad Company

The McCloud River Railroad Company, established in 1896, transported timber from woodlands circling the base of Mount Shasta for more than a century. According to one source, in the 1950s and 1960s, more than 6,000 rail cars loaded with timber made the trip from Burney to the sawmill in McCloud annually, with finished lumber and wood chips ready for pulping sent on to Mount Shasta City and the connection with the Southern Pacific Railroad main line. The McCloud railroad also transported foodstuffs grown and harvested in the region; diatomaceous earth used in a variety of industrial applications including as nontoxic pesticide; and people on sightseeing excursions, including a popular dinner train pulled by a refurbished steam locomotive.

In the late twentieth century, after a new owner purchased the line and renamed it the McCloud Railway, the company was beset by a number of challenges, including a devastating forest fire, diminished passenger traffic, and challenges maintaining financially viable rail transport of timber from the area. The railway ceased operations on the line east of McCloud in 2005, and began pulling up the tracks to Hambone and to Burney—the first steps in an abandonment process that would open the door to development of the Great Shasta Rail Trail.

The Great Shasta Rail Trail Association, a coalition composed of local advocacy groups, envisioned transformation of the unused railbed into a recreational trail, but initially the nonprofit limited that vision to the short section connecting Burney to McArthur–Burney Falls State Park. Given opportunity, creativity, teamwork, and perseverance—and nearly ten years of hard work and negotiation—the vision expanded to include the entire 80-mile stretch of rail line that the McCloud Railway sought to abandon. With the support of the Shasta Land Trust, the National Park Service's Rivers, Trails and Conservation Assistance Program, the California Transportation Commission, the Rails-to-Trails Conservancy, and others, the Great Shasta Rail Trail Association is halfway there, having created a remarkable recreational resource in the region.

The section of the Great Shasta Rail Trail that connects Burney to Lake Britton is remote and showcases the region's volcanic legacy, including the red cinder railbed and jumbled black lava rock.

Completing the Burney section of the trail as an out-and-back hike or mountain-bike ride will take a full day and full commitment. The cinder surface is not compacted, which makes for strenuous walking or cycling; no water sources are available; and stretches of the track are open to what may be brutal exposure to the summertime heat. Be prepared, don't over-estimate your physical abilities, seek shade when it's available, and turn around if you need to. No matter how far you go, the seclusion is divine.

3 BIZZ JOHNSON NATIONAL RECREATION TRAIL

The legendary Bizz Johnson National Recreation Trail links dense woodlands in the high country surrounding Lassen Peak and Lake Almanor to the spectacular Susan River canyon, treating trekkers to historic sites, trestles, and tunnels along the way.

Activities:

Start: Mason Station Trailhead in Westwood

Distance: 25 miles one way

Difficulty: Strenuous

Seasons/schedule: This trail can be used year-round, although travel can be difficult when the route is muddy. The Westwood end of the trail generally has snow on it Dec–Mar.

Fees and permits: None

Trail surface and conditions: The well-maintained and well-used trail is mostly gravel/original ballast and broken into doubletracks in segments.

Accessibility: The 7 miles of trail between Devils Corral and Susanville is accessible to people using wheelchairs once trail maintenance is completed in spring. The route is rougher between Devils Corral and Westwood.

Canine compatibility: Leashed dogs permitted

Amenities: Restrooms, parking, and information signboards are available at the Susanville Depot, Devils Corral, in Goumaz, and at Mason Station. Water is available at the Susanville Depot, in Goumaz, and at Devils Corral. All other services are available in Susanville, and groceries/water are available in Westwood. Information is available at the Susanville Depot, open on Sat only.

Trail contacts: Bureau of Land Management, Eagle Lake Field Office, Susanville; (530) 257-0456; www.blm.gov/visit/bizz-johnson. Lassen National Forest—Eagle Lake Ranger District, 477-050 Eagle Lake Rd., Susanville; (530) 257-4188; www.fs.usda.gov/recarea/lassen/recarea/?recid=11389.

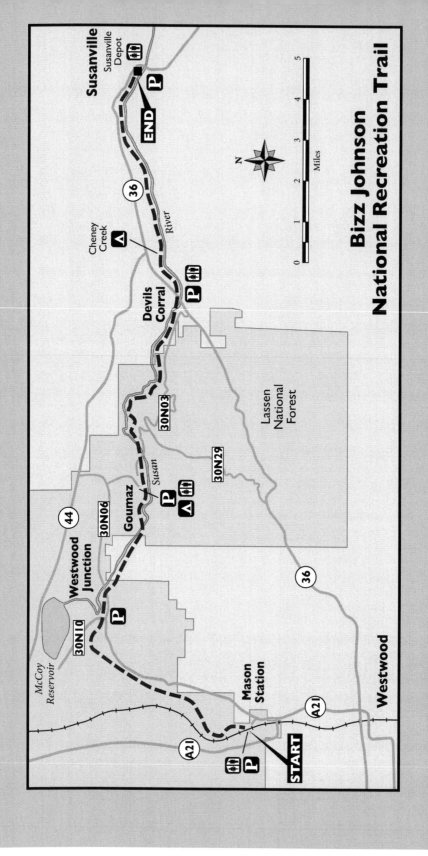

Bizz Johnson
National Recreation Trail

Lassen Land & Trails Trust, Susanville Depot, 601 Richmond Rd., Susanville; (530) 257-3252; https://lassenlandandtrailstrust.org/bizz-johnson-trail.

Nearest towns: Westwood, Susanville

Maps: The BLM and the US Forest Service have compiled a good, download-able map and brochure for the trail at www.blm.gov/visit/bizz-johnson.

Cell service: Good in Susanville; don't count on it along the route

Transportation: The Lassen Rural Bus provides a shuttle between Susan-ville and Westwood Mon–Sat. Bus schedules are available at www.lassen-transportation.com or by calling (530) 252-7433.

Finding the trailhead: To reach the western end point at the Mason Sta-tion trailhead outside Westwood, turn north off CA 36 onto Lassen County Road A–21. Follow CR A–21 north for 3 miles to the intersection with Las-sen County Road 101, which breaks off to the right (northeast) before the railroad tracks and is signed for the Bizz Johnson Trail. Follow CR 101 for about a quarter of a mile to the trailhead, which is on the left (northwest) side of the dirt road.

To reach the Goumaz trailhead, continue east on CA 36 from Westwood to the summit of Fredonyer Pass and turn left (north) onto Lassen Forest Road 30N29. Follow this road north for 6 miles to the Goumaz trailhead.

The well-signed Devils Corral trailhead is on the south side of CA 36 just east of where the highway crosses the Susan River at the base of the pass.

To reach the eastern end point at the Susanville Depot, follow Main Street to Weatherlow Street and turn south on Weatherlow, which becomes Richmond Road. The depot is on the left (southeast) side of Rich-mond Road; more parking and a formal trailhead are located across the street by the caboose.

Parking is abundant at both the Mason Station trailhead in Westwood and the Susanville Depot, and at the trailheads at Goumaz and Devils Cor-ral. All trailheads can be reached from CA 36, which runs between Chester and Susanville.

Trailhead GPS: Susanville Depot: N40 24.693 / W120 39.601; Devils Corral: N40 23.885 / W120 46.418; Mason Station: N40 21.710 / W120 59.934

The Main Line

Of all the jewels in the rail-trail system of California, the Bizz Johnson National Recreation Trail is arguably the brightest and most beautiful, and without question one of the best loved.

Like any quality gem, the attraction of the Bizz has many facets. Up high, near Westwood, the meditative track cuts a straight line through thick woodlands east of Lassen Volcanic National Park, though some of those woods burned in the 2021 Dixie Fire. The route passes stations that once bustled with the loggers and millers who supplied the business of the railroad; these stations are now lonely outposts marked by white signs.

The trail picks up speed, much as the trains used to, after it meets the Susan River near Westwood Junction. The river dives into a canyon and out of sight as the descent steepens, and the trail whistles past spills of black talus and cliffs of orange rock. Beyond the Goumaz station, at about the midpoint of the trail, the pitch mellows and the trail slips out of the forest into a broad valley, then down to meet the river again at Devils Corral.

On its easternmost leg, the rail trail runs alongside the Susan River, a broad waterway that has sliced a lovely canyon through the foothills. The railroad's parallel path plunges through rock outcrops that barred its passage, necessitating the construction of long, dark tunnels that add mystery and history to the journey.

The trail rides atop the former Fernley and Lassen branch of the Southern Pacific Railroad. This line, and a number of spurs in the high country, served the thriving lumbering community that worked the dense forests of Lassen County in the early part of the twentieth century. Established in 1914, the railroad operated for more than forty years, transporting logs, milled lumber, and people from Westwood to Fernley, Nevada, and points in between.

The last train ran on the line in 1956, and Southern Pacific abandoned the line in 1978. That was when the Rails-to-Trails Conservancy, along with Congressman Harold "Bizz" Johnson (for whom the trail is named), the Bureau of Land Management, the US Forest Service, and a number of community groups set to work converting the corridor into a trail. Their hard work paid off in a big way, resulting in one of the best long-distance trails in the state.

A pair of mountain bikers head out of Susanville on the Bizz Johnson National Recreation Trail.

The entire trail can be ridden one way via mountain bike or horseback comfortably in a single day, especially if you head downhill from Westwood to Susanville, a gradual descent of more than 1,300 feet on a 3% grade. If you are on a bike, you can take advantage of the Lassen Rural Bus or make other arrangements for a shuttle back to the original trailhead. You can also enjoy the trail in segments on foot, wheels, or hooves. The most popular short route heads west out of Susanville into the Susan River canyon, where you will find the railroad tunnels and a number of swimming holes that are especially inviting in late summer when the weather is warm and the river is placid.

The trail is described in its entirety as a downhill run from Mason Station in Westwood to the Susanville Depot. A short connector trail leads from the Mason Station parking area to the trail and Mason Station proper, which is adjacent to the existing tracks of the Burlington Northern Santa Fe Railroad.

Head east along the trail through the woods, passing Facht Station and Lasco Station and crossing a couple of Forest Service roads. The trail climbs almost imperceptibly as it follows long straightaways and sweeping turns through the forest, arriving at Westwood Junction at the 7.3-mile mark. Southern Pacific had a maintenance station at this junction from 1923 to 1930. Not quite a half mile beyond this marking, you will pass the Westwood Junction trailhead. A broad meadow stretches to the north, in the direction of McCoy Reservoir.

Pass Blair Station at about the 8-mile mark. Snowmobilers play on the maze of roads in these woods in winter, but staying on the Bizz is easy: Go straight (east) on the flat, obvious railroad grade. The rail trail continues through seemingly endless forest until it reaches a bridge over the fledgling Susan River at about the 10-mile mark. Cross the bridge and pass through the gate; this is a turning point, where the trail's aspect goes from predictable to enlivening.

The river is placid in its willow-lined bed on the right (south) side of the trail, then it dives into a canyon. The route, bordered by cliffs and black talus, drops past an old shack, "Frank's House," at 11 miles. Pass another gate, then arrive at the Goumaz station site at 12.3 miles.

At Goumaz you will find restrooms, a parking area, campsites, and water in the summer season. Located midway between Westwood and Susanville, this is a great place to rest and picnic. You'll also be in the midst of the Dixie Fire scar again, exposed to the sun where once there was an evergreen canopy providing shade, and able to observe the slow but inevitable regreening of the landscape.

East of Goumaz, pass another gate and cross a bridge, then begin a steep downhill run cut into a mountainside, exposing the crumbly orange rock underlying the forest. Another gate, at 17 miles, marks the trail's

The Mason Station trailhead for the Bizz Johnson Trail is tucked along active tracks outside Westwood.

passage through private property, where you must remain on the railroad grade to avoid trespassing. The broad river valley opens to the left (north) as you descend, and the ranch buildings of the lucky souls who work this high-country paradise are visible across the grassy valley floor.

The forest and its undergrowth pick up a more desertlike quality as you pass through ranchland via another gate at 18.1 miles. Continue down and across a spectacular and thrilling bridge at 18.7 miles; the Susan River lies far below. An old bridge spans the river on the north side; the highway, on a sturdy and modern bridge, runs to the south.

Beyond the span, the trail veers sharply down to the right (south) and plunges under the highway bridge, then climbs just as steeply to Devils Corral at 19.3 miles. Devils Corral, like Goumaz, is host to parking, an information kiosk, and restrooms. The trail skirts the corral on its south side and proceeds eastward into the Susan River canyon, with the river a tempting companion.

The primitive Cheney Creek camping area lies riverside at about the 21-mile mark; beyond it you will encounter the first tunnel. It's dark and creepy inside, and reflective posts keep you safely away from the tunnel walls. A bridge lies on the east side of the tunnel. Another bridge

The Susanville Depot

Located at the eastern end point of the Bizz Johnson Trail, the Susanville Depot is a great place to learn more about the history of the rail line that served the area. Built in 1913, the depot was destroyed by fire in 1989, but an addition built in 1927 survived the blaze and now serves as both depot and visitor center. Inside, you'll find educational displays and an abundance of information about the area, as well as souvenirs and a friendly and knowledgeable staff.

The Lassen Land & Trails Trust (LLTT), a nonprofit organization that helps preserve land and restore historic sites throughout Lassen County, operates out of the depot, which is on the National Register of Historic Places. The LLTT and the city of Susanville, along with the Bureau of Land Management and the US Forest Service, have invested a lot of energy in the development and promotion of the Bizz Johnson National Recreation Trail, and they celebrate the trail annually with the Rails-to-Trails Festival. This popular autumn event features great food, railroad handcar racing, arts and crafts, and, of course, hiking and cycling activities on the rail trail. The festival is a fundraiser for the land trust.

The depot is open on Saturday year-round and can be reached by calling (530) 257-3252; the LLTT website is https://lassenlandandtrailstrust.org.

and tunnel follow, the tunnel again a cool and intriguing addition to the experience. As you continue down the canyon, you'll also pass a seasonal waterfall and several swimming holes.

Hobo Camp, with trail connections and picnic facilities, is near the Susanville end of the trail. Pass the Miller Street trailhead, cross the bridge spanning South Lassen Street and the Susan River, follow the tracks past the caboose, then cross Richmond Road to the quaint depot and the end of the line.

BONUS TRACK: ALMANOR RAIL TRAIL

The country surrounding Lassen Peak and Lake Almanor is a delight year-round, and the Almanor Rail Trail offers an easy way to sample the peace and quiet of this beautiful landscape. The trail is a work in progress, and the only section with a formal trailhead is at the east end of Chester at the Olsen Barn Meadow, an expanse of greenery bordered on one side by the lakeshore and on another by the Feather River. The meadow offers a short loop—a little over a mile—that heads down past the majestic old barn to the riverside, then curls back along the railroad grade to CA 36 and back to the trailhead. It's perfect for a morning walk with the doggo.

The rail trail, on the bed of the Almanor Railroad, which once served the local timber industry and is now owned by Collins Pine Company, begins in downtown Chester. Arguably the best parking is where the route crosses 1st Avenue; from there the railbed heads northeast along the border of the little mountain town. A trestle, in disrepair in the summer of 2023, crosses the river to link to the Olsen Barn Meadow Trail. Hitching the in-town portion to the meadow loop makes for another nice option—and one that allows you to enjoy Chester. Hit hard by the Dixie Fire, which burned much of Lassen Volcanic National Park and the woods on the

The Almanor Rail Trail runs through the meadow surrounding the old Olsen Barn.

south and east shores of the lake, supporting local businesses and tourism in Chester will be important for years to come.

From the meadow the route continues east, parallel to the highway, to the Lake Almanor Peninsula. It can be accessed from near the North Shore Campground, though there's no trailhead here, and (full disclosure) when I was scouting, a mountain lion crossed in front of me, prompting a careful retreat. The track traces the shoreline for a stretch, offering wonderful views of the lake and the high country of Lassen Volcanic National Park. It bends away from the shoreline at Bailey Creek and gently climbs to cross County Road A13. From there a wooded stretch leads to trail's end on CA 147 near Clear Creek.

Plans call for connecting the Almanor Rail Trail to the Bizz Johnson National Recreation Trail, creating even more opportunities for long, awesome rambles and short day-hiking options. This is wild, beautiful country, and linking the unused railroad grades seems a good way to reuse what's no longer used by the area's timber industry.

Activities:

Start: Olsen Barn Meadow Trailhead in Chester

Distance: 12 miles one way from Chester to Clear Creek; 1.3 miles for the Olsen Barn Meadow loop

Difficulty: Strenuous in its entirety; easy for the Olsen Barn Meadow loop

Seasons/schedule: Year-round, sunrise to sunset

Fees and permits: None

Trail surface and conditions: Gravel and ballast in town and along lakeshore; mowed grass. The route is poorly maintained and rustic in parts, requiring users to negotiate fallen trees and other obstacles.

Accessibility: The grade is appropriate for people using wheelchairs but is not maintained.

Canine compatibility: Leashed dogs permitted

Amenities: Parking is available at the Olsen Barn Meadow Trailhead and all services can be reached from the route through downtown Chester.

Trail contact: Almanor Recreation and Park District, 101 Meadowbrook Loop, Chester; (530) 258-2562; www.yourarpd.org

Nearest town: Chester

Maps: The best online map is at www.traillink.com/trail-maps/almanor -rail-trail.

Cell service: Good in Chester; scarce as you get farther out

Transportation: None

Finding the trailhead: The Olsen Barn Meadow Trailhead is located on CA 36 at the western edge of Chester. Access to the rail trail is also available on the other side of the Lake Almanor causeway near North Shore Campground, County Road A13, and CA 147 at Clear Creek, but no formal trailheads exist at these locations as of summer 2023.

Trailhead GPS: Olsen Barn Meadow Trailhead: N40 18.739 / W121 13.330

The Almanor Rail Trail is a work in progress with a lot of potential.

Modoc Line Rail Trail

The Modoc Line Rail Trail tucks itself firmly into the "out there" extreme of the rails-to-trails spectrum. Stretching more than 80 miles through remote landscapes in rural northeastern California, the Modoc Line, like so many other long-distance rail trails, is a work in progress. As well as appealing to the usual suspects, it also offers recreational opportunities to off-highway vehicle (OHV) enthusiasts—and honestly, unless you are prepared as a hiker or a mountain biker to spend multiple nights in a high desert wilderness, those on OHVs are probably the only folks who can comfortably travel long distances on this route.

Three disconnected sections of the trail, which extends from near Wendel in the south to Likely in the north, are open for travel and, according to the Lassen Land & Trails Trust (LLTT), traverse "some of northeastern California's most dramatic rangeland, views of the Skedaddle and Warner mountain ranges, and opportunities to see wildlife, including herds of pronghorn antelope." The sections include a run from Wendel to US 395; the stark and stunning 22-mile Snowshoe Canyon segment, featured in a story map on the LLTT website (https://lassenlandandtrailstrust.org/modoc-line-rail-trail); and the Likely section.

The rail trail rides atop a railbed abandoned by the Union Pacific in 1996, but according to the Rails-to-Trails Conservancy TrailLink website for the route, in the early twentieth century, the line was a narrow gauge called the Nevada-California-Oregon (N-C-O), also known as the "narrow, crooked, and ornery."

For more information and trail maps, visit the LLTT website or the Rails-to-Trails Conservancy TrailLink site for the Modoc Line at www.traillink.com/trail/modoc-line-rail-trail.

4 SACRAMENTO RIVER RAIL TRAIL

This well-loved route, part of a greater trail system exploring the fire-scarred terrain surrounding Shasta County's Keswick Reservoir, stretches along the wide, green Sacramento River from near the Keswick Dam to the foot of Shasta Dam.

Activities:

Start: Rock Creek trailhead outside Redding

Distance: 18 miles round-trip

Difficulty: Moderate due to length

Seasons/schedule: Year-round, sunrise to sunset

Fees and permits: None

Trail surface: Pavement

Accessibility: The entire route can be traveled by people using wheelchairs.

Canine compatibility: Leashed dogs permitted

Amenities: Restrooms are at the Keswick Reservoir boat ramp trailhead and at the Chappie-Shasta Off-Highway Vehicle trailhead. Camping is also available at the Chappie-Shasta OHV Recreation Area. There is no food or water along the route. This is a long, hot ride or hike in summer, so pack plenty of water. Do not drink from the reservoir or river without treating the water first.

Trail contact: Bureau of Land Management, Redding Field Office, 6640 Lockheed Dr., Redding; (530) 224-2100; www.blm.gov/office/redding-field-office

Nearest town: Redding

Maps: The City of Redding's Parks and Recreation Department hosts a GIS-enhanced trail-mapping system that includes the Sacramento River National Recreation Trail; visit www.cityofredding.gov/government/departments/parks_and_recreation/index.php. A map of the rail trail, along with other trails along the Sacramento River, Keswick Reservoir, and

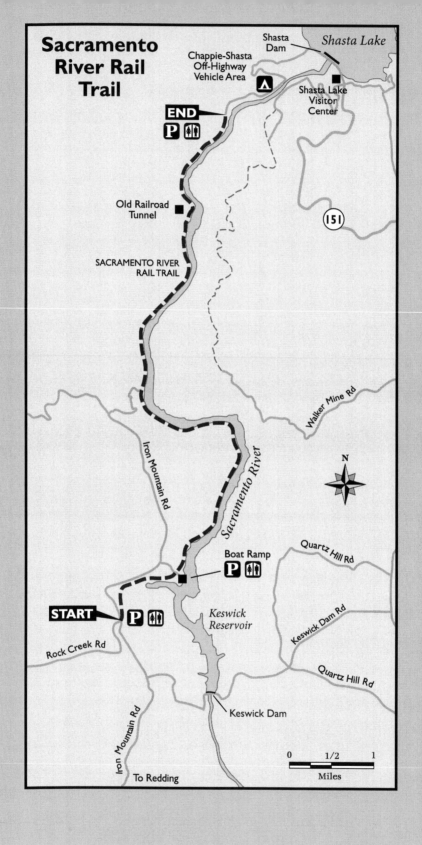

Sacramento River Rail Trail

Shasta Dam

Shasta Lake

Chappie-Shasta Off-Highway Vehicle Area

Shasta Lake Visitor Center

END

151

Old Railroad Tunnel

SACRAMENTO RIVER RAIL TRAIL

Iron Mountain Rd

Walker Mine Rd

Sacramento River

N

Boat Ramp

Quartz Hill Rd

START

Keswick Reservoir

Rock Creek Rd

Keswick Dam Rd

Quartz Hill Rd

Iron Mountain Rd

Keswick Dam

To Redding

0   1/2   1
Miles

up to Shasta Dam, is available online through the Bureau of Land Management; search www.blm.gov. Another good source is the Rails-to-Trails Conservancy TrailLink map at www.railstotrails.org.

Cell service: Good in town, marginal to none on the trail

Transportation: None

Finding the trailhead: To reach the Rock Creek trailhead from I-5 in Redding, head west on CA 299 (Eureka Way) for about 3.7 miles to Iron Mountain Road. Turn right (north) on Iron Mountain Road and head north 2.2 miles to the Rock Creek trailhead on the right (east). There is parking for four or five cars at this trailhead.

There is ample parking at the Keswick Reservoir boat ramp trailhead, which is about 1 mile north of the Rock Creek trailhead on Iron Mountain Road. Drop to the right down the paved access road for 0.3 mile to the large parking area.

The Chappie-Shasta Off-Highway Vehicle (OHV) trailhead and campground, at the north end of the trail, are accessible via Lake Boulevard and Shasta Dam Boulevard heading west from I-5 and across the Shasta Dam. There is ample parking at the Chappie-Shasta trailhead, as well as camping facilities.

Trailhead GPS: Rock Creek trailhead: N40 37.486 / W122 27.963; Keswick Boat Ramp trailhead: N40 37.944 / W122 27.151; Chappie-Shasta OHV trailhead: N40 42.777 / W122 26.223

The Main Line

In the battle for primacy of North Country rail trails, the Sacramento River Rail Trail and the nearby Bizz Johnson National Recreation Trail would be leading contenders. The Sacramento River route is home to the best that wilderness rail trails have to offer: superb views, river frontage, a railroad tunnel, an easy grade, and enough length to get travelers "out there."

The trail stretches along the shores of Keswick Reservoir and the swirling Sacramento River to the outlet of Shasta Lake at massive Shasta Dam. The 18-mile out-and-back endeavor described here requires

The Sacramento River Rail Trail offers a view of the Shasta Dam.

strength and perseverance. It also opens an accessible window on how wildfires alter landscapes and the experiences of the people traversing those impacted landscapes through time.

It also took strength and perseverance to build the railbed upon which this trail lies. Constructed in the heyday of the iron horse, the line first belonged to the Central Pacific Railroad, which also built the west-to-east leg of the fabled transcontinental railroad. Later the rails fell under the purview of the Southern Pacific, which ran express trains from Oregon to California through the Sacramento River canyon on the Shasta Route, dubbed the "Road of a Thousand Wonders." The line was rerouted with the construction of Shasta Dam; the original rails lie beneath the deep blue water of Shasta Lake.

After the line was abandoned in the 1980s, and the rails and ties were salvaged, the Bureau of Land Management, the city of Redding, and other private and public partners set about converting the line into a trail system. That system has since been designated a National Recreation Trail.

Beginning at the Rock Creek trailhead, head north on the paved trail. Cross a levee at 0.3 mile: Above and to the left (west) is the Spring Creek Dam, and below and to the right (east), Spring Creek widens into a narrow arm of Keswick Reservoir. The trail rides the slope above the sparkling water of the lake, curving east to the gate at the Keswick Reservoir boat ramp trailhead at 1.1 miles. You'll find restrooms, trash cans, and lots of parking at this point.

You'll also have passed through the burn scar of the 2018 Carr Fire, which originated along CA 299 in the nearby Whiskeytown National Recreation Area and blew out in every direction, including into Redding. The community of Keswick was devastated by the blaze, but in the years since the fire, some of the residents have rebuilt and nature has begun to rebound.

From the boat ramp the route continues to shadow the reservoir, but don't expect much in the way of shade, even once you leave the wildfire's footprint. The grade passes through cuts and overfilled ravines, with chaparral growing close on its edges. In the stillness of an autumn morning, the reservoir is a mirror, inviting travelers on the trail to splash through its smooth surface to cool off.

At about 3.5 miles, the reservoir narrows to river and bends westward, and the vegetation alongside the trail grows a little more riparian in nature. You can also see the volcanic rock that makes up the base of the railbed at the trail's edges. Dirt tracks open to off-highway vehicles (OHVs) occasionally intersect the paved rail trail, but the path ahead is clear. Continue on the obvious rail trail.

At 6.7 miles the route leaves the railroad grade to drop through a little creek that's dry by late summer; a narrow bridge spans the waterway. At 7.3 miles you'll reach the railroad tunnel: It's just long enough to get spookily dark at the middle, its roof arching high and cathedral-like overhead.

Side trails interrupt the route at 8.3 miles; stay straight on the railroad grade. The river swirls around little islands of dark rock, some capped with hearty vegetation; the currents and eddies trace intricate patterns in the water's surface, hinting at the dangerous power of the flow.

As you near the 9-mile mark, you'll reach the Chappie-Shasta trailhead for the Sacramento River Rail Trail. Shasta Dam looms to the northeast. There are ample parking, an information kiosk, and restrooms at the trailhead. Travel 0.1 mile down the pavement to reach the Chappie-Shasta OHV area proper, with a day-use area, camping, more restrooms, additional parking, and shaded benches and picnic tables.

Unless you've acquired a permit and made arrangements to be picked up here, return as you came.

5 HORNBECK TRAIL

On the Hornbeck Trail, narrow gauge has evolved perfectly into singletrack. The route zips through narrow cuts and along exposed hillsides, with views across Keswick Reservoir and the Sacramento River drainage toward the high peaks of the Trinity Alps.

Activities:

Start: Trailhead on Quartz Hill Road outside Redding

Distance: 8 miles round-trip

Difficulty: Hard. It's not long, but the route is winding and features more ups and downs than a typical rail trail.

Seasons/schedule: Year-round, sunrise to sunset. Heavy rain or summer heat may preclude a hike or ride.

Fees and permits: None

Trail surface: Dirt and gravel

Accessibility: Not accessible to people using wheelchairs

Canine compatibility: Leashed dogs permitted

Amenities: Restrooms, parking

Trail contact: Bureau of Land Management, Redding Field Office, 6640 Lockheed Dr., Redding; (530) 224-2100; www.blm.gov/office/redding-field-office

Nearest town: Redding

Maps: The City of Redding's Parks and Recreation Department hosts a GIS-enhanced trail-mapping system that includes the Sacramento River National Recreation Trail. Visit the site at www.cityofredding.gov/government/departments/parks_and_recreation/index.php. A map of the rail trail, along with other trails along the Sacramento River, Keswick Reservoir, and up to Shasta Dam, is available online through the Bureau of Land Management; search www.blm.gov. Another good source is the Rails-to-Trails Conservancy TrailLink map at www.railstotrails.org.

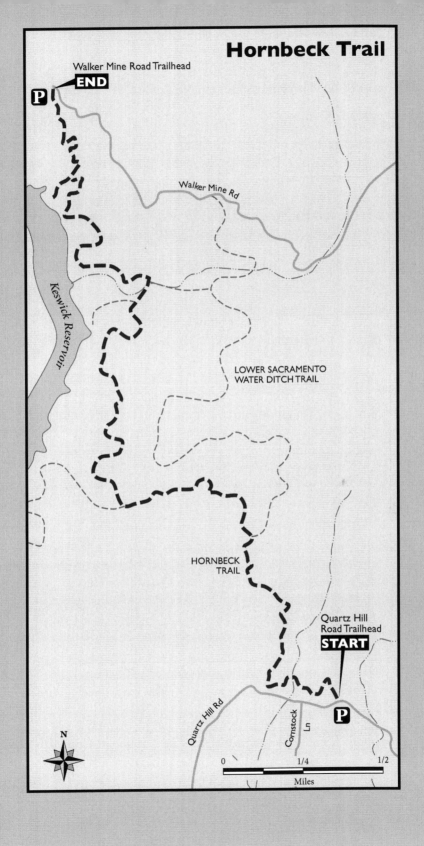

Hornbeck Trail

Walker Mine Road Trailhead
END
P

Walker Mine Rd

Keswick Reservoir

LOWER SACRAMENTO
WATER DITCH TRAIL

HORNBECK
TRAIL

Quartz Hill
Road Trailhead
START

P

Quartz Hill Rd

Comstock Ln

N

0   1/4   1/2

Miles

Cell service: Good in town; marginal to none on the trail

Transportation: None

Finding the trailhead: To reach the Quartz Hill parking area from I-5 in Redding, head west on CA 299 (Eureka Way in the town of Redding) for about 3.7 miles to Iron Mountain Road. Turn right on Iron Mountain Road and head north for 1.9 miles to Keswick Dam Road. Go east 2.2 miles on Keswick Dam Road, across Keswick Dam, to Quartz Hill Road, and turn left (north). The trailhead is 1.7 miles up Quartz Hill Road on the left (north) side of the road.

Trailhead GPS: Quartz Hill Road Trailhead: N40 38.151 / W122 25.320

The Main Line

Narrow-gauge railbed to superb singletrack: The Hornbeck Trail is a standout example of how perfectly the former can become the latter. The route doesn't stay true to the former rail line in its entirety, sometimes curling through manzanita and oak woodlands before rejoining the line, but with steep-sided cuts and sublime views of Keswick Reservoir, mountain bikers will love the route, and hikers and equestrians will enjoy it as well.

But all users should take note: This is not your typical rail trail, as it is narrow and involves steep pitches and switchbacks. You'll be sharing the trail, so stay right and single file to let other users pass. If you are on a mountain bike, make sure you are well versed in gearing up and down.

The rail trail follows the onetime Quartz Hill narrow-gauge line, which supplied quartz to nearby copper-smelting operations. You can find remnants of that quartz, sparkling white amid the reds and deep browns of the surrounding soil, along the route. The trail was named in honor of engineer Chuck Hornbeck, a volunteer who was active in development of the route.

The route is described heading north from the Quartz Hill Road trailhead. A gate blocks the service road for the adjacent power line corridor; the trail is on the left (west) side of the parking area, where you'll also find an information signboard (with maps) and a distinctive trail mile marker. The marker, about 2 feet high and fashioned of stamped metal, is one of

The singletrack Hornbeck Trail rolls on and off an old narrow-gauge rail line, offering a wonderful long hike or moderate mountain bike ride.

several along the route; the Hornbeck, intersected by drainages and
other paths, is also identified by slen-
der metal posts topped with painted
green metal knobs.

The initial section of the trail
lies off the grade and winds uphill
through a forest of manzanita, the
blood-colored branches providing
spindly shade.

At about 0.5 mile the trail curls
onto what appears to be the former railroad grade, a straight swath
through the oak woodland. At 0.7
mile you reach a trail intersection; a
trail marker directs you straight on the
grade. Follow the trail post around a
switchback at the 1-mile mark (pass-

*Nuggets of quartz can still be found
along the Hornbeck Trail; be sure to follow Leave No Trace principles and let the
stones remain for others to enjoy.*

ing one of the low stamped-metal trail posts as well).

The route levels after a nice quarter-mile downhill run; the railroad
grade proper is visible through the brush to the right. Regain the grade
at 1.3 miles, where you can also spy what appear to be leftover railroad
ties. Mountain views open at about 1.6 miles as you follow the contour
of the hillside. Reach a bench in the shade of oak and manzanita at 1.8
miles; the quartz for which the hill was named is scattered about the trail
at this point.

The 2-mile marker is beyond a cut in the hillside. At 2.3 miles stay on
track by following the markers and heading left through the cut. Reservoir
views open by the 2.5-mile mark, then the route veers away from the lake.
A series of trail markers directs you through a winding section until you
rejoin the railroad grade at about 2.8 miles.

Reservoir views open again at the 3-mile mark; from here you can see
the Sacramento River Rail Trail winding through the scrub on the western
shore of the lake. At 3.5 miles pass the 0.1-mile-long side trail to the Freitas
Overlook on the left (west). The rail trail climbs gently through the woods
to the Walker Mine Road trailhead, with parking and restrooms, at 4 miles.
Unless you have a ride waiting at Walker Mine, return as you came.

6 SACRAMENTO RIVER NATIONAL RECREATION TRAIL

This trail heads up the Sacramento River on one side to a striking stress ribbon bridge, and then back down the other side to a historic railroad bridge. Add a turn through Turtle Bay Exploration Park to see a third bridge—the remarkable Sundial.

Activities:

Start: Court Street/South Diestelhorst Trailhead

Distance: 5.5 miles round-trip, plus an optional lollipop loop through the arboretum

Difficulty: Moderate. Although the portion of the trail on the railroad grade is easy, the portion that's not features several steep hills. The length of the route also precludes an easier rating.

Seasons/schedule: Year-round, sunrise to sunset

Fees and permits: None for the trail; a fee is charged to enter Turtle Bay Exploration Park

Trail surface and conditions: The trail is paved (asphalt and concrete), well maintained, and well traveled, but when the Sacramento River runs high, portions may be flooded.

Accessibility: The entire route is accessible to people using wheelchairs.

Canine compatibility: Leashed dogs permitted

Amenities: Restrooms are located 0.2 mile upstream from trailhead, at the ribbon bridge, in Lake Redding Park, and at Turtle Bay Exploration Park. No food is available along the trail, but you'll find plenty of restaurants and markets nearby in Redding and in Turtle Bay. Water fountains are few and far between on the path and Redding is notorious for its summertime heat, so bring plenty to drink with you.

Trail contact: City of Redding Park and Recreation Department, 20055 Viking Way, Building #4, Redding; (530) 224-6100; www.cityofredding.gov/government/departments/parks_and_recreation/index.php

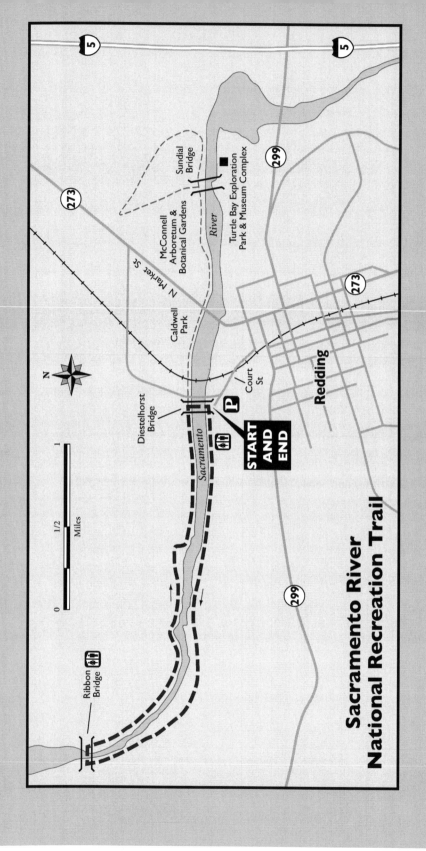

Sacramento River
National Recreation Trail

5

5

299

273

273

299

N

Miles
0   1/2   1

Sundial
Bridge

River

McConnell
Arboretum &
Botanical Gardens

Turtle Bay Exploration
Park & Museum Complex

N Market St

Caldwell
Park

Court
St

Redding

P

Diestelhorst
Bridge

START
AND
END

Sacramento

Ribbon
Bridge

Nearest town: Redding

Maps: The City of Redding's Parks and Recreation Department hosts a GIS-enhanced trail mapping system that includes the Sacramento River National Recreation Trail. Visit the site at www.cityofredding.gov/government/departments/parks_and_recreation/index.php. A map of the rail trail, along with other trails along the Sacramento River up to Shasta Dam, is also available online through the Bureau of Land Management; search www.blm.gov. Another good source is the Rails-to-Trails Conservancy TrailLink map at www.railstotrails.org.

Cell service: Good

Transportation: No public transportation serves the trail specifically, but the Redding Area Bus Authority provides transit throughout the city. For schedules and routes, visit www.rabaride.com.

Finding the trailhead: To reach the trailhead from I-5 in Redding, take the CA 299/CA 44 exit and head left (west) on CA 299. The highway leads into downtown Redding, where the freeway ends. Signs mark the passage of CA 299 as it winds through town, first heading west on Shasta Street, then right (north) on Pine Street, then left (west) on Eureka Way. Follow Eureka Way/CA 299 to Court Street. Turn right (north) on Court Street and follow it for a half mile to the parking lot on Middle Creek. The lot is on the left (west) side of Court Street just before the bridge over the Sacramento River.

You can also reach the trail from Turtle Bay Exploration Park at 844 Sundial Bridge Dr. From I-5, take the CA 299 exit and head west on CA 299 to the Sundial Bridge Drive exit in about 0.5 mile. Cross the bridge and access the trail on the north side of the river through the arboretum.

The Main Line

The Sacramento River, green and swift, has carved a gentle canyon that curls through the center of Redding and waters the strip of riparian habitat on either shore that cradles this classic rail trail. The Sacramento River Trail Bridge, a simple, graceful, 400-foot-long arc of concrete known as a ribbon bridge, lifts the trail over the river at the western end point of this

The iconic *Sundial Bridge* isn't on the Sacramento River rail trail proper, but it's close enough, and it's not to be missed.

route. At the eastern end the historic and more traditional Diestelhorst Bridge ties the trail into a pleasing, 5.5-mile loop.

And as if to emphasize this is a rail trail, the pedestrian Diestelhorst is mirrored by the Court Street bridge, which in turn is overshadowed by the high trestle that supports an active Union Pacific line. Watching a train pass over this trestle will thrill more than railroad buffs.

Interpretive signs along the route describe the natural and man-made history of the area and add to the trail's charm. Views westward are of the Trinity Mountains; heading east on the north side of the river affords vistas of Lassen Peak, one of two Cascade volcanoes that dominate Redding's skyline. The other, Mount Shasta, can't be seen from the river valley.

But that's not all. Follow the river east of the Diestelhorst Bridge, and you will reach the Turtle Bay Exploration Park and the McConnell Arboretum & Botanical Gardens, home to an oak savanna of unrivaled beauty and rich with the legacy of the Wintu tribe, which lived in the area prior to the arrival of Europeans.

Only a mile of the trail is on a former railroad grade, with the rest of the route on historic roads that served mining operations along the river. That mile of former railway, installed in the 1880s as part of the Southern Pacific system in the area, was incorporated into the portion of the trail on the south side of the river when the path was built in 1986.

The route, described here heading upstream along the southern bank of the Sacramento from the Court Street trailhead and then downstream on the north side of the river on the return, begins at the western end of the parking area. Pass the Court Street water fountain; restrooms lie 0.2 mile ahead. The path overlooks the turquoise river and is overhung with trees and bushes that bloom pink and white in spring and are alive with darting hummingbirds and butterflies. Memorial benches and mile markers line the route. The railroad grade runs alongside and out of sight of the paved path on the south side.

At 1.5 miles the trail breaks out from under the canopy of trees and views open to the western mountains. Climb a short hill onto the railroad grade, which runs above the exposed and rocky shoreline. Cross a bridge over a small creek, then cross the bridge spanning Middle Creek. The Middle Creek Rail Trail breaks off to the left, heading up Middle Creek Canyon and offering another rail trail out-and-back option (or addition).

At 2.5 miles the gray ramparts of Keswick Dam and the silver strand of the Sacramento River Trail Ribbon Bridge come into view. The formal trail

Turtle Bay Exploration Park

Redding takes great pride in its Sacramento River frontage, and that pride has found perfect expression in both its lovely riverside trailways and in Turtle Bay Exploration Park.

The park's centerpiece is the Sundial pedestrian bridge, a spectacular structure that spans the river between the McConnell Arboretum & Botanical Gardens and the Turtle Bay Exploration Park's museum complex. Its sail-like pylon soars 220 feet, the frosted green glass that paves its deck mirrors the color of the water below, and its railings offer bird's-eye views of the Sacramento's whorls and swirls.

Though the railroad portion of the trail doesn't extend into this complex, Turtle Bay is worth exploring. From the Diestelhorst Bridge, continue east on the concrete path for about 1 mile, passing the playgrounds, ballfields, swimming complexes, and picnic grounds of Lake Redding Park and Caldwell Park. The path drops under the Market Street bridge and meanders into the 200-acre McConnell Arboretum & Botanical Gardens. You've arrived at Turtle Bay.

The gardens are planted with species from Mediterranean climates around the world, including South Africa, Chile, and Australia. Within the arboretum you can explore a fantastic oak savanna that rings with birdsong and dances with shadows at sunset, as well as a children's garden and a medicinal garden. A 3-mile paved loop winds through the arboretum and links to the Sundial Bridge.

On the south side of the bridge, you'll find more to explore in the Turtle Bay museum complex, including a river aquarium, a butterfly exhibit, a historic railroad exhibit, and Paul Bunyon's Forest Camp, which showcases the area's rich forestry and logging history.

More information on Turtle Bay Exploration Park is at www.turtlebay.org; or call (530) 243-8850.

The Diestelhorst Bridge is at the east end of the Sacramento River National Recreation Trail loop.

bears right (east) across the bridge, but you can continue upstream on the Sacramento River Rail Trail from here, traveling approximately 10 miles north to Shasta Dam (see route #4).

Across the bridge and now headed downstream on the north shore of the river, the trail bends east and mimics a roller coaster as it undulates past trail signs, a restroom, and junctions with trails that head north into hills. Lassen Peak, often snow-covered into early summer, dominates the eastern horizon as you continue.

Climb a rather steep hill and the rail trail arcs through a drainage in the midst of a cluster of madrone and oak. At 4 miles the trail reaches the Harlan Drive trailhead and hops onto a quiet residential street. Go about 400 yards down the street to the continuation of the trail, which heads for the river through a small meadow on the right (south) side of the road.

The trail is now more suburban, passing the yards of lovely riverfront homes. The train trestle, Diestelhorst pedestrian bridge, and Court Street Bridge are at the 5.5-mile mark. To return to the trailhead, head left (north), away from the concrete riverside path and onto the bridge approach, then turn right (south) to cross the bridge.

For a longer excursion, stay on the riverside path, which continues downstream, passing under the triad of bridges, to Turtle Bay Exploration Park and the Sundial Bridge.

7 PARADISE MEMORIAL TRAILWAY

This rail trail connects neighborhoods in a mountain town that's rebuilding after a wildfire.

Activities:

Start: Pentz Road trailhead

Distance: 5.2 miles one way

Difficulty: Easy on a bike if you coast downhill with a shuttle back to the trailhead; moderate to hard as an out-and-back ride or hike

Seasons/schedule: Year-round, sunrise to sunset

Fees and permits: None

Trail surface and conditions: Asphalt

Accessibility: The trail is accessible to people using wheelchairs.

Canine compatibility: Leashed dogs permitted

Amenities: No water is available along the route, so bring what you need. Restrooms are available in the Paradise Community Park near the route's south end point. Food and other services are a block or two away from the trail along the Skyway.

Trail contact: Paradise Recreation and Park District, 6626 Skyway, Paradise; (530) 872-6393; www.paradiseprpd.com

Nearest town: Paradise

Maps: The best online trail map is available on TrailLink: www.traillink.com/trail-maps/paradise-memorial-trailway.

Cell service: Good

Transportation: Butte Regional Transit (B-Line) provides bus service in the area but doesn't run regularly from trailhead to trailhead. For schedule information, visit www.blinetransit.com or call (530) 342-0221 or (800) 822-8145.

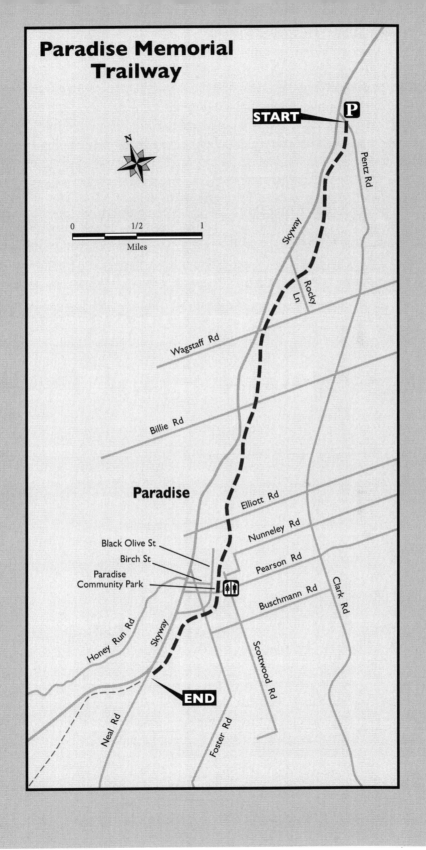

Paradise Memorial Trailway

START

P

Pentz Rd

Skyway

Rocky Ln

N

0   1/2   1
Miles

Wagstaff Rd

Billie Rd

Paradise

Elliott Rd

Nunneley Rd

Black Olive St

Birch St

Pearson Rd

Paradise
Community Park

Buschmann Rd

Clark Rd

Honey Run Rd

Skyway

Scottwood Rd

Neal Rd

END

Foster Rd

Finding the trailhead: To reach the southern trailhead, follow the Skyway, the main route through Paradise, to its intersection with Neal Road, which is at the southernmost end of town. There is a small parking lot at this location. To reach the upper, northernmost trailhead, follow the Skyway through town to its intersection with Pentz Road. The trail heads south from this intersection. There is limited parking off the roadway at this end point, with on-street parking available on Pentz Road.

Trailhead GPS: Pentz Road trailhead: N39 48.019 / W121 34.855; Neal Road trailhead: N39 44.764 / W121 38.241

The Main Line

Rewriting the entry in this guidebook for the Paradise Memorial Trailway is emotional. The entry from my previous FalconGuide for this rail trail starts this way:

> With a name like Paradise, it had better be good. Fortunately, like the town through which it runs, the Paradise Memorial Trailway lives up to its billing. Climbing into the pine-shrouded foothills that buckle up where California's great Central Valley meets the Sierra Nevada, the trail is gentle but rugged, on the safe side of untamed. It is mostly wooded, with evergreens dominating the landscape higher up, and more diverse oak woodland flourishing down low. Insulated for the most part by the curtain of the forest, the trail offers easy access to the Skyway, Paradise's main drag, and all the amenities of the town.

Some of this still holds true. The trailway remains a gentle but rugged climb through this foothills town, but things have changed drastically. In 2018 the Camp Fire ravaged Paradise. The superlatives about the woodlands no longer apply; much of the trail now runs through an open landscape, fire-scarred trees mingled with the remaining evergreens.

But it's still Paradise. And there's still a trail. And it's important to witness not only the recovery of the woodlands that once defined what's called the Ridge, but also the resilience of the people who continue to call it home.

The Diamond Match Company was the primary user of the Southern Pacific rail line upon which the trail was built. The company, like many other enterprises in the mountains of California, ran logging and milling operations that used railroads to haul raw timber and finished lumber. The company's logging town was located north of Paradise in Stirling City, and the railroad ran through Butte Canyon down into Chico. Southern Pacific eventually abandoned the line, opening the opportunity to transform the corridor into a rail trail.

The grade of the Paradise Memorial Trailway averages 3%, making for an easy downhill run, especially on a bicycle, and a more strenuous uphill trek. The trail is described here heading downhill from the Pentz Road end point, but if you don't plan to shuttle, you might want to reverse the direction so you aren't laboring uphill at the end of your adventure.

The trail is set a bit below the grade of the Skyway as it heads south from Pentz Road. Private homes and cabins were, or will be, on the left (southeast) side of the paved path, which rises to meet the Skyway at the 0.7-mile mark, then is separated again by a thin wedge of vegetation. Beginning at the 1-mile mark, the trail stretches uninterrupted by cross streets until its intersection with Rocky Lane at 1.7 miles.

Cross Wagstaff Road at 2.2 miles, and then Billie Road at 2.9 miles. Beyond Billie Road the trail becomes more of a town path, easily shared by hikers, cyclists, dog walkers, strollers, and squirrels. At 3.5 miles the route skirts Paradise High School, with its ballfields, and it's just a couple of blocks onto the Skyway through a neighborhood, demonstrating how the rail trail serves as a connector between homes, businesses, and public works.

From Cedar Street to Pearson Road, the trail passes through Paradise Community Park, with restrooms, a pavilion, a tot lot, and the railroad depot. The path makes a sharp right-hand (west) turn and climbs to Black Olive Street at about the 4-mile mark.

The final section passes through oak scrubland typical of lower elevations in the foothills; birdsong and wildflowers may accompany you to the trail's end at Neal Road. Unless you have arranged a shuttle, return as you came.

BONUS TRACK: CHICO AIRPORT BIKE PATH

The grassy expanses surrounding the Chico Regional Airport are surprisingly scenic, hosting a variety of songbirds that raise a pleasant ruckus in spring. This rail trail, set on a right-of-way abandoned by the Sacramento Northern Railway that linked Chico to cities in the Bay Area, runs from the airport south into downtown Chico, where it offers residents a shady alternative to walking or cycling on the streets.

Activities:

Start: The Chico Airport or anywhere along the path in Chico

Distance: 3.5 miles one way

Difficulty: Easy

Seasons/schedule: Year-round, sunrise to sunset

Fees and permits: None

Trail surface and conditions: Asphalt; the trail is well maintained.

Accessibility: The trail is accessible to people using wheelchairs.

Canine compatibility: Leashed dogs permitted

Amenities: No restrooms are available along the trail. While no stores or restaurants are available at the airport end of the trail, the other end is on Esplanade, which runs through the heart of town and provides access to a variety of eateries and markets. No water is available along the route, so pack all you will need.

Trail contact: City of Chico Parks, 411 Main St., Chico; (530) 896-7800; https://chico.ca.us

Nearest town: Chico

Maps: Excellent maps of bike trails in the area are available on the City of Chico website (https://chico.ca.us/post/experience-chico-bike) and the Butte County Association of Governments site (www.bcag.org/documents/transit/bike_maps/BCAG_BIKE_MAP_front_web.pdf).

Cell service: Good

Transportation: Butte Regional Transit (B-Line); www.blinetransit.com; (530) 342-0221 or (800) 822-8145

Finding the trailhead: To reach the Chico Regional Airport trailhead from CA 99 in Chico, take the Cohasset Highway/Mangrove Avenue exit. Head north on Cohasset Road for about 3 miles to Boeing Avenue and turn left (west). Follow Boeing for 0.2 mile to Fortress Street and turn left (south). Sikorsky Avenue intersects Fortress Street at about 0.1 mile; the rail trail is on the left (east) side of Fortress Street. No parking lot is available at this end point.

The southern end of the rail trail is at the intersection of Esplanade and 11th Avenue. To reach this from CA 99, take the Cohasset Highway/Mangrove Avenue exit and head west on Cohasset Road. Follow Cohasset Road for 0.5 mile to its intersection with Esplanade and turn left (south). Follow Esplanade for 0.3 mile to 11th Avenue. The rail trail is located just north of this junction, but there's no convenient parking here. You can find parking on nearby residential streets, however, including along Cohasset Road and Cohasset Lane.

Trailhead GPS: Chico Regional Airport: N39 47.634 / W121 50 53; downtown Chico end point: N39 44.914 / W121 51.198

BONUS TRACK: MIDWAY BIKE PATH

Walnut orchards—brilliant with pink and white blooms in spring, laden with fruit in summer and autumn, and naked in winter—line this rural bike path, which borders the Midway Road in southern Chico. Formerly called the Durham Bike Path, the route is popular with cyclists and links with other bike routes in this bike-friendly college town. Like the Chico Airport Bike Path, the trail rides atop a railbed abandoned by the Sacramento Northern Railway, which once offered commuter service between Chico, Sacramento, and cities in the Bay Area.

Activities:

Start: East Park Avenue trailhead

Distance: 2.5 miles one way

Difficulty: Easy

Seasons/schedule: Year-round, sunrise to sunset

Fees and permits: None

Trail surface and conditions: Asphalt

Accessibility: The trail is accessible to people using wheelchairs.

Canine compatibility: Leashed dogs permitted

Amenities: None; bring what you need. There's no formal trailhead at either end of the route, but street parking is available at the north end of the trail off East Park Avenue and at the junction of the trail with Hegan Lane, about 0.1 mile south. Eateries, markets, and restrooms can be found just a few miles north in central Chico.

Trail contact: City of Chico Parks, 411 Main St., Chico; (530) 896-7800; https://chico.ca.us

Nearest town: Chico

Maps: An excellent map of bike trails in the area is available on the City of Chico website (https://chico.ca.us/post/experience-chico-bike) and the Butte County Association of Governments site (www.bcag.org/documents/transit/bike_maps/BCAG_BIKE_MAP_front_web.pdf)

Cell service: Good

Transportation: Butte Regional Transit (B-Line), www.blinetransit.com; (530) 342-0221 or (800) 822-8145

Finding the trailhead: To reach the northern end point of the Midway Bike Path from CA 99 in Chico, take the Paradise/Park Avenue exit. Go east on East Park Avenue to Midway Road.

To reach the southern end point at Jones Avenue and Midway, continue south on Midway for 2.3 miles to its intersection with Jones Avenue. No parking is available at this end point.

Trailhead GPS: East Park Avenue and Midway Road: N39 42.829 / W121 48.822

8 MACKERRICHER HAUL ROAD TRAIL

Magical beaches with expansive views over the Pacific Ocean are the hallmark of the MacKerricher Haul Road Trail, a spectacular rail trail that runs the length of a state park.

Activities:

Start: Pudding Creek Trestle in Fort Bragg

Distance: 3.5 miles one way

Difficulty: Moderate due only to trail length

Seasons/schedule: Year-round, sunrise to sunset

Fees and permits: None for the trail. A fee is charged for day use and camping at MacKerricher State Park.

Trail surface and conditions: Asphalt, but the trail may be covered by sand in stretches or flooded/washed out by surf.

Accessibility: The trail is accessible to people using wheelchairs from Pudding Creek through the main part of MacKerricher State Park, but wheelchairs—or any other kind of wheeled machine, for that matter—will have a hard time if there's sand on the trail or a washout. Beach wheelchairs are available in the state park.

Canine compatibility: Leashed dogs permitted on the trail, but not on Ten Mile Beach.

Amenities: No food is available along the route, but you can find water in the campgrounds within the state park. The park also has areas for picnicking. Restaurants and a market can be found in Fort Bragg to the south of the park.

Trail contact: MacKerricher State Park, 24100 MacKerricher Park Rd., Fort Bragg; (707) 937-5804; www.parks.ca.gov (search for park by name)

Nearest town: Fort Bragg

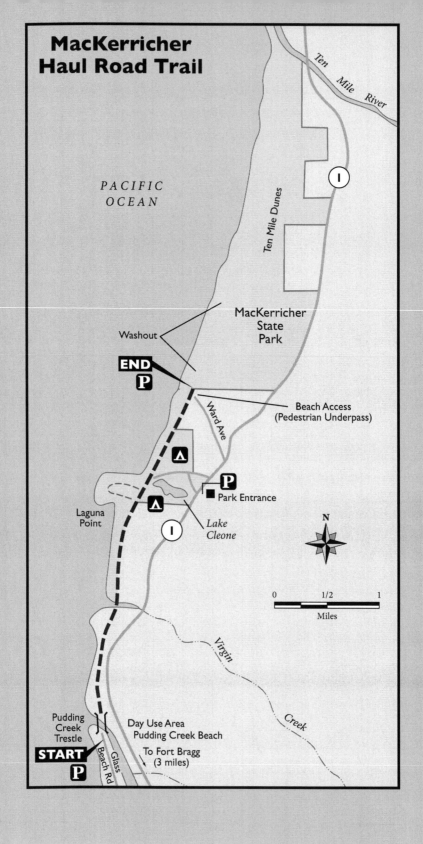

MacKerricher
Haul Road Trail

PACIFIC OCEAN

Ten Mile River

Ten Mile Dunes

MacKerricher State Park

Washout

END
P

Beach Access
(Pedestrian Underpass)

Ward Ave

Park Entrance

Lake Cleone

Laguna Point

N

0   1/2   1
Miles

Virgin Creek

Pudding Creek Trestle

Day Use Area
Pudding Creek Beach

To Fort Bragg
(3 miles)

START
P

Glass Beach Rd

Maps: MacKerricher State Park map, available on the park website at www .parks.ca.gov in the downloadable brochure.

Cell service: Marginal

Transportation: No public transportation serves the trail.

Finding the trailhead: To reach the southern end point at the Pudding Creek Trestle from CA 1 in Fort Bragg, head north from town toward the bridge that spans Pudding Creek. Turn left onto West Elm Street, then right on Glass Beach Drive. A large parking area and the trailhead are at the end of Glass Beach Drive.

The rail trail can also be reached via the main entrance of MacKerricher State Park, which is about 3 miles north of Fort Bragg on CA 1. Turn left (west) into the park, following Mill Creek Road past the entrance station and the campground access road. Mill Creek Road arcs around the west shore of Lake Cleone and forks. Take the right fork into the parking area for the main beach, the trailhead, and Laguna Point.

Trailhead GPS: Pudding Creek trailhead: N39 27.473 / W123 48.475; MacKerricher State Park trailhead: N39 29.341 / W123 47.948

The Main Line

Views from the MacKerricher Haul Road Trail are mesmerizing. The uncrowded beaches are washed with rhythmic insistence by waves, which fill tidal pools that grow warm and inviting under the summer sun and have sculpted sand dunes that offer refuge to seabirds and trail travelers alike.

The trail has also been called the Logging Road (as well as the Ten Mile Coastal Trail), but its formal name reflects the route's previous incarnation as a road used to haul lumber from woodlands in the Ten Mile River watershed to the Union Lumber Company mill in Fort Bragg. The railroad that originally occupied the route was established in 1916 by the lumber company, which operated the line until 1949. The tracks were ripped up in a single day, according to historian Gene Lewis of Fort Bragg, so that

Joggers head down the Haul Road rail trail in MacKerricher State Park.

‖|||||||||||||||||||||||||||||||||||||||||||||||||||||||||||||||||||||||||||||||||‖

Take a Ride on the Skunk Train

In addition to the Haul Road Trail and lovely MacKerricher State Park, Fort Bragg is also home to the western terminus of the famous California Western Railroad Skunk Train. This historic train service offers scenic excursions into the redwoods and oak woodlands of the Coast Ranges between the oceanside town and the inland town of Willits, including a climb to an elevation of 1,700 feet, an exploration of the estuary where Pudding Creek spills to the sea, and the opportunity to travel via railbike on sections of the historic lines.

Trains depart from the Fort Bragg Depot, located on Laurel Street 1 block west of CA 1. The excursions are extremely popular with families and railroad buffs, so it is recommended that you make reservations for your journey. For information and reservations, call (707) 964-6371 or visit www.skunktrain.com.

‖|||||||||||||||||||||||||||||||||||||||||||||||||||||||||||||||||||||||||||||||||‖

the lumber company could build a private "high speed" logging road that could accommodate special logging trucks.

The lumber company used the Logging Road until 1983, when rainwater spilling out of the dunes in MacKerricher State Park washed out nearly 7,000 feet of the route. The state parks department, which had acquired most of the land surrounding the haul road, didn't permit it to be rebuilt. It was subsequently abandoned and transformed into a lovely rail trail.

The trail runs through sensitive habitat occupied by three endangered species, including the snowy plover, a pretty little bird whose numbers have been in decline due to increased use of beaches by people. In the Ten Mile Dunes complex, north of Laguna Point and the trailhead, about 3 miles of remnant haul road was set to be removed to enhance habitat as this guide went to press. Ten Mile Dunes, sequestered over millennia by shifting dunes and changing sea levels, contains what the park calls "vegetative microclimates" fostering unique ecosystems including the

Inglenook Fen. If you venture into this spectacular but sensitive territory, tread with care, and obey all signs.

The route begins at the Pudding Creek trestle and heads north, passing between the backyard lawns of motels on the east side and the narrow beach on the west. At about the 1.5-mile mark, the rail trail crosses the bridge at Virgin Creek, then passes northward into the core of MacKerricher State Park.

At about 2.5 miles the paved rail trail breaks away from the ocean as it skirts Laguna Point. The point, a highlight of MacKerricher State Park, juts out into the ocean, and side paths and boardwalks lead through the woodlands to open areas on the promontory surrounding stations where visitors enjoy seal watching and whale watching.

North of the point, the elevated trail passes the main beach at the park, and side trails lead through the driftwood onto the soft sand. The Surfwood campground and Lake Cleone are on the right (east) side of the road.

The path is arrow-straight and abundantly scenic as it continues northward over the pedestrian tunnel that allows campers to reach the beach. At about the 3.5-mile mark, pass the beach access at Ward Avenue and head into the dunes. There is a small parking lot at this access point.

The washout is just north of Ward Avenue. You can leave the railroad grade and walk down onto the beach via a small trail, but the dunes along this stretch and headed north are off-limits: They are part of the Inglenook Fen–Ten Mile Dunes Natural Preserve. Retrace your steps to the trailhead.

SACRAMENTO AREA

9 SACRAMENTO NORTHERN BIKE TRAIL

The Sacramento Northern Railroad slices through a cross section of California's capital city, stretching from the old neighborhoods of Sacramento through the suburbs and then out into farmland.

Activities:

Start: 20th Street between C and D Streets

Distance: 10 miles one way

Difficulty: Hard due only to length; if taken in short sections, the difficulty can be reduced to easy.

Seasons/schedule: Year-round, sunrise to sunset. In spring, when the American River runs high, the trail between CA 160 and the Jedediah Smith Memorial Trail may be flooded.

Fees and permits: None

Trail surface and conditions: Pavement; the trail is well maintained and well traveled

Accessibility: The entire trail is accessible to people using wheelchairs.

Canine compatibility: Leashed dogs permitted

Amenities: Public restrooms are available at the Rio Linda–Elverta Community Center at the Rio Linda trailhead. Other amenities, including food and water, are available along the route in various neighborhoods. You can picnic in Discovery Park, in one of the gazebos along the route, or at Rio Linda's Depot Visitor Center.

Trail contact: City of Sacramento Public Works Bicycling Program, 915 I St., Room 2000, Sacramento; (916) 808-8434; www.cityofsacramento.org/Public-Works/Transportation/Programs-and-Services/Bicycling-Program

Nearest town: Sacramento

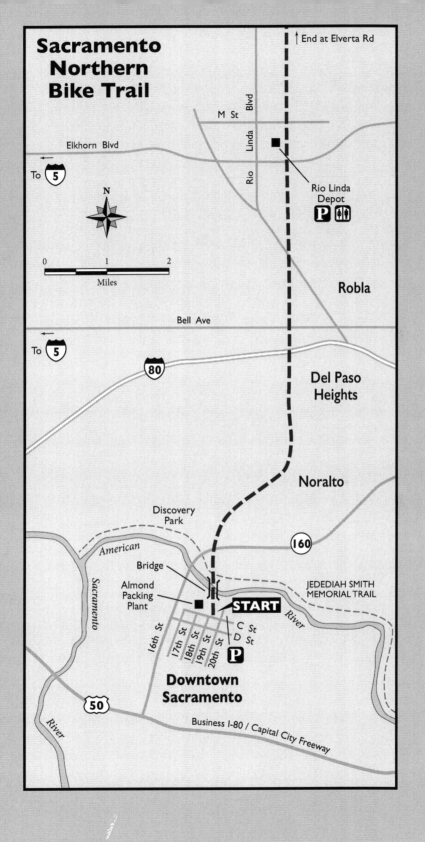

Maps: A detailed, downloadable bicycling map that includes Sacramento-area rail trails is available on the Bicycling Program website at www.cityof sacramento.org/Public-Works/Transportation/Programs-and-Services/ Bicycling-Program.

Cell service: Good

Transportation: Sacramento Regional Transit District, 1400 29th St., Sacramento; (916) 321-BUSS (2877); www.sacrt.com

Finding the trailhead: To reach the Sacramento end point from the westbound lanes of I-80 (Capital City Freeway), take the 15th Street (CA 160) exit (the 16th Street exit if you are headed eastbound). Go north on 16th Street to D Street. Go right (east) on D Street to 20th Street; turn left (north) on 20th Street to C Street. The trail is located between 19th and 20th Streets, on the north side of the road. There is plentiful streetside parking.

Trailhead GPS: N38 35.052 / W121 28.575

The Main Line

These 10 miles of rail trail offer snapshots of lifestyles and landscapes in California's capital city. The landscapes include grand Victorian homes in the old town area, industrial complexes, pleasant suburban neighborhoods, and rural farm communities in Rio Linda. The lifestyles are a bit more complicated: In addition to the families and commuters you might expect to find using the rail trail to get around, a healthy population of people experiencing homelessness also frequents the route, and chances are you'll encounter an encampment somewhere down the line.

The trail runs along the former Sacramento Northern Interurban Electric Rail line, which carried passengers between the two bustling agricultural communities of Sacramento and Chico. The trains stopped running in the mid-1940s, and the rail line was eventually abandoned. Construction on the trail, which has been upgraded and lengthened over the years, began in 1980.

The trail begins on C Street between 19th and 20th Streets, at the edge of a charming old neighborhood of classic homes and sycamore-lined

A metal trestle spans the American River on the Sacramento Northern Bike Trail.

street, adjacent to the railroad tracks on the east side of the Blue Diamond almond factory. Head north on the paved path, passing under the bridge of the active Union Pacific tracks, and meander through industrial complexes for a half mile to a trail intersection. Stay right (north) on the Sacramento Northern trail, which passes across the American River on a spectacular metal trestle, then drops into the riparian greenery on the north shore of the river.

At 1 mile pass under CA 160 and merge briefly with the Jedediah Smith Memorial Trail, which runs east to west along the American River. Follow the merged trails east for 0.3 mile to the next trail intersection and head left (north) across Del Paso Boulevard into Discovery Park. This section of the trail, along with the trails that border the ponds in this area of the park, may be flooded in spring.

Where the Jedediah Smith Trail branches off to the left (northwest), circling shady ponds that ring with birdsong, stay right on the Sacramento Northern trail, which takes the high road and climbs onto the raised bed overlooking the ponds. At about 1.5 miles the trail leaves the raised bed and drops down across railroad tracks, then continues north.

Industry gives way to homes as you cross a small bridge and enter the Noralto neighborhood. Paths accessing neighborhood streets break both right and left from the trail, and you'll cross a series of residential streets, most of which are quiet but require attention to traffic.

Homes border the trail to about the 3-mile mark; for the most part, you're traveling between backyard fences. At 3.9 miles cross Arcade Creek and its twin levees, then pass through the Redding Park greenbelt, which buffers the trail from the adjacent homes, and exit Noralto to enter Del Paso Heights. Archways announce the transitions; gazebos and benches also line the route, offering trail travelers a number of opportunities to rest and rehydrate in the shade.

In Del Paso Heights the linear greenbelt that buffers the trail widens and feels more parklike, with formal access points at street junctions. At about the 5-mile mark, at Harris Avenue, turn right (east) onto the Harris Avenue sidewalk for 25 yards to the crosswalk, cross busy Rio Linda Boulevard, and pick up the northbound trail on the other side. Cross a couple of side streets, then pass under the I-80 overpass.

You're now in the Robla neighborhood and at the 5.2-mile mark. A broad, exposed greenbelt borders the paved path; cruising here gives trekkers a hint of countryside, with widely spaced homes on large pieces of property bordered by rustic fences. Then you reenter suburbia, and a dirt footpath borders the paved rail trail.

Cross Marysville Boulevard at 6.7 miles. The trail now enters country proper, stretching between pastures that are richly green and dotted with wildflowers in spring, and bleached blond after the long, hot summer.

Cross a series of levees and a ditch at 7 miles. The canopies of broad-leaved trees shade the trail and insulate it from the nearby airport. At 7.6 miles cross Dry Creek; beyond, the oaks form a substantial and welcome bower of shade over the path. The waterway runs alongside the trail, adding its coolness to that of the trees.

Pass the horse arena on the right (east) side of the path, then cross Elkhorn Avenue, which can be busy, to a series of bridges spanning a braided creek or ditch that has cut ragged channels into raw-looking earth.

Trees again crowd the trail as you head into the park complex surrounding the Rio Linda Depot, which is near the 8-mile mark. The community center grounds include a tot lot, broad lawns, picnic facilities, and the depot itself, now a visitor center. This is a good turnaround spot for families on daylong cycling outings.

The trail was extended north to Elverta Road in 2006, offering recreationalists an additional 1.8 miles of paved path. The additional mileage offers access to local schools and neighborhoods and includes benches for rest and contemplation, drinking fountains, and a small forest of still-maturing shade trees, including native oaks. At the Elverta end point, a park-and-ride at Elverta Road and Rio Linda Boulevard, you'll find a shelter with benches, water, and a parking area. Though the railbed continues, unpaved and unimproved, beyond Elverta Road, this is the end of the line. Unless you've arranged a shuttle, return as you came.

10 SACRAMENTO RIVER PARKWAY TRAIL

The city center that was home to the first railroad in the state of California is a fitting setting for a rail trail. Saturated in history and culture, wedged between the Sacramento River and a working rail line, the Sacramento River Parkway Trail is a pleasure to walk or ride.

Activities:

Start: Trailhead at the California State Railroad Museum

Distance: 1.5 miles one way

Difficulty: Easy

Seasons/schedule: Year-round, sunrise to sunset

Fees and permits: None to use the trail; parking fees are levied on streets and in garages

Trail surface and conditions: Wooden boardwalk, concrete, asphalt

Accessibility: The entire route is accessible to people using wheelchairs.

Canine compatibility: Leashed dogs permitted

Amenities: Restrooms are at the trail's northern end point in Old Sacramento and at Miller Park at the southern end point. A plethora of eateries crowds the trail in Old Sacramento. From candy to crab, water to wine, take your pick.

Trail contact: City of Sacramento Public Works Bicycling Program, 915 I St., Room 2000, Sacramento; (916) 808-8434; www.cityofsacramento.org/Public-Works/Transportation/Programs-and-Services/Bicycling-Program

Nearest town: Sacramento

Maps: A detailed, downloadable bicycling map that includes Sacramento-area rail trails is available on the Bicycling Program website at www.cityof sacramento.org/Public-Works/Transportation/Programs-and-Services/Bicycling-Program.

Cell service: Good

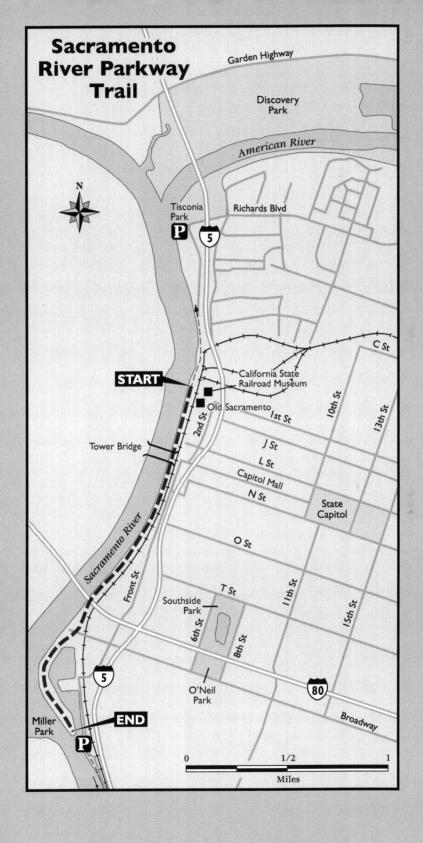

Transportation: Sacramento Regional Transit District, 1400 29th St., Sacramento, CA 95812; (916) 321-BUSS (2877); www.sacrt.com

Finding the trailhead: The northern end point of the trail is at the California State Railroad Museum in Old Sacramento. To reach Old Sacramento, take the J Street exit from I-5 and follow the signs. Both on-street parking and parking garages are available in the area; fees are charged.

Miller Park, at the south end point, is adjacent to the mazelike confluence of the Capital City's freeways. From Old Sacramento, head south on Second Street to Front Street, which is south of Capitol Mall, and continue south on Front Street to Broadway. Turn right (west) on Broadway; this becomes Marina View Drive and leads into the large parking areas for the park and the Miller Park Marina.

Trailhead GPS: N38 35.058 / W121 30.256

The Main Line

Culture and history envelop this section of this popular, well-loved rail trail. Sandwiched between the Sacramento River and a working rail line in the heart of California's capital city, the parkway lacks nothing: It allows trekkers to explore the California State Railroad Museum, skirts the historic buildings of Old Sacramento, and cruises the banks of the mighty river that links the Gold Country to San Francisco Bay. It also serves up restaurants, riverboat rides, tattoo parlors, candy shops, a broad promenade, a riverfront park, and the chance to see an old-time locomotive unleash a column of steam onto the pillars of a freeway bridge.

The trail runs adjacent to the tracks of the working Sacramento Southern Railroad, upon which the railroad museum runs weekend excursion trains. The railroad dates back to the turn of the twentieth century, when the Southern Pacific built the line to facilitate transportation of the bounty of the Central Valley's fields and orchards to port cities in the Bay Area. Both freight and passenger trains operated on the branch line, which ran south for 24 miles to Walnut Grove and beyond until the late 1970s, when floods destroyed miles of track. The Southern Pacific ceased operations on

The promenade offers stellar views of Sacramento's historic Tower Bridge.

Amenities of Old Sacramento

Old Sacramento and the capitol district are rich with cultural and historical amenities. Here's a short list of activities you can enjoy before or after your promenade on the Sacramento River Trail.

- Explore the historic district, where cobblestone streets and boardwalks front elaborate old buildings that house candy shops, ice cream parlors, cafes and restaurants, clothing boutiques and souvenir shops, toy stores and purveyors of antiques and jewelry, photographers, tobacconists, and fortune tellers. It's a feast for the eye, stomach, and pocketbook.

- Visit the many museums around downtown Sacramento, including the California State Railroad Museum, the California Capital Museum, the Crocker Art Museum, the California State Indian Museum, and Sutter's Fort State Historic Park.

- Visit the capitol, seat of the Golden State's government.

- Take a trip on the excursion train or a riverboat—or both.

   More information is available at www.oldsacramento .com. For information on tours of the state capitol, a California State Park, visit www.parks.ca.gov.

the rail line by the early 1980s; the state railroad museum began running the excursion trains on the Sacramento end of the route in 1984.

This tour encompasses a short section of the longer trail, beginning behind the railroad museum, near the freight yard and Central Pacific Railroad Depot, on the narrow paved path that runs atop the river levee. Head south along the riverfront; the levee gives way shortly to a boardwalk bordered by touristy shops and restaurants. The working tracks are on the left, and riverboats are docked along the waterfront to the right.

Excursion trains run along the track adjacent to the Sacramento River Parkway Trail.

At 0.25 mile reach the Capitol Mall intersection, with the yellow pylons of Tower Bridge rising on the right (west), and the capitol gracing the end of the mall on the left (east). Carefully cross the mall and continue south along the wide, lighted promenade, lined with flower-filled planters on pedestals bearing plaques that describe the colorful history of Old Sacramento. Benches overlook the river, where pleasure boats ply the deep green water. Keep in mind that the Sacramento is a big, dangerous river; no matter the temptation, no swimming is permitted.

The formal promenade ends at the 0.5-mile mark, but the trail, with the tracks on the left and the levee wall and river on the right, continues south. At 0.6 mile it's pinched between the levee wall and the tracks; the bikeway narrows at 0.8 mile. The focus is now on the river, which teems with recreational boaters and wildlife, including flocks of waterfowl that perch on timber structures along the riverbank. The uneasy juxtaposition of the urban and the untamed is on display here, with the Capital City Freeway, a man-made span of concrete and metal, arcing over the powerful waterway that preceded it and will no doubt long outlast it.

At 1.4 miles pass a field of oil tanks, and reach trail's end at the intersection of Broadway at 1.5 miles. Turn right and head down toward the river into Miller Park, a linear stretch of lawn dotted with trees and picnic tables that stretches to the mouth of the Sacramento Marina. Return as you came.

Though this route is bookended by the railroad museum and Miller Park, you can extend your exploration from either end point. The trail formally begins about a mile north of Old Sacramento in Tisconia Park and hitches to the American River Parkway, a spectacular trail that stretches from Discovery Park to the powerhouse below Folsom Dam. It continues south of Miller Park as well, with the trail picking up again in the Miller Park Marina, reached via an on-street walk down Ramp Way. From the marina, the paved trail is wedged between the river, the active rail line, and the interstate for a long stretch before ending in a parking lot at the end of Captain's Table Road. Another short section of trail, disjointed from the rest, begins at Garcia Bend Park and continues south to the Bill Conlin Sports Complex.

11 EL DORADO TRAIL

The Missouri Flat to Forni Road section of the El Dorado Trail, another exceptional long-haul rail trail, winds through the woodlands south of central Placerville.

Activities:

Start: The small parking lot on Missouri Flat Road in Placerville

Distance: 5.4 miles out and back

Difficulty: Easy

Seasons/schedule: Year-round, sunrise to sunset

Fees and permits: None

Trail surface and conditions: Pavement; the trail is popular and well maintained

Accessibility: This section of the El Dorado Trail is accessible to people using wheelchairs, but other sections are dirt, gravel, and ballast.

Canine compatibility: Leashed dogs permitted

Amenities: Trash cans, information signboards at trailheads

Trail contacts: El Dorado County Transportation Commission, 2828 Easy St., Suite 1, Placerville; (530) 642-5260; www.edctc.org. Friends of El Dorado Trail, PO Box 1388, Placerville, CA 95667; http://eldoradotrail.com.

Nearest town: Placerville

Maps: USGS Coloma CA online at http://eldoradotrail.com/trail-map

Cell service: Good at either end point; sketchy in between

Transportation: El Dorado Transit, (530) 642-5383; https://eldorado transit.com

Finding the trailhead: From Sacramento, take US 50 west to Placerville. Take the Missouri Flat Road exit and go right on Missouri Flat Road for

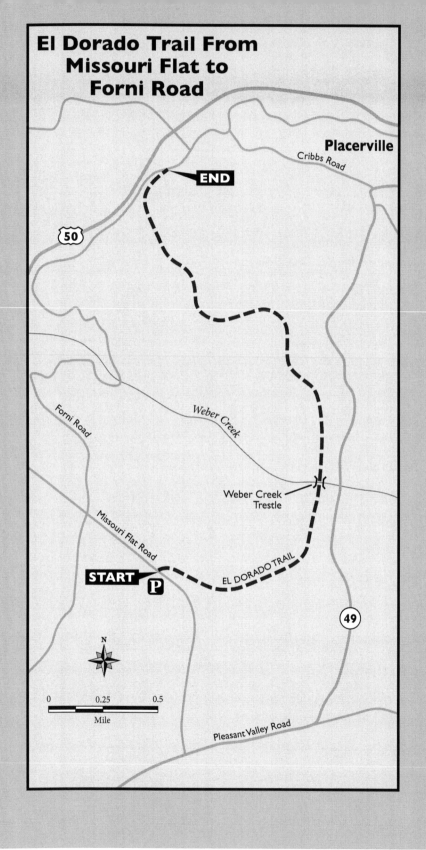

El Dorado Trail From Missouri Flat to Forni Road

Placerville

Cribbs Road

50

END

Weber Creek

Forni Road

Weber Creek Trestle

Missouri Flat Road

START

P

EL DORADO TRAIL

49

N

0   0.25   0.5

Mile

Pleasant Valley Road

about 0.8 mile, past the shopping centers on the right, to the fenced parking area for the Missouri Flat trailhead on the left. There is parking for about fifteen cars.

Trailhead GPS: N38 42.217 / W120 49.551

The Main Line

Midway across the trestle bridge that spans Weber Creek on this scenic stretch of the El Dorado Trail, the guardrails are secured with dozens of locks inscribed with the names of lovers who have come to this high place to secure the commitments with lock and key—or a combination, as the case may be.

The views from the high trestle, a main draw along this section of the 35-mile-long El Dorado Rail Trail, are as inspiring as the sentiments expressed by the locks. The span towers above the forested gorge, with the stream running out of sight and earshot far below. The trail occupies the former rights-of-way of two defunct lines—the Sacramento-Placerville Transportation Corridor and the Michigan-California rail corridor—and currently stretches from the El Dorado county line on the west to Camino, about 7 miles east of Placerville, where this section begins and ends. The hope is that one day the rail trail will reach over the crest of the Sierra Nevada into the Lake Tahoe basin.

This 2.5-mile stretch is essentially an urban route in a mostly rural setting. The gentle, paved lane winds through woodland and grassland but is never far from development and never truly free of road noise from nearby highways. Nonetheless, it offers walkers and cyclists a chance to stretch their legs and clear their minds, whether they've got just enough time to make it to the bridge and back or can spend all day walking or riding for miles through California's scenic Gold Country. Parcourse installations add an alternative fitness option to the walk. And you might be pleasantly surprised to find yourself alone for long stretches, particularly if you take to the trail on a weekday.

Begin at the trailhead on Missouri Flat Road, a busy thoroughfare offering access to shopping and other services. Though development is

The section of the El Dorado Trail between Missouri Flat and Forni Road in Placerville has busy urban end points, but the middle is all about country.

The Weber Creek Trestle spans a deep gorge and is decorated with locks left by lovers.

obvious on either side of the path, it is gradually screened by curtains of brush and woodland.

By the time you reach the Weber Creek trestle at about the 1-mile mark, signs of civilization have thinned out considerably. On the far side of the bridge, it's all about the countryside, with meadows and stands of oaks bordering the route. As for the climbing, even as the pitch increases, it remains minimal; this is a rail trail, after all.

The trail is bisected by a roadway at 1.6 miles, and again the incline increases by a few degrees. Signs of civilization begin to encroach on the route again at the 2.2-mile mark—parcourse installations, houses, and finally commercial lots. The turnaround at the Forni Road trailhead is at 2.7 miles. Retrace your steps to the trailhead, or continue on up the trail into the historic Placerville downtown, where you'll find all the amenities. And then carry on, if you'd like, climbing farther into the evergreen skirts of the Sierra Nevada.

12 DELTA MEADOWS RAIL TRAIL

This straight-ahead walk follows an old railroad grade through dense riparian habitat along sleepy Railroad Slough. Blackberry, wild grape, and fig are twined with the native willow and cottonwood that thrives alongside the abandoned railbed.

Activities: 🚶 🏃 🧗 🦌

Start: The gate behind Chuck Tison Memorial Park in Locke

Distance: 3.4 miles out and back, including short detour along a second levee road

Difficulty: Easy

Seasons/schedule: Year-round, sunrise to sunset

Fees and permits: None

Trail surface and conditions: Unmaintained dirt and gravel. The trail may be muddy in winter.

Accessibility: None

Canine compatibility: Leashed dogs permitted

Amenities: None

Trail contact: California Department of Parks and Recreation, Contra Solano Sector Office, 96 Mitchell Canyon Rd., Clayton; (925) 673-2891; www.parks.ca.gov (search for park by name)

Nearest town: Locke

Maps: USGS Isleton CA, Courtland CA, Bruceville CA. A map is not necessary as there is, essentially, only one trail in the park.

Cell service: None

Transportation: None

Finding the trailhead: From Sacramento, follow I-5 south about 20 miles to the Twin Cities Road exit. Take Twin Cities Road west about 4 miles to River Road, which is perched on the levee. Turn left on River Road and

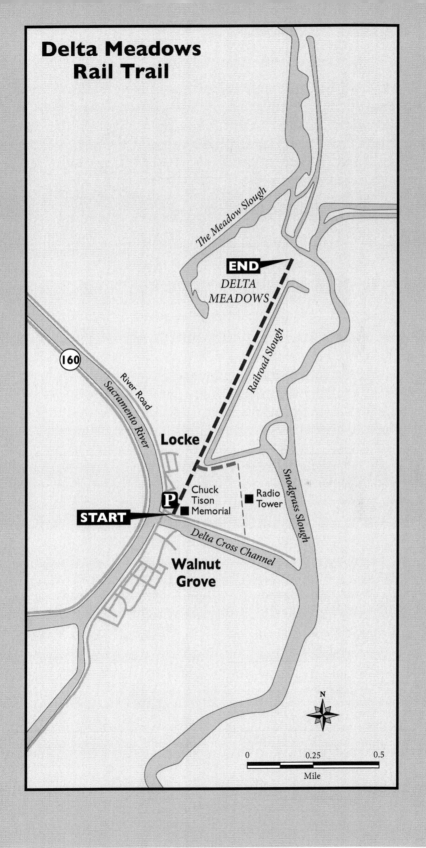

Delta Meadows
Rail Trail

The Meadow Slough

END

*DELTA
MEADOWS*

Railroad Slough

160

River Road

Sacramento River

Locke

Snodgrass Slough

P

Chuck
Tison
Memorial

Radio
Tower

START

Delta Cross Channel

**Walnut
Grove**

N

0   0.25   0.5

Mile

drive through the historic town of Locke. Look for the sign for Chuck Tison Memorial Park on the left just outside town, before River Road makes a sweeping turn toward Walnut Grove. Turn left on the unsigned paved road at Tison Park, then quickly left again toward a gate, where there is parking for about five cars. There is a Delta Meadows River Park sign, but it is partially obscured by foliage.

Trailhead GPS: N38 14.832 / W121 30.528

The Main Line

|||||||||||||||||||||||||||||||||||||||||||||||||||||||||||||||||||||||||||||||||||||||||||||||||||||||||||||||||||||||||||||||||||||||||||||||||||||||||||||||||||||||||||

Obscurity lends Delta Meadows a unique feel. Even the most minimal of amenities are nonexistent. Toward trail's end, lush, untamed riparian plants and grasses encroach on the route. It's one of California's neglected parks, a bit sad and a bit shabby, but it feels content and grandmotherly. Perhaps those very qualities—placidness, gentleness, a sense of hidden depths—drew park planners to acquire the property in the first place.

This little park has been closed since 2010, the result of budget constraints and fiscal strife that resulted in the closure of many more of California's state parks in 2012. But a single trail, built on a former Southern Pacific railroad grade, is still open to foot traffic. Obscurity means the trail is little used: You may find yourself alone on the broad track. There are no crowds, despite the fact that Locke and Walnut Grove, with their historical sites, quaint shops, and cozy eateries, are nearby.

The trail has a decidedly undistinguished start, with the trailhead and dirt parking area surrounded by rusting shipping containers and other industrial flotsam and jetsam. The railroad grade shoots straight ahead, with the cottonwoods and willows that line the nearby waterways pushed back so that the sun bakes the trail surface. The sound of cars driving on nearby River Road wafts into the park, cell towers rise from open meadows to the right, and you can look down on the backyards of trailer park homes through openings in the trailside brush to the left.

But within a quarter of a mile, all that is left behind. Grand old oaks reach boughs over the track, and the blackberries, poison oak, wild grape, and other scrubby plants thicken in the understory. At your first glimpse of Railroad Slough at 0.25 mile, take the short path that breaks right—this

The rail trail through Delta Meadows River Park burrows through thick brush watered by neighboring sloughs.

out-and-back spur dead-ends at a gate and a service road that leads back to the cell tower, but not before passing figs that, instead of growing into majestic trees, have adopted a bush-and-vine form, their giant leaves unmistakable amid the less flashy oak and grape. Where the spur track climbs onto a mound, you'll encounter a stand of sycamore—and possibly, if the tides (or the owner) haven't taken it away, a hard-used skiff, its red-and-white paint chipped and peeling.

Retrace your steps to the junction with the rail trail at 0.7 mile and go right, passing a gate and a fenced-off utility station, the last man-made items you'll encounter for a stretch. The trail becomes more remote-feeling the farther you walk. The slough flows to your right, feeding into the more substantial Snodgrass Slough, but the brush is so dense it's hard to get a clear view. Meditative if you are on your own, and an easy walk-and-talk if you have a companion, the setting is quieting.

A meadow opens on the left at the 1.25-mile mark, and a gate blocks passage onto an intersecting roadway that leads into private property. Farther on, ponds can be glimpsed to the left, their surfaces obscured by water lilies with vibrant purple blooms in season.

The trail, now distinctly overgrown, with noxious star thistle erupting along the centerline and thick on the verge, ends not far beyond the ponds. A berm and sign mark the end point at 1.7 miles; beyond the berm the path is overwhelmed by a bank of blackberry. From here, retrace your steps to the trailhead.

Making Up for Funding Shortfalls

More than seventy sites in the California State Parks system were targeted for closure in 2012. The parks department faced a $22 million shortfall due to a statewide budget crisis, and that meant shutdown and neglect. In a handful of cases, private and nonprofit organizations stepped in to cooperatively manage and operate a beleaguered park, and with that grassroots support those parks have thrived.

Delta Meadows was not so lucky. It remains a state park with a comforting wildness, but the lack of state funding translates to a certain frustration, especially given the scandal that erupted just months after the closures were announced. Parks officials had squirreled away more than enough money to cover the shortfall. Even with funding in hand, however, bureaucracy failed its mandate.

Thankfully, Delta Meadows's proximity to the historic town of Locke has buoyed the park with impromptu support. Locke was built in 1915 by Chinese residents uprooted when fire consumed Walnut Grove's Chinatown. Five years later the region experienced an "asparagus boom," and the Southern Pacific Railroad built a line into the region (a section of which later became the park's rail trail). The little Chinese enclave was briefly an agricultural boomtown, with more than 600 residents who ran markets, a theater, and a community garden, and also could, if they chose to, patronize speakeasies, opium dens, and brothels. The town's decline began in the 1930s and continued in the wake of World War II, as second-generation Chinese Americans opted out of agricultural livelihoods. Despite the decline, and in recognition of its cultural significance, the town, now with only about a hundred permanent residents, is on the National Register of Historic Places. It's also become a tourist attraction, which bodes well for the future of Delta Meadows. For more information on the town and its history, visit www.locke-foundation.org.

The Delta Meadows park property is unimproved; there are no services. The property is patrolled by state park peace officers and game wardens from the California Department of Fish & Game.

BONUS TRACK: FAIRFIELD LINEAR TRAIL PARK

Primarily a commuter route that leads from the Solano Mall and the subdivisions of urban Fairfield to Solano Community College, a portion of this rail trail runs through a nicely landscaped greenbelt featuring small playgrounds and benches; another portion is separated from busy I-80 by little more than a hedge of flowering oleander; the northeastern-most section, which connects the mall to Dover Avenue, is used mostly as an off-street route into town. The trail epitomizes how diverse a rail trail in an urban setting can be, and how a city can integrate a former rail line like this one into the fabric of its recreational and transportation options.

Activities:

Start: Solano Mall

Distance: 4 miles one way

Difficulty: Easy

Seasons/schedule: Year-round, sunrise to sunset

Fees and permits: None

Trail surface and conditions: Well-maintained asphalt and concrete

Accessibility: The trail is fully accessible to people using wheelchairs

Canine compatibility: Leashed dogs permitted

Amenities: You can find just about anything in the Solano Mall at the trail's east end, from water to food to shoes. Other restaurants are available throughout Fairfield. Portable toilets are available at the ballfields on the Solano Community College campus at the trail's western terminus. There's plenty of parking at the Solano Mall, but only a small dirt lot at the west end point and no parking at the Dover Avenue trailhead.

The Many Bonus Tracks of the Valley

Pulling together a guide to the "best" rail trails has meant whittling out the functional but critically important "almost best." For better or worse, urban rail trails that didn't make the cut based on my subjective criteria are often the best rail trails for other folks based on equally valid criteria. They may not have the scenic punch of the Bizz Johnson or the MacKerricher Haul Road, but they do something utilitarian and essential that those paths can't: They link people to the places they need to go to, and enable them to get there under their own power.

Think about it. Getting from point A to point B anywhere in California without a car, even in urban environments, is next to impossible. Just getting to public transit can involve a motor and the greenhouse gasses those motors emit.

There's also the fact that every rail trail offers green space—or the promise of green space—and exercise, no matter how fast you walk or ride. Well-being springs from green space and exercise; well-being springs from rail trails. Walk to school. Bike to work. Skate to the park. Stretch your legs. Breathe fresh air. Say hi to your neighbor, or a fellow jogger, or the dog and her human. Add nothing to the air around you but what you exhale.

Urban and suburban neighborhoods in Sacramento and other Central Valley cities harbor a number of rail trails that, were this a comprehensive guide rather than a "best of," would have made the cut. I'm giving them brief mention here hoping they'll spark curiosity, because there might be a rail trail near where you work or go to school, and if there's not, there might be an abandoned track that could be transformed.

- The Clarksburg Branch Line Trail, built on an abandoned Sierra Northern Railroad right-of-way, is one of five designated segments of the planned Great California Delta Trail. Described by one writer as a good choice for people who want to get out into nature without getting too far out into nature, the gravel and paved trail, 3 miles one way, is located in West Sacramento, with trailheads at the junction of Locks Drive and Jefferson Boulevard in the north and at the South River Road River access in the south.

- The Folsom Parkway Rail Trail connects downtown Folsom with the Lake Natoma Trail on the American River. The 3-mile-long (one way) paved route, which parallels Folsom Boulevard and an active rail line, features areas of greenbelt as well as access to light rail stations, office parks, and an outlet mall. You can hop onto the route at any of the light-rail stations or at the historic Folsom Station parking area at the north end, where you can link up with the fabulous American River/Jedediah Smith Memorial Trail.

- The Manteca Tidewater Bikeway runs through the city of Manteca from north to south, offering connections to parks, places of work, and residential neighborhoods. Built on the former bed of the Tidewater Railway, the route is paved, about 3.5 miles long, and parallels an active rail line as it nears its southern end point at the intersection of Moffat Boulevard and Spreckels Avenue. The northern end point is on West Lathrop Road, with good parking and easy access from nearby Northgate Park.

- The Virginia Corridor Trailway serves the citizens of Modesto, connecting neighborhoods to schools, businesses, workplaces, and more. The paved route is 4.2 miles long and rides atop the right-of-way of the former Tidewater Southern Railway. For much of its length, it is buffered by mature landscaping or a generous greenbelt, and offers access to shelters, picnic facilities, and small gardens. The trail runs from near the Modesto Junior College Campus northeast to Lions Park junction, where it turns straight north. At Woodrow Avenue the pavement ends, but the trail, now gravel and unimproved, continues to Bang Avenue.

- The Southside Bikeway in Vacaville is only 1.2 miles long, but it still provides everything a suburban rail trail should: connections amid a dollop of countryside. Built on a stretch of abandoned Sacramento Northern Railway corridor, the paved path is buffered by greenbelt and runs from Al Patch Park to all the amenities of Vacaville near I-80. The best place to start is at the south end at Al Patch Park, located on California Drive; you'll find plenty of parking around the ballfields here.

The Rails-to-Trails Conservancy's TrailLink app is a good source for more information on these and other rail trails throughout California and beyond. You can also contact your local parks department to find out more.

Trail contact: City of Fairfield Public Works Dept., 1000 Webster St., Fairfield; (707) 428-7485; www.fairfield.ca.gov/government/city-departments/public-works

Nearest town: Fairfield

Maps: The best trail map is on the TrailLink website at www.traillink.com/trail-maps/fairfield-linear-park.

Cell service: Good

Transportation: Fairfield Transit (FAST), (707) 422-2877; https://fasttransit.org

Finding the trailhead: To reach the southwestern end point from I-80, take the Abernathy Road exit. Go north on Abernathy Road for 0.5 mile to Rockville Road. Turn left (west) on Rockville Road and go 1.7 miles to Suisun Valley Road. Turn left (south) on Suisun Valley Road and go 0.3 mile to Solano Community College. Circle the college to the southeast section; the trail begins between the soccer field and the baseball diamond.

To reach the Solano Mall end point from I-80 in Fairfield, take the Travis Boulevard exit. Follow Travis Boulevard east to Solano Mall and park in the mall parking lots fronting Travis Boulevard. The trailhead is opposite the mall, on the south side of Travis Boulevard between 2nd Street and Pennsylvania Avenue.

Trailhead GPS: Solano Mall end point: N38 15.479 / W122 03.132; Solano Community College end point: N38 14.003 / W122 07.137

The Fairfield Linear Park path is one of many utilitarian rail trails in the region.

SAN FRANCISCO BAY AREA

13 FOSS CREEK PATHWAY

The 71-mile SMART Pathway will be a work in progress for years to come, but the Foss Creek Pathway in Healdsburg offers a good sampling of what's in place and what's in store.

Activities:

Start: Healdsburg Parking Lot A

Distance: 1.8 miles one way

Difficulty: Easy

Seasons/schedule: Year-round, sunrise to sunset

Fees and permits: None

Trail surface and conditions: Well-maintained pavement

Accessibility: The trail is accessible to people using wheelchairs.

Canine compatibility: Leashed dogs permitted

Amenities: Other than parking, no public amenities are available at the downtown Healdsburg end point, but restaurants, groceries, and splendid shopping are available throughout the downtown area. Abundant parking, restrooms, and water are available at the Healdsburg Community Center end point.

Trail contact: City of Healdsburg Planning and Building Dept., 401 Grove St., Healdsburg; (707) 431-3348; www.ci.healdsburg.ca.us/370/Foss-Creek -Pathway-Plan

Nearest town: Healdsburg

Maps: An interactive map is available at https://sonomamarintrain.org/ smart_pathway

Cell service: Good

Transportation: Sonoma County Transit, (707) 585-7516; https://sctransit .com. Healdsburg Shuttle offers in-town service: www.ci.healdsburg.ca.us/ 871/Public-Buses.

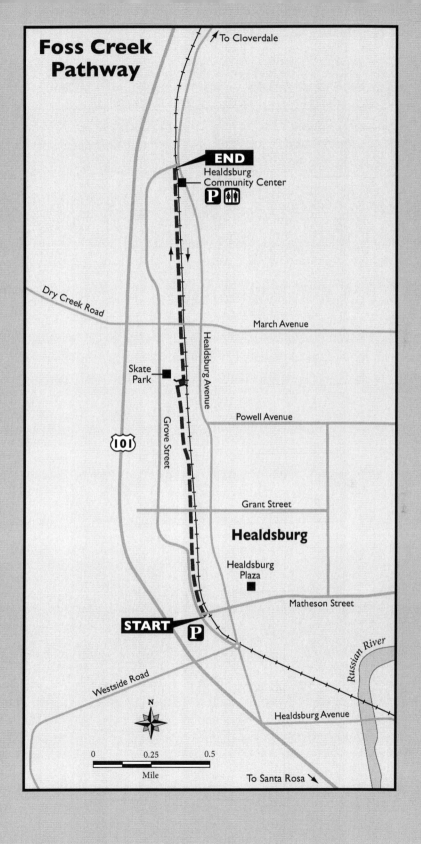

Finding the trailhead: From US 101, take the downtown Healdsburg exit. At the roundabout take the Vine Street exit and continue for about 0.1 mile (a long city block) to Lot A on the right. You can access the trail from the lot, or backtrack to the roundabout—or even to the Russian River, if you want to tag the whole thing.

Trailhead GPS: N38 36.639 / W122 52.336

The Main Line

||||||||||||||||||||||||||||||||||||||||||||||||||||||||||||||||||||||||||||||||||||||||||||||||||||||||||||||||||||||||||||||||||||||||||||||||||||||||

Healdsburg is a beloved Wine Country destination, offering easy access to wineries in the Dry Creek Valley, Alexander Valley, and Russian River Valley, and a historic plaza lined with swanky restaurants, galleries, and boutiques. It'll also one day be home to a Sonoma-Marin Area Rail Transit (SMART) station, and already boasts a section of rail trail that's part of the SMART Pathway.

This section of the Foss Creek Pathway begins a couple of blocks west of the plaza in a narrow greenbelt tucked between Grove Street and the

Public art lines the Foss Creek Pathway in Healdsburg.

now-unused rail line. The corridor was part of the historic Northwestern Pacific Railroad before acquisition by SMART, and the rail right-of-way extends to the Mendocino County line and beyond. The setting is decidedly urban at the outset, but the trail is lighted, shady, well landscaped, and features interesting public art displays.

At 0.3 mile the pathway crosses Foss Creek and breaks from the roadway, with the defunct rails running alongside on the right and an industrial district on the left. Cross Grant Street at 0.5 mile, and the greenbelt widens. The rail trail begins a gentle climb to a catch basin for flood control and rides on the raised bed alongside to a junction at the 1-mile mark. Go right, across the bridge that spans the creek, to continue on the Pathway; the bridge ahead and to the left leads to the Carson Warner Memorial Skate Park. Continue to the Dry Creek Road crossing at 1.2 miles.

Cross the tracks on the far side of Dry Creek Road and continue with the future SMART rail on your left. The pathway is more exposed and a little wilder as it shoots straight northward; though still lighted, you've left public art and formal landscaping behind. At 1.6 miles the shade returns in the form of redwoods bordering the ballfields at the Healdsburg Community Center. The end of the line as of September 2023 is at the 1.8-mile mark at the junction of Grove Street and Healdsburg Avenue.

The Foss Creek Pathway is part of what planners envision as a 70-mile-long rail trail stretching from Cloverdale in Sonoma County to Larkspur in Marin County—and beyond.

The Great Redwood Trail

The Great Redwood Trail Agency has a dream that's already starting to take shape in the SMART Pathway, the Humboldt Bay Trail, and other North State rail trails but still has a long way to go—250 miles, that is, give or take.

If the vision becomes reality, the Great Redwood Trail will stretch 316 miles through some of Northern California's most scenic wildlands, combining the SMART Pathway in Marin and Sonoma Counties with the North Coast Railroad Authority's rail corridor through Mendocino, Trinity, and Humboldt Counties. The intent

The Foss Creek Pathway in Healdsburg is one link in a rail trail that, if all goes as planned, will stretch from Marin County to Humboldt County.

is to connect San Francisco Bay to Humboldt Bay via a long-distance route that will satisfy any hiker, backpacker, or cyclist with a hankering for long-distance adventuring.

According to the agency website, when completed, "the legacy trail will travel through some of the wildest and most scenic landscapes in the United States, traversing old-growth redwood forests, running alongside oak woodlands and vineyards, and winding through the magnificent Eel River Canyon." It will also serve as an "economic engine" fueling tourism in the North State.

There are, of course, challenges ahead, not the least of which is raising enough money to convert the rail corridor into either a trail corridor or a rail-with-trail corridor. That said, the effort has the backing of California legislators, the Coastal Conservancy, representatives from counties and jurisdictions along the way, and others. You can read all about it, offer your comments, and follow the planning process by visiting https://thegreat redwoodtrail.org.

Return as you came. And stay tuned: Plans call for the Foss Creek segment of the SMART Pathway to extend a total of 4.1 miles, from the northern border in Healdsburg south to the city of Windsor.

BONUS TRACK: THE SMART PATHWAY

When completed, the SMART Pathway will mirror the SMART railway for more than 70 miles, enabling commuters to ride the rails from city to city between the northernmost station in Cloverdale, Sonoma County, and the southernmost station in Larkspur, Marin County, as well as travel the trails between stations or from stations to their homes or businesses. As of summer 2023, nearly 30 miles of Pathway were complete, but in discontinuous segments scattered up and down the Sonoma-Marin Area Rail Transit (SMART) line.

The Foss Creek Pathway is among the most scenic of the segments in place thus far; most of the Pathway is urban and utilitarian, offering views when possible and sheltered by whatever greenery grows or has been planted in the corridors. Much of the Pathway consists of (or will consist of) Class I routes, or dedicated bike lanes/trails in the rail corridor but separate from motorways. The Pathway will also offer links to regional scenic trails, as well as both on-street and off-street commuter routes.

Dedicated Pathway segments presently connect two downtown Santa Rosa SMART stations and continue south into Roseland; another segment connects the Rohnert Park and Cotati SMART stations; short, discontinuous segments are available in Petaluma and Novato; and a generous length of Class I trail links the Marin Civic Center SMART Station with the station in downtown San Rafael, and then with the last station at Larkspur Landing, where commuters can board the ferry to San Francisco.

The Cal Park Hill Tunnel is a highlight along the southern section of the trail, funneling cyclists and walkers through a bore in the hillside separating San Rafael from Larkspur. The TrailLink website describes how the tunnel, which dates back to the late nineteenth century, had collapsed at both ends by the 1980s, before the right-of-way was acquired for use by SMART. To make it safe for both the passenger trains and Pathway users, the original timbers were replaced with steel arches and reinforced with "shotcrete"—concrete fired at the walls with such force that it sets hard and fast.

The downloadable SMART Pathway map highlights the sections in place, in progress, and in planning (https://sonomamarintrain.org/smart_pathway).

14 JOE RODOTA AND WEST COUNTY REGIONAL TRAILS

Springtime green and summertime gold highlight the oak woodlands that border sections of the linked West County Trail and Joe Rodota Trail, which connects downtown Santa Rosa to the rural community of Forestville.

Activities:

Start: Railroad Square in Santa Rosa

Distance: 13 miles one way

Difficulty: Strenuous due to length

Seasons/schedule: Year-round, sunrise to sunset

Fees and permits: None

Trail surface and conditions: Asphalt; the trail is well maintained. People experiencing homelessness may establish camps near the trail.

Accessibility: The trail is accessible to people using wheelchairs.

Canine compatibility: Leashed dogs permitted

Amenities: No public restrooms are available along the trail proper. Water, restaurants, grocery stores, and just about anything else you might need, including restrooms, are available in Railroad Square, Sebastopol, and Forestville.

Trail contact: Sonoma County Regional Parks Department, 2300 County Center Dr., Suite A120, Santa Rosa; (707) 565-2041; https://parks.sonoma county.ca.gov/visit/find-a-park/joe-rodota-trail; https://parks.sonomacounty .ca.gov/visit/find-a-park/west-county-regional-trail

Nearest towns: Santa Rosa, Sebastopol, Graton, Forestville

Maps: A map is available for download at https://parks.sonomacounty.ca .gov/visit/find-a-park/west-county-regional-trail.

Cell service: Mostly good; a sure thing as you pass through towns along the way

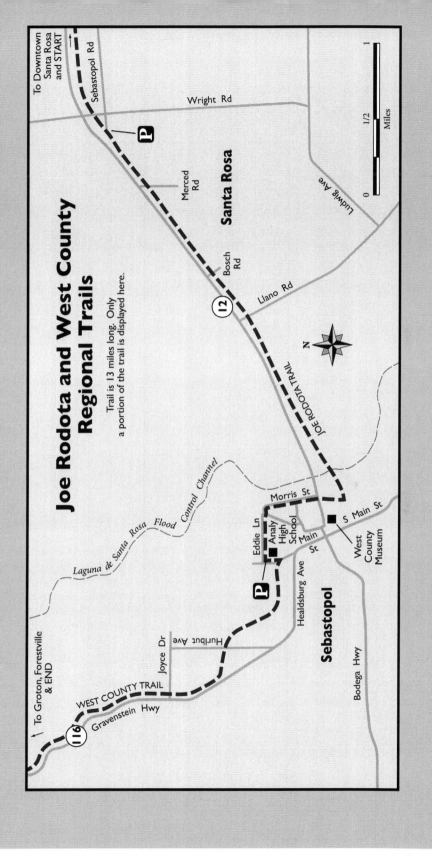

Joe Rodota and West County Regional Trails

Trail is 13 miles long. Only a portion of the trail is displayed here.

To Downtown Santa Rosa and START

Sebastopol Rd

Wright Rd

P

Merced Rd

Santa Rosa

Bosch Rd

Ludwig Ave

Llano Rd

12

N

JOE RODOTA TRAIL

Laguna de Santa Rosa Flood Control Channel

Morris St

Eddie Ln

Analy High School

Main St

S Main St

West County Museum

P

Healdsburg Ave

Sebastopol

To Groton, Forestville & END

Hurlbut Ave

Joyce Dr

WEST COUNTY TRAIL

Gravenstein Hwy

116

Bodega Hwy

0   1/2   1

Miles

Transportation: Sonoma County Transit, (707) 576-7433; https://sctransit.com

Finding the trailhead: There's plenty of street parking at the trail's end point in Railroad Square; the trail's end point is on West 3rd Street just west of the railroad tracks on the banks of Santa Rosa Creek. A small, unimproved parking lot is available at the Sebastopol Road trailhead, located off CA 12 on the western edge of Santa Rosa, near the Wright Road stoplight. Turn left (south) on Wright Road and go 0.2 mile to Sebastopol Road. Turn right (west) on Sebastopol Road for 0.2 mile to the road's end in the trail's parking area.

In Sebastopol proper, trailhead parking is along the road fronting Analy High School. To reach this trailhead, follow CA 12 to its intersection with CA 116 in Sebastopol. Turn right (north) on CA 116, and proceed to its intersection with North Main Street. Go 0.1 mile north on North Main Street to the trailhead, which is on the left (west) side of the road opposite the high school.

A small trailhead parking lot is in Graton, at the junction of Graton Road and Bowen Street/Ross Road, and there's a small parking lot at the Forestville end point on Ross Station Road.

Trailhead GPS: Railroad Square in Santa Rosa: N38 26.106 / W122 43.293; Sebastopol trailhead: N38 24.396 / W122 49.628; Forestville trailhead: N38 27.513 / W122 53.155

The Main Line

Sonoma County is synonymous with Wine Country, but this trail passes through a landscape that harkens back to the county's orchard and ranching roots, and even further back than that. For a couple of miles, the route is adjacent to expanses of oak woodland and grassland, with nary a vineyard or orchard in sight, and probably comes as close to what the regional indigenous tribes—the Coast Miwok, Wappo, and Pomo peoples—cultivated prior to European invasion.

That said, the remnant pastoral terrain surrounding the trail is under enormous threat of development of homes and businesses and by the

Signage keep users on track as the West County Trail passes through rural Graton and Forestville.

vineyards that have supplanted dairies and apple orchards as the mainstay of Sonoma County agriculture.

The trail follows the bed of the Petaluma and Santa Rosa Railroad, an electric line that carried passengers between Santa Rosa and Forestville. The first part of the trail, from downtown Santa Rosa to Petaluma Avenue in Sebastopol, is named for Joe Rodota, the first director of the Sonoma County Regional Parks Department.

The route can be done as a single one-way (or out-and-back, for the hardy cyclist) excursion or separated into sections. The first section, from Santa Rosa to downtown Sebastopol, is utilitarian, both for people walking or cycling to work or local businesses, or for skaters and cyclists looking for a workout. The section that heads west out of Sebastopol, and especially once west of the little town of Graton and heading into Forestville, is more rural, lending itself nicely to hiking and walking.

The trail begins in busy downtown Santa Rosa, just south of the Railroad Square shopping district, where it links to the Santa Rosa Creek Trail. Parking here will cost you a small fee. The route crosses to the south side of CA 12, then heads west, with the freeway and busy roads constant companions. The setting is distinctly urban/industrial, bursting with strip malls. Cross Dutton Avenue at about 0.3 mile, then Stony Point Road at about 1.2 miles. *Note:* The stretch of the Joe Rodota Trail west of Stony Point Road has repeatedly been the site of encampments set up by people experiencing homelessness, and on occasion those camps may impede or preclude recreational use.

Continue for about 1.5 miles to the trailhead parking area at Sebastopol and Wright Roads, where the route changes temperament, taking on a more pastoral demeanor. Continuing west, the path parallels the highway and is shaded by oaks and eucalyptus. Less than a half mile farther, the trail crosses Merced Avenue; beyond, the trail is separated from the road by oak trees and shoulder-high cow parsnip, and the land to the south is open pastureland dotted with the occasional oak. Blackberry brambles border the path; look for the tasty berries in late summer and early fall.

Cross Bosch Road at 3.7 miles and Llano Road at 4 miles. The trail begins a slow arc to the south, away from the highway, until distance and a buffer of earth and trees muffle the road noise. At 6.2 miles cross a small bridge; at 6.5 miles a larger bridge spans the Laguna de Santa Rosa Flood Control Channel.

Homes border the trail as you near Sebastopol, the western terminus of this trail section, which ends on CA 116 in town, opposite the West County Museum and an old railroad car on a disembodied section of track.

To reach the second section of the path, follow bike lanes along Sebastopol's city streets. A paved path that breaks right before the CA 116 end point connects the Rodota Trail to Morris Street. Head north along Morris Street for almost 0.4 mile to Eddie Lane; stay on Eddie Lane for 0.3 mile, passing the ballfields of Analy High School, to High School Road. The trail resumes about 0.1 mile south (left) of the Eddie Lane outlet.

The next section of trail heads west from Analy via a tree-shrouded corridor between lovely homes. The summer scents of blackberry, eucalyptus, and ripening apples alternate as you cross two quiet residential streets. About 0.5 mile from the Analy trailhead, the rail trail crosses East Hurlbut Avenue and passes the Sebastopol Charter School. This section ends at CA 116 after about 1 mile.

CA 116 marks the end of what most locals know as the Joe Rodota Trail; from here on out to Forestville, it's the West County Trail. Follow the paved path north along the east side of CA 116, also known as the Gravenstein Highway, for about 0.9 mile to Occidental Road. The trail leaves the railroad grade at this point, bearing left (west) along the shoulder of Occidental Road for nearly 0.9 mile. Turn right (north) on the signed paved

Autumn colors paint the West County Trail near Graton in rural Sonoma County.

Walkers, cyclists, and equestrians frequent the West County Trail, which links to the Joe Rodota Trail in Sebastopol and rolls through vineyards and orchards to Forestville.

path at the gate, heading north into the vineyards. You have traveled about 9 miles from Santa Rosa at this point.

As the trail nears the little town of Graton, at about 9.7 miles, it parallels a shady street called Railroad. Turn right on Grey Street, then hook quickly left onto Bowen Street and follow it for 0.2 mile to Graton Road. Cross the main thoroughfare through town and go a bit left (west) of the fire station; you'll find a parking lot with restrooms behind the station at the Graton trailhead.

The path rejoins the railroad grade north of Graton Road, tracing rural Ross Road for 0.7 mile north to a junction at Green Valley Road. Travel west (left) along the shoulder of Green Valley Road for about 0.3 mile to where the route picks up again, heading north. The path crosses boardwalks and unpaved sections as it passes through the Atascadero Creek Marsh Ecological Reserve.

The next major street crossing, at Ross Station Road, is 1 mile north of Green Valley Road. Travel east on Ross Station Road a short distance; the trail continues from here. It's not quite another mile north to the trail's end near Forestville. By the time you reach this end point, you will have traveled about 13 miles. Unless you've made other arrangements, return as you came.

15 SONOMA CITY TRAIL

This rail trail presents a pleasant walk through the city of Sonoma, a celebrated Wine Country destination. The popular path passes several historic sites, including the home of General Mariano Vallejo, Mission San Francisco Solano (Sonoma Mission), and the Depot Park Museum, where you can peruse exhibits focused on both railroad and other aspects of local history.

Activities:

Start: Trailhead on Lovall Valley Road

Distance: 3 miles round-trip

Difficulty: Easy

Seasons/schedule: Year-round, sunrise to sunset

Fees and permits: None

Trail surface and conditions: Well-maintained pavement

Accessibility: The entire trail is accessible to people using wheelchairs.

Canine compatibility: Leashed dogs permitted

Amenities: The trail is located only blocks from Sonoma Plaza, where fine dining establishments abound. A grocery store is located within easy walking distance of the trail's end at Maxwell Farms Regional Park; restrooms and picnic facilities are available there too. There are picnic tables at the park. Restrooms are also available at Depot Park, near the midpoint of the trail, and on the Plaza.

Trail contact: City of Sonoma, No. 1, The Plaza, Sonoma; (707) 938-3681; www.sonomacity.org

Nearest towns: Sonoma, El Verano

Maps: A downloadable map of City of Sonoma bike trails is available at www.sonomacity.org/documents/sonoma-bicycle-map.

Cell service: Good

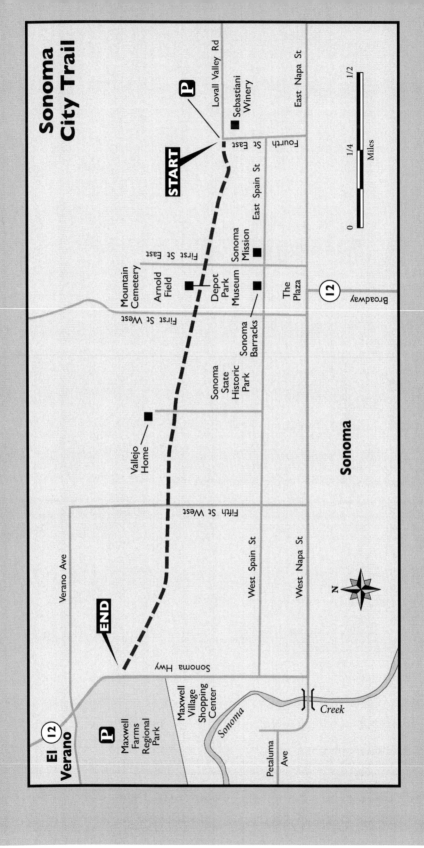

Sonoma City Trail

START

END

Lovall Valley Rd

■ Sebastiani Winery

Fourth St East

East Napa St

East Spain St

First St East

Sonoma Mission ■

Mountain Cemetery

Arnold Field ■

Depot Park Museum ■

First St West

The Plaza

■ Sonoma Barracks

12

Broadway

Sonoma State Historic Park

Sonoma

Vallejo Home ■

Fifth St West

West Spain St

West Napa St

N

Verano Ave

El Verano 12

P

Maxwell Farms Regional Park

Maxwell Village Shopping Center

Sonoma Hwy

Sonoma Creek

Petaluma Ave

0   1/4   1/2

Miles

Transportation: Sonoma County Transit, (707) 576-7433; https://sctransit .com

Finding the trailhead: To reach the eastern end point from Sonoma Plaza at the intersection of CA 12 and Napa Street, go right (east) on Napa Street for less than 0.5 mile to 4th Street East. Turn left (north) and follow 4th Street East for about 0.5 mile to Lovall Valley Road. There is limited parking along the street. You also may find parking in the lot for the Sebastiani Winery.

To reach the western end point from CA 12 at Sonoma Plaza, follow Napa Street/CA 12 west to where CA 12 veers north near Petaluma Avenue (follow the signs). Follow CA 12 about 1 mile to Verano Avenue, and turn left (west). The entrance to Maxwell Farms Regional Park is on the left (south) side of Verano Avenue. Abundant parking is available at Maxwell Farms; a parking fee is levied.

Trailhead GPS: Lovall Valley Road trailhead: N38 17.678 / W122 26.963; Maxwell Farms Regional Park: N38 18.043 / W122 28.486

The Main Line

|||||||||||||||||||||||||||||||||||||||||||||||||||||||||||||||||||||||||||||||||||||||||||||||||||||||||||||||||

Aah, the Wine Country. Bunches of fragrant grapes, deep red and gold-green, ripen on orderly vines. The smells of gourmet delicacies waft from restaurants with doors flung open to the warm summer breezes. Hills shaded by stately oaks roll up to a sky painted a perfect California blue. The Sonoma City Trail captures all this in a neat package.

The paved rail trail begins adjacent to a vineyard, passes through quaint Depot Park, where the old depot serves as a historical museum, then rolls through the former estate of Spanish landowner General Mariano Vallejo, now part of the Sonoma State Historic Park. Wander south from the midpoint of the trail down a quiet neighborhood street and you'll find yourself on the Plaza, where you can shop, eat, take in a bit of California history at the Sonoma Barracks or Mission San Francisco Solano (Sonoma Mission), then relax and unwind in the Plaza's rose garden.

The Sonoma Valley Railroad Company, organized in 1879, operated passenger and freight trains that ran on what was initially a narrow-gauge

The Sonoma City Trail rolls through grasslands surrounding the historic home of General Mariano Vallejo, who founded the city, served as governor of what was then called Alta California, and was unseated in the Bear Flag Revolt.

line through the valley. The line ran from Vineburg to Sonoma Plaza and was later extended north to Glen Ellen. After the track was changed to standard gauge, the SVRR became part of the Northwestern Pacific Railroad complex, which in turn was purchased by Southern Pacific.

The railroad began its decline in the early 1940s, when passenger service north to Kenwood was discontinued and the tracks torn up. Trains stopped running on the main line by 1960. Historical information about the Sonoma Valley Railroad and other regional rail lines can be explored at the Depot Park Museum.

The trail begins opposite the Sebastiani Winery at the intersection of 4th Street East and Lovall Valley Road. The path passes grapevines, then a community garden, as it rolls toward the center of town. At 1st Street East you enter Depot Park; here you'll find picnic sites and ballfields busy with baseball games in spring and soccer games in autumn. The Depot Park Museum, complete with a Southern Pacific Railroad car on a salvaged strip of track, is the park's centerpiece. The museum is open Saturday and Sunday from 1 to 4 p.m.; learn more at https://sonoma valleyhistory.org. First Street East also offers great access to the Plaza.

The historic Sonoma Depot serves as home to the Depot Park Museum.

At about the half-mile mark, cross 1st Street West, pass the Depot Hotel and more ballfields, then enter the near-pristine meadow serving as a buffer to the Vallejo Home. Called Lachryma Montis, Latin for "mountain tear," it's difficult to imagine being sad amid all the beauty surrounding the place.

After crossing the historic site's paved driveway, the trail enters a residential area. Cross the busiest street intersection at 5th Street West at about 1 mile; beyond, the trail passes petite Olsen Park and becomes distinctly residential in nature. A series of street intersections follows. Most are quiet neighborhood drives, but cross with care.

Beyond the intersection with Robinson Road, the trail splits. Stay right (north) on the bike path. At the 1.5-mile mark, reach CA 12. The trail ends here, but Maxwell Farms Regional Park, with a series of paved paths, frontage on Sonoma Creek, a playground, ballfields, a skate park, and other amenities, is just across the street from trail's end. This is a busy crossing: It's best and safest to head south along the sidewalk to the signal and crosswalk at Maxwell Village Shopping Center, then backtrack north to the park. Return as you came.

16 VALLEY OF THE MOON TRAIL

The rail trail linking Sonoma Valley Regional Park to the historic campus of the former Sonoma Developmental Center rests on the abandoned bed of the Sonoma Valley Railroad Company line that once ran the length of the Valley of the Moon.

Activities:

Start: Valley of the Moon Trailhead in Sonoma Valley Regional Park

Distance: 4 miles out and back

Difficulty: Easy

Seasons/schedule: Year-round, sunrise to sunset

Fees and permits: A parking fee is charged.

Trail surface and conditions: Pavement and dirt/gravel. The unpaved portion may be sticky muddy in winter after rainstorms.

Accessibility: The paved Valley of the Moon Trail section of the route is accessible to people using wheelchairs.

Canine compatibility: Leashed dogs permitted

Amenities: Restrooms, water, and picnic tables are available at the main entrance to Sonoma Valley Regional Park; more picnic tables are located along the Valley of the Moon Trail. There's also a fenced dog park. Nearby Glen Ellen is famous for the saturation of fine restaurants and specialty grocery stores in its tiny "downtown."

Trail contact: Sonoma County Regional Parks Department, 2300 County Center Dr., Suite A120, Santa Rosa; (707) 565-2041; https://parks.sonoma-county.ca.gov/visit/find-a-park/sonoma-valley-regional-park

Nearest town: Glen Ellen

Maps: A downloadable park map is available at https://parks.sonoma-county.ca.gov/visit/find-a-park/sonoma-valley-regional-park.

Cell service: Good

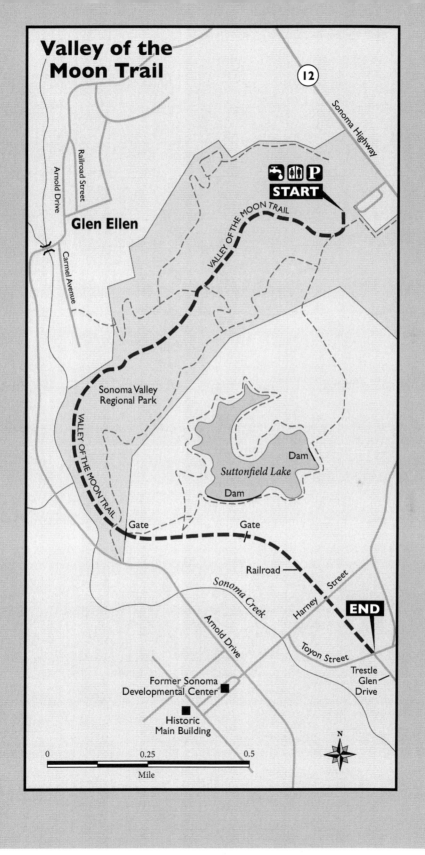

Valley of the Moon Trail

12

Sonoma Highway

START

VALLEY OF THE MOON TRAIL

Arnold Drive

Railroad Street

Carmel Avenue

Glen Ellen

Sonoma Valley
Regional Park

VALLEY OF THE MOON TRAIL

Dam

Suttonfield Lake

Dam

Gate

Gate

Railroad

Street

Harney

END

Sonoma Creek

Arnold Drive

Toyon Street

Trestle
Glen
Drive

Former Sonoma
Developmental Center

Historic
Main Building

N

0   0.25   0.5

Mile

Transportation: Sonoma County Transit, (707) 576-7433; www.sctransit
.com

Finding the trailhead: From Sonoma Plaza, head west on West Napa
Street/CA 12 for about 1 mile. Keep right at the stoplight at the junction with Petaluma Avenue to stay on CA 12 toward Boyes Hot Springs
and Santa Rosa, and continue 5.5 miles to the entrance of Sonoma Valley
Regional Park in Glen Ellen.

Trailhead GPS: N38 21.858 / W122 30.736

The Main Line

In 1891 the first residents of what was then called the California Home for
the Care and Training of Feeble-Minded Children disembarked at the Santa
Rosa & Carquinez Railway's depot in tiny Eldridge, just south of the village

*The railroad grade–turned–Valley of the Moon Trail runs through Sonoma Valley Re-
gional Park.*

The railroad grade that runs through Sonoma Valley Regional Park leaves the pavement as a dirt spur leading into Glen Ellen.

of Glen Ellen. Their new home was in the green heart of what author Jack London would call the Valley of the Moon, at the foot of Sonoma Mountain on the west and the Mayacamas range on the east.

A lot has changed since those children arrived more than a century ago, but a few things remain. The home is now known as the Sonoma

Rail Trails and Wildfire

Fortunately, rail trails in Northern California have weathered wildfire relatively well. They are durable, whether paved or gravel or ballast, and often traverse urbanized landscapes, giving them some protection from the ravages of the mega-fires that have transformed wildlands throughout the American West.

That said, rail trails in Northern California have been burned over in spectacular ways. Witness the Sacramento River Rail Trail, which passes through the 2018 Carr Fire scar. Down in Redding, that fire generated a fire whirl—a tornado of flame—that incinerated a neighborhood and took a handful of lives. Witness the Paradise Memorial Trailway, deep inside the Camp Fire burn. That infamous blaze incinerated most of an entire city and took scores of lives in the process. Witness the Bizz Johnson National Recreation Trail and the nearby Almanor Rail Trail, clipped by the 2021 Dixie Fire that destroyed Greenville, torched much of Lassen

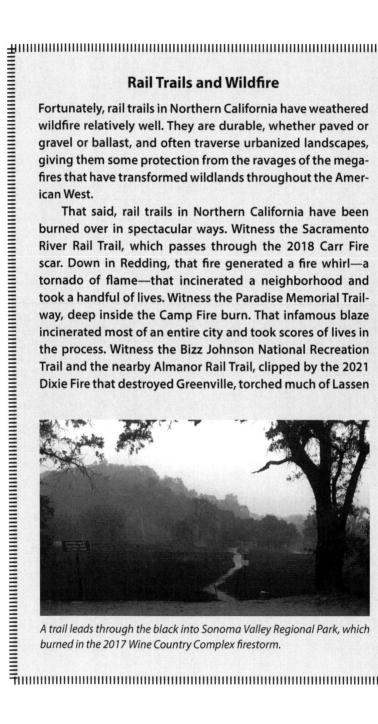

A trail leads through the black into Sonoma Valley Regional Park, which burned in the 2017 Wine Country Complex firestorm.

Volcanic National Park, and left the woodlands surrounding Chester a wasteland, at least temporarily.

And finally, witness Sonoma Valley Regional Park's Valley of the Moon Trail. The entire park burned in the 2017 Wine Country firestorm, which destroyed thousands of homes and killed dozens of people. This last rail trail runs through my hometown. I know personally the toll wildfire takes on a community and its recreational anchors.

But trails, like the communities they serve, are resilient. The word may be overused, but resilience best describes what comes after the fire in both natural and human communities. For me, a survivor, the elements of resilience—renewal, recovery, rediscovery—seem as natural as wildfire. Whether plants whorling up from ashes or people rebuilding their homes, resilience is real; resilience is hopeful.

Perhaps I embrace resilience because I've experienced it so intimately. From day one, even as I watched fire sweep across the regional park, I knew the park would endure. The trees, the grasses, the animals, the trails . . . this wasn't an end. It was a remaking. Whether humans like what it looks like or not, after the fire, nature carries on. And so do we.

All that said, communities recovering from wildfire, whether large cities like Redding or small towns like Chester, need people to visit, and to walk and ride their rail trails. They need the tourism, the investment, and the caring to survive. Heading out on these fire-scarred trails also offers a chance for hikers and riders to give back as they use the routes. Everything helps—purchasing your trail snack at the local market; having your bike repaired by the local shop; simply appreciating the community (natural and human) that brought you to the trail you enjoy and saying thank you for carrying on.

Developmental Center, and its grand redbrick main building still stands. You can see it from the abandoned rail corridor, which survives as a roadway and trail that runs through the abandoned campus and the adjoining regional park.

Just as the Santa Rosa & Carquinez line became the Sonoma Valley Railroad, and then the Southern Pacific, the home became known as the Sonoma State Home and finally what the locals call the SDC. The rail corridor marks the eastern edge of the campus, which is slated for redevelopment; the rolling hills and wetlands between the campus and CA 12 became state parkland in January 2024. Walking the rail line is literally walking the wildland-urban interface. It's also building constituency for right-sized redevelopment that does no harm to the surrounding parkland and the wildlife corridor that runs through it, but rather enhances it.

The route described here begins off the rails, so to speak. The paved Valley of the Moon Trail starts near the highway and winds down through the oak-shaded hollow cradling the seasonal Black Canyon Creek. Side trails are tempting diversions, but it's easy to stay on track—just stick to the pavement.

As the Valley of the Moon Trail leaves the canyon and arcs southward at about the 0.8-mile mark, it climbs aboard the abandoned rail line. Sonoma Creek, which flows year-round, parallels the route for the next 0.3 mile but is mostly out of sight, shrouded by the canopy of oak, buckeye, and bay.

At the trail junction at the 1.2-mile mark, the paved trail goes right over the rise, and the Woodland Star Trail breaks left, climbing onto the ridge. The railroad grade, now unpaved, continues straight. A gate marks the SDC boundary. You can walk around it if it's closed.

The trail is a straight shot through the meadow that opens below the dam of Suttonfield Lake—another tempting diversion. The unpaved service road that leads to the top of the dam crosses the railbed at the 1.3-mile mark. Beyond, the dirt track is bowered by oaks until it drops onto paved Railroad Street at another gate.

Now on the SDC campus proper, you can walk down Railroad to the junction with Harney; look west to see the brick Main Building. Railroad becomes Trestle Glen at the junction with Toyon at the southern boundary of the campus. This is the turnaround point. Return as you came.

BONUS TRACK: NAPA VALLEY VINE TRAIL

When completed, the Napa Valley Vine Trail, a rail with trail, will be 47 miles long, connecting American Canyon in the south, where the Napa River opens into San Pablo Bay, to trendy Calistoga and St. Helena in the north. A 12.5-mile-long paved section is currently in place, starting in Kennedy Park alongside the river in the south and then hitching up alongside the Napa Valley Wine Train line to travel through downtown Napa and then out into the vineyards.

Busy CA 29 also runs alongside, so the path never feels secluded, but the views up onto the vineyard-covered slopes of the Vaca and Mayacamas ranges are stunning, especially in autumn. As you might expect, the trail offers access to an abundance of wineries and fine dining establishments. The northernmost end point as of summer 2023 was in Yountville, where you'll find parking, restrooms, and a bus stop in the event you opt out of an out-and-back journey.

Activities:

Start: Kennedy Park

Distance: 12.5 miles one way

Difficulty: Strenuous given the distance

Seasons/schedule: Year-round, sunrise to sunset

Fees and permits: None

Trail surface and conditions: Pavement. The path shares the rail and highway corridor, so there is no shade.

Accessibility: The entire trail is accessible to people using wheelchairs.

Canine compatibility: Leashed dogs permitted

Amenities: Restrooms, parking, and other facilities are available at both end points. You can also find anything you might desire—water, groceries, a fine pinot noir—in downtown Napa as you pass through, as well as at restaurants and wineries along the trail.

Trail contact: Napa Valley Vine Trail, 3299 Claremont Way, Suite 5, Napa; (707) 252-3547; www.vinetrail.org

Nearest towns: Napa, Yountville

Maps: Detailed downloadable maps are available online at www.vinetrail .org/pub/htdocs/route.html.

Cell service: Mostly good

Transportation: Napa Valley Transit Authority (The Vine), (707) 251-2800; https://vinetransit.com

Finding the trailhead: Kennedy Park is at 3291 Streblow Dr. in Napa. From central Napa, take Soscol Avenue south for about 3 miles to Streblow Drive and turn right into the park. The northern end point is in Yountville Community Park, 2900 Lincoln Ave., Yountville, off CA 29 about 9 miles north of downtown Napa.

Trailhead GPS: Kennedy Park: N38 16.048 / W122 16.927

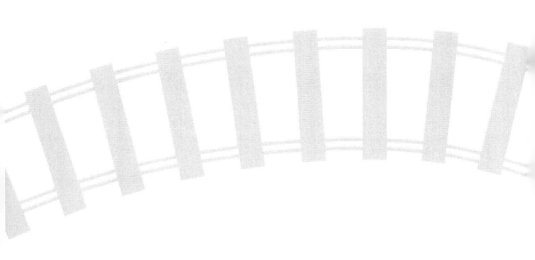

17 SONOMA BAYLANDS TRAILS

This rail with two trails features the dog-friendly Sears Point Trail, which runs alongside the active line through grasslands filled with bird-song, and the longer, pet-free Eliot Trail, which rides the levee above the tracks, tracing the San Pablo Bay waterfront. On a clear day the views from either path are stunning, encompassing some of the Bay Area's most iconic peaks.

Activities:

Start: Sonoma Baylands Trailhead

Distance: 2.6 miles out and back on the Sears Point Trail; 5 miles out and back on the Eliot Trail

Difficulty: Easy

Seasons/schedule: Year-round, sunrise to sunset

Fees and permits: None

Trail surface and conditions: Dirt and ballast

Accessibility: The Eliot Trail, composed of well-maintained gravel, is accessible to people using wheelchairs. The Sears Point Trail to the headquarters complex is accessible as well, but not so much heading out to the power station end point.

Canine compatibility: Leashed dogs permitted on the Sears Point Trail; no dogs allowed on the Eliot Trail

Amenities: Ample parking is available at the trailhead; restrooms are available at the junction with the active rail line at 0.2 mile.

Trail contact: Sonoma Land Trust, 822 5th St., Santa Rosa; (707) 526-6930; https://sonomalandtrust.org

Nearest towns: Petaluma, Novato, Sonoma

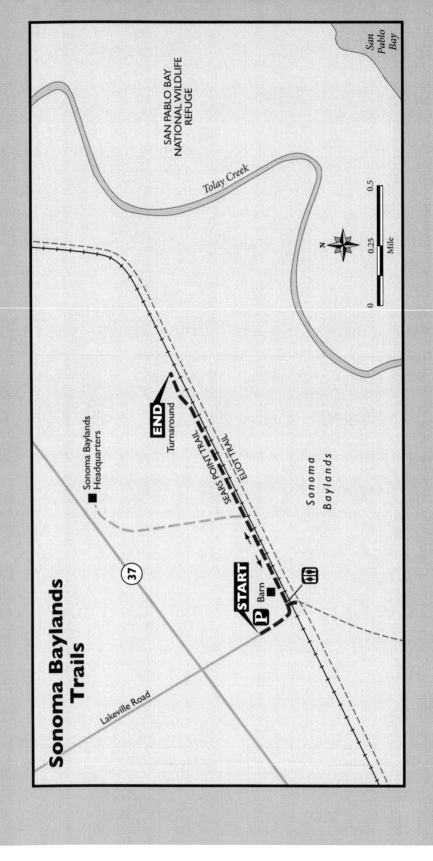

Sonoma Baylands Trails

San Pablo Bay

San Pablo Bay National Wildlife Refuge

Tolay Creek

Sonoma Baylands Headquarters

37

Lakeville Road

START

P

Barn

END

Turnaround

SEARS POINT TRAIL

ELIOT TRAIL

Sonoma Baylands

N

0   0.25   0.5

Mile

Maps: A downloadable brochure with a map is available at https://sonomalandtrust.org/wp-content/uploads/2019/01/BaylandsMap-Hex-WEB-2.pdf.

Cell service: Good

Transportation: No public transit serves the trail.

Finding the trailhead: Access to the trailhead is off CA 37 at Sears Point, about equidistant from Petaluma, Novato, and the city of Sonoma. From the intersection of CA 37 and the Lakeville Highway, go south on Reclamation Road for about 0.2 mile to the trailhead parking area.

Trailhead GPS: N38 07.844 / W122 28.415

The Main Line

Yes, the trails running through the Sonoma Baylands are technically rail trails but, to be honest, when it comes to reasons why you should visit the Baylands, the active rail line plays a distant second fiddle to the bird-watching and wildlife viewing. The routes lie within the San Pablo Bay National Wildlife Refuge, traversing open space parcels preserved and managed by the Sonoma Land Trust, which helped spearhead an ecological restoration success story that has not only enhanced ecosystems for birdlife, wildlife, and aquatic species, but also for humans.

And then there are the viewscapes. The twin trails feature stellar vistas across the water to some of the hallmark peaks of the North Bay, including Mount Tamalpais, Mount Burdell, Cougar Mountain (part of the Sonoma Mountains) and, on a clear day, Mount Diablo.

The wetlands surrounding the trails, like so many other wetlands around San Francisco Bay, had been drained over more than a century to advance development of towns, farmlands, and commercial enterprises, including railroads: The Northwestern Pacific and Southern Pacific Railroads used the tracks back in the day and now Sonoma-Marin Area Rail Transit (SMART) runs freight on the line. The land trust, in partnership with the wildlife refuge, began the tidal marsh restoration project in 1995. A pivotal dike on the Dickson Ranch was breached in 2015, and in the years

Fog begins to creep over the ridgelines of Mount Tamalpais, one of the iconic Bay Area peaks visible from the Sonoma Baylands rail trails.

since, the wetlands and all the flora and fauna that depend on that eco-system have flourished.

The Eliot Trail is also part of the much longer San Francisco Bay Trail, providing a critical linkage in what will one day be a showcase trail around the shoreline of the bay. The Sears Point Trail offers access to the wildlife refuge headquarters as well as a peaceful wander through a landscape where some farming (haying) takes place.

A single path, alongside a gated, paved farm road, leads to the active rail line at 0.2 mile, where trails diverge. The Sears Point Trail is on the north side of the tracks and cruises past the old barn and surrounding hayfields, which ring with birdsong—red-winged blackbirds, sparrows and other little brown birds, crows, and raptors are common sights. At 0.6 mile the formal trail bends north toward the headquarters complex, but you can continue along the trackside path for 1.3 miles, where it dead-ends at a power station. Return as you came; it's all about the views of Mount Tamalpais, Mount Burdell, and the ridges between on the way back to the trailhead.

Leashed dogs are permitted on the Sears Point Trail within the Sonoma Baylands preserve, but they are not allowed across the tracks on the parallel Eliot Trail.

The viewscapes along the Eliot Trail, perched atop the levee protecting the rail line, are more expansive. From the trail junction at 0.2 mile, cross the tracks and climb briefly to the levee top, where the Sonoma Baylands Trail (also a trail alongside the rails), the Dickson Trail (short and sweet), and the Eliot Trail meet. When the tide is in, you can launch your kayak or canoe and paddle about. Hikers and cyclists can meander 2.4 miles one way to the trail's end at a bench overlooking the Napa-Sonoma Marshes Wildlife Area. The ultimate in a walk-and-talk route, the Eliot Trail features benches and overlooks for chatting, snacking, or just taking it all in. Return as you came.

18 CROSS MARIN TRAIL

This spectacular rail trail in western Marin County runs alongside scenic Lagunitas Creek from a historic bridge through Samuel P. Taylor State Park. Sunny meadows and rolling hills overlook the waterway, and dark, cool redwood groves rise alongside the path.

Activities:

Start: The old highway bridge in Tocaloma

Distance: 4.5 miles one way

Difficulty: Moderate due only to length

Seasons/schedule: Year-round, sunrise to sunset

Fees and permits: None. Fees are charged to park or camp in Samuel P. Taylor State Park.

Trail surface and conditions: Asphalt for 3 miles, from Tocaloma to the Irving Group Picnic Area; dirt and ballast for the last 1.5 miles, from the picnic area to Shafter Bridge. The dirt/ballast section of the trail may be muddy in winter and early spring.

Accessibility: The paved segment of the trail is accessible to people using wheelchairs. Hardy wheelchair users may attempt the dirt section to Shafter Bridge, but it's fairly rough and can be muddy in wet weather.

Canine compatibility: Leashed dogs permitted on the trail outside the state park. Leashed dogs are only permitted in developed areas within the park.

Amenities: None at either trail end point, but water and restrooms are available in the state park. You will find all the amenities in the nearby town of Point Reyes Station, restaurants at the crossroads in Olema, and a small grocery store in Lagunitas.

Trail contacts: For information about the section of trail within Samuel P. Taylor State Park, call (415) 488-9897 or visit the website www.parks .ca.gov and search for the park by name. For the trail section in the Golden

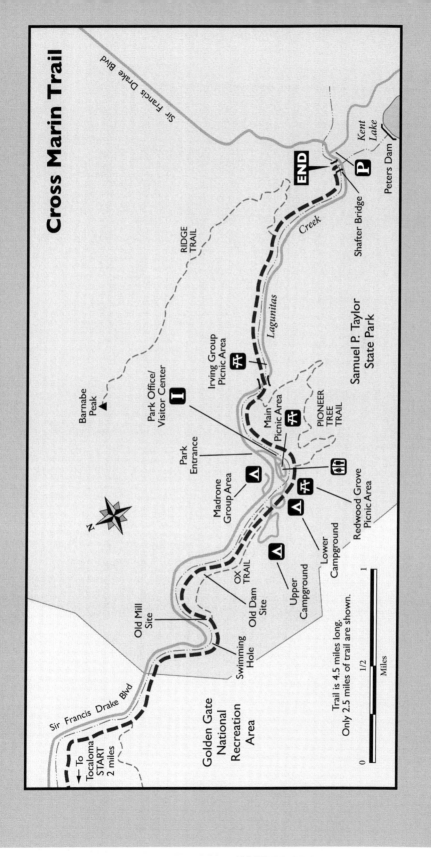

Gate National Recreation Area, contact the visitor center at Point Reyes National Seashore at (415) 464-5100 ext. 2, or visit www.nps.gov/things todo/walk-the-cross-marin-trail.htm.

Nearest towns: Lagunitas, Olema, Point Reyes Station

Maps: Because the trail spans different jurisdictions, no single map other than the one on the Rails-to-Trails Conservancy's TrailLink app shows the route in its entirety. For the section in the Golden Gate National Recreation Area, a downloadable map is at www.nps.gov/pore/planyourvisit/upload/map_trailssouth.pdf. For the section in Samuel P. Taylor State Park, download the brochure from the park's site at www.parks.ca.gov.

Cell service: Marginal to none

Transportation: No public transportation serves the trail specifically. Bus routes serving surrounding communities are offered by Marin Transit (415-226-0855).

Finding the trailhead: To reach the trail from US 101 in Larkspur/Corte Madera, take the Sir Francis Drake Boulevard exit and head west on Sir Francis Drake Boulevard through the towns of Kentfield, San Anselmo, and Fairfax, and then through the pastoral San Geronimo Valley. Shafter Bridge is 15.5 miles from US 101. The Tocaloma parking area at Platform Bridge Road is at 20 miles.

The best parking and access outside Samuel P. Taylor State Park is at the Tocaloma end point. At the intersection of Sir Francis Drake Boulevard and Platform Bridge Road, turn right (north) onto Platform Bridge Road; roadside parking is in a pullout on the left (west), at the east end of the old bridge about 100 yards from the intersection. Parking at Shafter Bridge is limited, located in a small lot off Sir Francis Drake Boulevard.

You may also reach the rail trail through Samuel P. Taylor State Park. The park entrance is midway between Shafter Bridge and Tocaloma. Pay the fee and follow the park road to parking adjacent to the trail.

Trailhead GPS: Tocaloma trailhead: N38 03.022 / W122 45.564; Shafter Bridge trailhead: N38 00.282 / W122 42.503

The Main Line

|||||||||||||||||||||||||||||||||||||||||||||||||||||||||||||||||||||||||||||||||||||||||||||||||||||||||||||||||||||||||||||||||||||||||||||||||||||||||||||||||||||||||||||||||||

A gentle, inviting creek with a swimming hole; sun-drenched views onto rolling pastureland; cool, dark redwood groves; a scenic cascade filling rock basins with clear water . . . the Cross Marin Trail serves up all of this and more.

The soul of the trail is Lagunitas Creek, also known as Papermill Creek, which played an important role in the history of western Marin County. In the mid-nineteenth century, Samuel Penfield Taylor, for whom Samuel P. Taylor State Park is named, used the proceeds of a gold-mining operation to purchase property along the pastoral creek. Instead of logging the land, a logical endeavor for entrepreneurs of the period given the building boom in San Francisco, Taylor established two mills along the creek, one manufacturing paper and the other black powder.

The powder mill was short-lived: It blew up in 1874. The paper mill, however, thrived, especially after construction of a narrow-gauge railroad

Redwoods, buckeyes, bay laurels, and oaks shade the Cross Marin Trail in west Marin County.

that made shipment of Taylor's goods easier. It also made Taylorville, the small town that grew up around the mill and railroad, a popular destination for weekenders from the 1870s through the turn of the twentieth century. Camp Taylor was outfitted with both a resort hotel and more rustic accommodations, as well as an abundance of natural beauty.

The 4.5-mile Cross Marin Trail follows the abandoned bed of the North Pacific Coast Railroad, which began in Larkspur, ran through Camp Taylor, and continued up the coast to Tomales and beyond. This line was eventually purchased by the Northwestern Pacific Railroad.

Beginning at the Platform Bridge Road parking area, cross the lovely old bridge that spans Lagunitas Creek and turn left (south) onto the signed trail. The path dives under Sir Francis Drake Boulevard, then cruises through buckeye, bay laurels, and scattered redwood groves to a long, narrow meadow with views across the valley onto the hills of neighboring ranchland. Towering eucalyptus trees guard the southern reach of the meadow.

Just beyond, at 1.4 miles, you'll reach the Jewell Trail intersection. From here, if you choose to leave the rail trail, you can climb steeply onto the Bolinas Ridge Trail. Pass the gate that marks the state park boundary near the 2-mile mark; now the trail follows a park road through lovely stands of redwoods. Stay straight on the park road, ignoring roads that branch left and right to housing and other park facilities. On the north (creek-side) border of the trail, in a tiny clearing, a historic marker commemorates the Pioneer Paper Mill, built by Samuel Taylor in 1856. The Ox Trail takes off to the east opposite the marker.

Pass another creek-side marker at the 2.5-mile mark, at the site of the first fish ladder on Lagunitas Creek. At 3 miles another gate marks a park boundary. Now you are in the heart of the park, passing campsites, picnic areas, and restrooms. Stay straight on the park road, again ignoring any roads that depart right or left, passing the Redwood Grove Picnic Area and then through yet another gate. The Pioneer Tree Trail takes off to the south just past the gate. In 2022 the namesake tree fell following a fire.

The rail trail's surface changes from asphalt to gravel as it bends across a bridge spanning the highway and creek at 3.5 miles and passes the Irving Group Picnic Area. Now with a wilder feel, the trail is separated from the highway by the creek and dense walls of redwood and bay laurel. The Ridge Trail, which leads to the summit of Barnabe Peak, leaves from the north side of the railroad grade a half mile beyond the picnic grounds.

The old bridge spanning Lagunitas Creek serves as the western gateway to the Cross Marin Trail.

A gate and the Kent Lake trailhead mark the end of the route at 4.5 miles. Take the narrow trail on the south side of the grade down to the creek and head upstream about 100 yards to the cascades that fill swimming holes known as the Ink Wells beneath Shafter Bridge. This ideal picnic spot is also a great place to watch steelhead spawn in winter. Take a dip, then return as you came to return to the Tocaloma trailhead.

19 OLD RAILROAD GRADE

Climbing nearly 2,000 feet to the summit of Mount Tamalpais, the Old Railroad Grade boasts some of the best views in the San Francisco Bay Area. The steady grade of the winding dirt track is now a popular mountain bike route, but back in the day the railroad was a weekend destination for upper-class ladies and gentlemen who would travel by ferry from San Francisco to spend a day in the country.

Activities:

Start: Blithedale Summit Trailhead

Distance: 9 miles one way

Difficulty: Strenuous. As railroad grades go, this one is steep but wonderfully rewarding.

Seasons/schedule: Year-round, sunrise to sunset. The route may be muddy or impassable when it rains. Also, the mountain may be swathed in cool—sometimes Minnesotan—fog, even in summer, so be prepared for changing weather conditions.

Fees and permits: None

Trail surface and conditions: Ballast and dirt

Accessibility: The trail is not accessible to people using wheelchairs.

Canine compatibility: Leashed dogs are permitted on lower portions of the route but not in Mount Tamalpais State Park.

Amenities: Restrooms are available at the West Point Inn and at the summit of Mount Tamalpais. No food or water is available along the trail proper, but you can pack a picnic lunch to eat at the inn or at the summit. Grocery stores are available near the trailhead in Mill Valley, along with fine restaurants and shopping.

Trail contact: Marin Municipal Water District; (415) 945-1180; www.marin water.org—click on the Mount Tam Watershed link

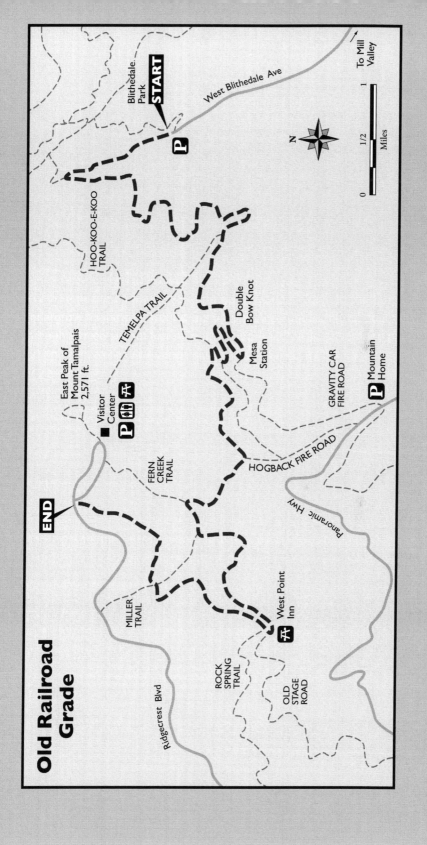

Old Railroad Grade

START

Blithedale
Park

West Blithedale Ave

To Mill
Valley

N

Miles

0   1/2   1

HOO-KOO-E-KOO TRAIL

TEMELPA TRAIL

East Peak of
Mount Tamalpais
2,571 ft.

Visitor
Center

Double
Bow Knot

Mesa
Station

GRAVITY CAR
FIRE ROAD

Mountain
Home

HOGBACK FIRE ROAD

FERN
CREEK
TRAIL

END

Panoramic Hwy

MILLER
TRAIL

West Point
Inn

ROCK
SPRING
TRAIL

OLD
STAGE
ROAD

Ridgecrest Blvd

Nearest town: Mill Valley

Maps: A detailed downloadable map of the trail starting at Mountain Home is available from the Marin Municipal Water District at www.marin water.org/sites/default/files/2020-09/Watershed%20Visitor%20Map.pdf. One Tam, a nonprofit coalition of land management agencies on the mountain, also has an excellent downloadable map at www.onetam.org/media/pdfs/ONE_TAM_Map_Web_Jan2015_1.pdf.

Cell service: Good near the trailhead, marginal as you climb to the summit

Transportation: Golden Gate Transit, 511 (toll-free in the Bay Area) or (415) 455-2000; www.goldengate.org

Finding the trailhead: To reach the Blithedale Park trailhead from US 101 in Mill Valley, take the East Blithedale Avenue exit and follow East Blithedale Avenue into downtown Mill Valley, where it ends at the intersection of Throckmorton and West Blithedale Avenue. Turn right (north) on West Blithedale Avenue and follow the narrow road up through neighborhoods into Blithedale Park. The Blithedale Summit Trailhead is on the right (east) side of the road at a green gate.

To reach the summit of Mount Tamalpais from US 101 in Mill Valley, take the CA 1/Stinson Beach exit and head west on CA 1 (Shoreline Highway) to its intersection with the Panoramic Highway. Turn right (north) on the Panoramic Highway and climb to Pantoll Road. Turn right (north) on Pantoll Road and keep climbing to its end at the Rock Spring picnic area on Ridgecrest Boulevard. Turn right (east) on East Ridgecrest Boulevard and follow this to its end in the East Peak parking lot.

Adequate parking is available at both end points, but lots may be packed on weekends or during the summer.

Trailhead GPS: N37 55.255 / W122 33.321

Remnants of track are visible atop the Old Railroad Grade on Mount Tamalpais.

The Main Line

⁣||||||||||||||||||||||||||||||||||||||||||||||||||||||||||||||||||||||||||||||||||||||||||||||||||||||||||||||||||||||||||||||||||||||||

The tempestuous Pacific Ocean sets the mood on Mount Tamalpais. When the sea pulls back her blanket of fog, views from the summit sweep for miles in every direction—north up the ragged, emerald California coast; east to the snowcapped Sierra Nevada; south across San Francisco Bay and its glittering city; and west past the shadowy Farallon Islands to the horizon. Sun bathes the peak's forested slopes, and the Old Railroad Grade offers the perfect opportunity to enjoy these gifts.

But when the fog rolls in, enveloping the mountain in cold mists and brisk winds, conditions can feel downright arctic. Even then, though, Mount Tam delivers an unexpected gift. Though civilization sprawls below, a traveler on a fog-shrouded ridge may suddenly find themself alone in a whispering wilderness, lost in time, the mountain's long natural history quietly unfurling all around.

The history of the Old Railroad Grade stretches back only a moment in time on that scale. At the turn of the twentieth century, the Mill Valley & Mount Tamalpais Scenic Railway Company operated "The Crookedest Railroad in the World" on the mountain. Passengers rode the winding line— more than 280 curves—to the summit, savored the views and perhaps took a hike along the rolling crest, then rode the rails back down to Mill Valley. The line was abandoned in 1930, and the grade is now popular with both hikers and mountain bikers.

The trailhead is at Blithedale Park on the gated Blithedale Summit/ Northridge Fire Road, and the route begins by following the course of Arroyo Corte Madera del Presidio northward. The grade climbs steadily for the duration, so set your pace, and prepare for the long haul.

At the first trail intersection, H-Line Fire Road switchbacks up and right (northeast); stay left on the railroad grade. At the next intersection, with Horseshoe Fire Road, go left (southwest), down and over the creek, then continue climbing through a forest of bay laurel, oak, madrone, and manzanita that grows more open as you ascend.

At about 1.5 miles the trail passes a gate and the Temelpa Trail junction as it merges with paved Summit Avenue/Fern Canyon Road. Go right (north) on Fern Canyon, enjoying lovely views of San Francisco and the

One of the old gravity cars that delivered tourists from Mount Tamalpais to Muir Woods makes an appearance on a siding at the top of the peak.

bay. The pavement ends at a gate posted with watershed signs. Pass the gate to the right (the left road is a driveway) and continue upward on the Old Railroad Grade.

At about the 3-mile mark, near the site of Mesa Station and the junction with the Gravity Car Grade (another rail trail that links to a trailhead at Mountain Home), the road reaches a T intersection. Go right (east) and up on the switchbacking rail trail, which negotiates the Double Bow Knot, where the grade gains an incredible 600 feet in elevation. Less than a half mile beyond, pass the Hoo-Koo-E-Koo Trail, which breaks off to the right; stay left (west) on the obvious railroad grade.

As you climb, the forest gives way to low-growing coastal scrub, thick with the blooms of sticky monkey flower and scotch broom in the spring, dry and silvery in summer and fall. At the Hogback Road intersection, at about the 4-mile mark, stay right (west). Beyond, as you cruise through moist draws that boast waterfalls in winter and spring, pass the Fern Canyon Trail, a water tank, and the Miller Trail, all on the right (north) side of the grade.

At about 6 miles the trail switches back around the West Point Inn. The inn has offered hospitality to mountain visitors since it was built in 1904. It provides the perfect setting for hikers or cyclists to stop, rest, enjoy the spectacular views and, if you are done climbing, picnic before heading back down the mountain. A number of other trails also depart from this spot, including the Matt Davis Trail and the Old Stage Road. With a good map and some time, you can explore these other routes.

To continue on the Old Railroad Grade, round the broad switchback, passing behind the West Point Inn's cabins, and head east, climbing above wooded canyons that stretch down toward Mill Valley. Another couple miles of easy climbing, during which you pass the Miller and Tavern trail junctions, lead to the end of the grade on East Ridgecrest Boulevard. Go right (east) on the paved highway, which climbs steeply in spots, to the summit area parking lot. A fragment of the railroad is on the west side of the East Peak; in the barn on East Peak, you can also check out a replica of a gravity car. Cap your journey with an ascent to the summit and bask in vistas and a profound feeling of accomplishment.

Unless you've arranged for a shuttle, you must return the way you came, or you can choose one of many alternative trails for the descent.

20 NWP RAILROAD PATH

From the banks of estuarine Corte Madera Creek to the tangled undergrowth wrapped around the unused Alto Tunnel, this rail trail runs through a lovely slice of Marin County. It is primarily a neighborhood path, but one with stellar views and links to additional rail trails with more stellar views.

Activities:

Start: Larkspur trailhead off Doherty Drive

Distance: 1.4 miles one way

Difficulty: Easy

Seasons/schedule: Year-round, sunrise to sunset. The dirt section may be muddy during and following winter rains.

Fees and permits: None

Trail surface and conditions: Most of the trail is paved, but the southern end of the trail is dirt and narrows to overgrown singletrack as you approach the Alto Tunnel end point.

Accessibility: The paved segment of the trail is accessible to people using wheelchairs.

Canine compatibility: Leashed dogs permitted

Amenities: The trail passes through downtown Larkspur, where you can find grocery stores, restaurants, and restrooms in the depot.

Trail contact: Town of Corte Madera Department of Parks and Recreation, 240 Tamal Vista Dr., Corte Madera; (415) 927-5057; www.townof cortemadera.org/199/Parks-Recreation

Nearest towns: Larkspur, Corte Madera

Maps: The best map is on the Rails-to-Trails Conservancy TrailLink app at www.traillink.com/trail-maps/nwp-railroad-trail.

Cell service: Good

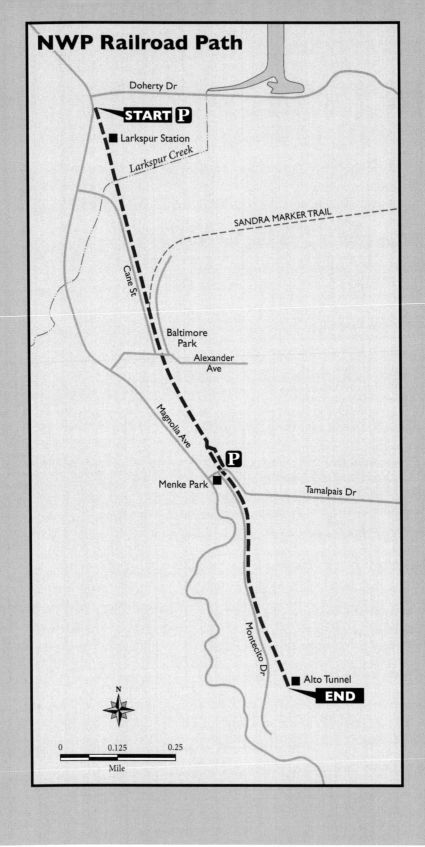

NWP Railroad Path

Doherty Dr

START P

Larkspur Station

Larkspur Creek

SANDRA MARKER TRAIL

Cane St

Baltimore Park

Alexander Ave

Magnolia Ave

P

Menke Park

Tamalpais Dr

Montecito Dr

Alto Tunnel

END

N

0   0.125   0.25

Mile

Transportation: Golden Gate Transit, 511 or (415) 455-2000; www.golden gate.org

Finding the trailhead: To reach the Doherty Drive trailhead from US 101, take the Sir Francis Drake Boulevard exit and go west on Sir Francis Drake Boulevard to Bon Air Drive. Turn left (south) on Bon Air Drive and go over the bridge; a paved trail takes off to the north from the right (west) side of the road. The rail trail begins on the left (east) side of Bon Air Drive on the far side of the bridge, heading south. Parking is available in a municipal lot near the junction of Doherty Drive and Magnolia Avenue, and the trail begins behind (east of) the parking lot.

Trailhead GPS: N37 56.195 / W122 32.077

The Main Line

The NWP Railroad Path connects charming downtown Larkspur with neighboring Corte Madera, both enclaves in wealthy Marin County near the San Pablo Bay waterfront. Paved in town and dirt as it approaches the long-unused Alto Tunnel, the rail trail rides on abandoned right-of-way that once belonged to the Northwestern Pacific Railroad (hence the NWP), which ran passenger lines to a number of then-small agricultural and log-ging towns dotting the North Bay countryside.

Though the track is buffered by trees and landscaping, it is suburban, linking neighborhoods with the amenities of Larkspur. It has strong nat-ural features as well, offering connections with a number of waterways in the area, including Larkspur Creek and to trails following tidal Corte Madera Creek. Take a turn on another rail trail, the Sandra Marker (aka the Larkspur Path), and you can link to the Redwood Highway/San Clemente rail trails. Cruise out and back on all three of these routes in sequence for a longer excursion with lovely waterfront views.

Beginning at the northern trailhead at Doherty Drive, the rail trail parallels Magnolia Avenue as it heads south, never more than a couple of blocks off the main drag through town. That's where you'll find shops and restaurants, as well as Larkspur Station, once a stop on the now-defunct Northwestern Pacific.

Larkspur Station on the Larkspur rail trail is a classic small-town railroad depot.

Shaded and quiet, the rail trail slides between the backyards of an expensive neighborhood for about 0.6 mile before entering the town of Corte Madera. At 0.8 mile the trail hooks through a parking lot and navigates the complicated intersection where Tamalpais Drive meets Redwood Avenue meets Corte Madera Avenue meets Montecito Drive. It sounds worse than it is—the rail trail cuts straight through via crosswalks and passes through little Menke Park on a sidewalk.

Beyond the junction the trail surface transitions to gravel. Continue southward between backyard fence lines toward the hills. As you near trail's end, the track narrows and burrows through overgrown woodland for 0.1 mile to a clearing at the closed Alto Tunnel. Advocates hope to one day open the tunnel so hikers and cyclists can connect the NWP line from Larkspur through Mill Valley and into Sausalito. Return as you came.

Option: On your way back down from the tunnel to the Doherty Drive trailhead, take a right onto the Sandra Marker Rail Trail where it diverges just north of the Alexander Avenue bridge. The paved path curves slowly east and becomes a straight shot toward the bayshore, passing ballfields and backyards through a widening marshland intersected by water channels. Cross Tamal Vista Boulevard at about the 0.9-mile mark and the path dives under busy US 101 adjacent to Wornum Drive. On the east side of the freeway, the trail ends at its junction with rail trails that border Redwood Highway and San Clemente Drive, running alongside the waterfront for 1.2 miles and offering lovely views across the bay. Trail's end is on Paradise Drive; return as you came. Hitch the three paths together for an out-and-back journey from Doherty Drive of about 7.8 miles.

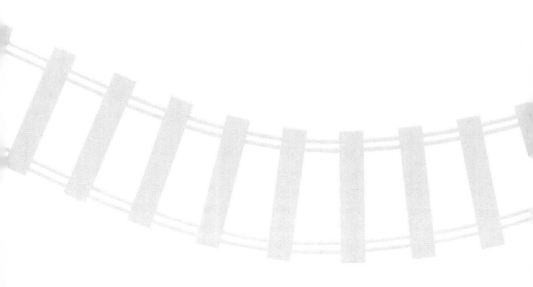

21 OLD RAIL TRAIL

Scanning the western and southern horizons from this shoreline rail trail, you'll be treated to views of Mount Tamalpais, the wooded hills of Sausalito, and the shimmering skyline of San Francisco.

Activities:

Start: Blackie's Pasture trailhead in Tiburon

Distance: 2.1 miles of the 2.7-mile-long trail (one way) are on the abandoned railroad grade.

Difficulty: Easy

Seasons/schedule: Year-round, sunrise to sunset

Fees and permits: None

Trail surface and conditions: Asphalt with a walkway of crushed stone alongside

Accessibility: The entire path is accessible to people using wheelchairs.

Canine compatibility: Leashed dogs permitted

Amenities: Parking is available in the lot at Blackie's Pasture trailhead but can be difficult to find in downtown Tiburon, especially on busy weekends. No food is available along the trail itself, but once you arrive in Tiburon, restaurants, delis, and markets offer a variety of gastronomic temptations. Restrooms are available at the Blackies Pasture trailhead and at South of the Knoll Park. Public restrooms are also available in the ferry terminal for the Blue and Gold Fleet in Tiburon.

Trail contact: Town of Tiburon Public Works Department/Parks Division, 1505 Tiburon Blvd., Tiburon; (415) 435-7354; www.townoftiburon.org/201/Public-Works

Nearest town: Tiburon

Maps: The best trail map is on the Rails-to-Trails Conservancy site at www.traillink.com/trail-maps/old-rail-trail-/.

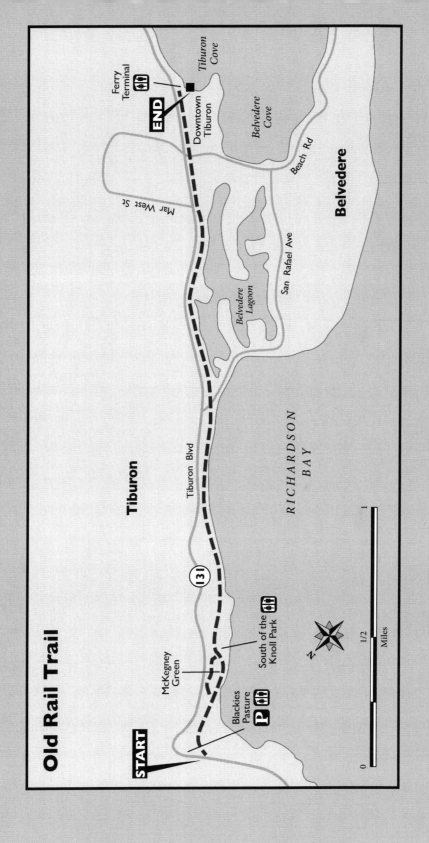

Old Rail Trail

START

Tiburon

Blackies Pasture

McKegney Green

South of the Knoll Park

Tiburon Blvd

131

RICHARDSON BAY

Mar West St

Ferry Terminal

END

Downtown Tiburon

Tiburon Cove

Belvedere Cove

Beach Rd

San Rafael Ave

Belvedere Lagoon

Belvedere

N

0   1/2   1
Miles

Cell service: Good

Transportation: Golden Gate Transit, 511 or (415) 455-2000; www.golden gate.org

Finding the trailhead: From US 101 in Mill Valley, take the Tiburon Boulevard (CA 131) exit. Go east on Tiburon Boulevard to Blackies Pasture Road, which is on the right (south) side of the highway along the waterfront. The Tiburon end point is about 3 miles farther south, also on the waterfront.

Trailhead GPS: N37 53.825 / W122 29.360

The Main Line

The views from this rail trail, which winds through what's also known as Tiburon Linear Park, couldn't be any richer. As you head down the trail toward the tip of the Tiburon peninsula, following the shoreline of Richardson Bay, the windows of homes tucked into the dark woods of Sausalito reflect sunlight like sparklers. The tips of the towers of the Golden Gate Bridge rise above these hills, simple and elegant. Beyond Belvedere, its gentle slopes garnished with lavish homes, the jagged skyline of San Francisco glitters across the waters of San Francisco Bay.

Traveling back along the path from downtown Tiburon to Blackies Pasture, the reclining profile of the Sleeping Lady—Mount Tamalpais—dominates the view. The mountain's lower flanks sparkle with sunlight reflected off the windows of homes tucked into the dark hollows of Mill Valley, and Richardson Bay laps calmly on the beach to the west.

And to the north, the posh homes of Tiburon are perched over the trail and bay, allowing the town's wealthy residents to revel in spectacular views that visitors can only enjoy for a short time.

The path follows the old-time route of the Northwestern Pacific Railroad, which provided passenger service through Marin and Sonoma Counties from the early 1900s through the 1930s. At the south end of the trail, in downtown Tiburon, you will pass the historic depot, just one of many stops on the rail line and its spurs, which connected San Francisco

The Old Rail Trail offers views of Richardson Bay and the surrounding hills.

to Larkspur, Fairfax, the logging town of Duncan Mills on the Russian River, and other way stations in the North Bay.

The route is described beginning in Blackies Pasture, named for a beloved horse who wandered the shoreline meadow back in the day. The broad path leads across Shapero Bridge at 0.1 mile to McKegney Green, where the trail forks, leading either bayside around the green or up and to the northeast of the broad lawn. A series of interpretive signs lines the path, which is also called the Tiburon Historical Trail; the signs are maintained by local nonprofits dedicated to preserving the history of the peninsula.

McKegney Green is the perfect place to kick a soccer ball around, throw a Frisbee, fly a kite, or just sit and watch the bay waters shimmer. The bayside trail hosts benches that look out over Belvedere and San Francisco Bay. The rail trail proper sticks to the pavement on the high road and passes South of the Knoll Park, tucked in the lee of a hill. The park offers visitors a tot lot, a restroom, and another large grassy area.

The trail is tucked between Tiburon Boulevard and the bay beyond South of the Knoll Park. A strip of beach allows trail users to fish, sunbathe, launch their paddle sport of choice or, again, just contemplate the views.

Benches, garbage cans, and a couple of water fountains line the trail as it continues south, offering virtually unbroken views for the next mile or so.

At about the 1.5-mile mark, cross San Rafael Avenue at a stoplight. The path continues on the south side of the road, leaving the bay views behind as it dives into a bower of trees and oleander that buffers it from the adjacent boulevard. At 1.9 miles pass a roadside parking lot, the small green of the Tiburon Dog Park, and adjacent tennis courts. Just 0.2 mile beyond, the path splits; stay right and proceed to the end of the rail trail proper, at Mar West Street.

You can turn around here, but if you've come this far, you ought to sample the pleasures of downtown Tiburon. Now a bike route, the trail continues alongside the boulevard, and sidewalks offer pleasant road-side walking. At 2.4 miles cross Beach Road, and at 2.6 miles reach the train depot. At trail's end, at 2.7 miles, you arrive at the ferry terminal for the Blue and Gold Fleet and other transbay lines. Yet another small green overlooks Angel Island and San Francisco in the distance. Follow the same route back to the trailhead.

22 MILL VALLEY–SAUSALITO MULTIUSE PATH

The rail trail hitching Mill Valley, at the base of Mount Tamalpais, to the Sausalito shoreline traverses the wetlands of Richardson Bay, where egrets, herons, and other seabirds forage at low tide. The path also passes the San Francisco Bay Model, a fascinating exhibit illustrating the dynamics of the bay.

Activities:

Start: Edna Maguire School parking lot in Mill Valley

Distance: 3.5 miles one way

Difficulty: Moderate due to length

Seasons/schedule: Year-round, sunrise to sunset

Fees and permits: None

Trail surface: Asphalt with a parallel path of crushed stone in some sections

Accessibility: The entire trail is accessible to people using wheelchairs.

Canine compatibility: Leashed dogs permitted

Amenities: Restrooms are available in the various parks along the bike path, including Bayfront Park in Mill Valley and Earl F. Dunfy Park in Sausalito. Both Mill Valley and Sausalito harbor eateries that range from fast-food outlets to upscale restaurants. It's a diner's delight.

Trail contact: Marin County Parks, Marin County Civic Center, San Rafael; (415) 473-6388, ext. 4; www.parks.marincounty.org/parkspreserves/parks/mill-valley-sausalito-pathway

Nearest towns: Mill Valley, Sausalito, Marin City

Maps: A downloadable map of the Bothin Marsh Preserve, available at www.parks.marincounty.org/parkspreserves/preserves/bothin-marsh, shows most of the trail.

Cell service: Good

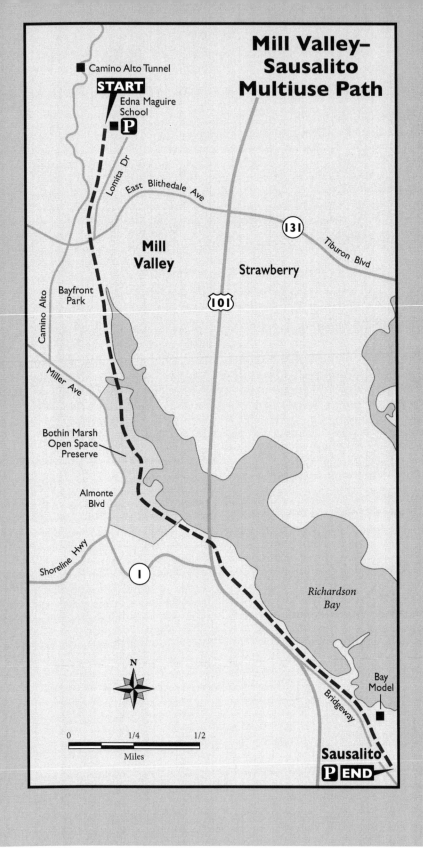

Mill Valley–
Sausalito
Multiuse Path

Camino Alto Tunnel

START

Edna Maguire
School

P

Lomita Dr

East Blithedale Ave

131

Tiburon Blvd

**Mill
Valley**

Strawberry

Camino Alto

Bayfront
Park

101

Miller Ave

Bothin Marsh
Open Space
Preserve

Almonte
Blvd

Shoreline Hwy

1

Richardson
Bay

N

0   1/4   1/2
Miles

Bridgeway

Bay
Model

Sausalito
P END

Transportation: Golden Gate Transit, 511 or (415) 455-2000; www.golden gate.org

Finding the trailhead: From US 101 in Mill Valley, take the East Blithedale Avenue exit and follow East Blithedale for 0.7 mile to Lomita Drive. Turn right (north) on Lomita Drive and follow it for 0.6 mile to Edna Maguire School. The parking area is on the left (west), but you can also park on the streets nearby.

To reach the southern end point in Sausalito from US 101, take the Sausalito exit and follow Bridgeway through the heart of town to the parking lot at Plaza Vina Del Mar. Because of the town's popularity with tourists, it is often full.

Trailhead GPS: N37 54.497 / W122 31.484

The Main Line

This rail trail illustrates the interplay between natural areas and developed settings along lengthy trail corridors. Bordered by a tangle of blackberry and poison oak at the outset, the paved path skims the manicured lawns of a neat suburban park, passes through the Bothin Marsh Preserve, where snowy egrets and other waterfowl do their best to ignore the hum of nearby traffic as they forage, and then slams into urbanization, paralleling busy US 101 before plunging into the heart of historic Sausalito. It ends with postcard views of the bay and city of San Francisco, amid the sights and sounds that draw tourists from around the world to the cosmopolitan enclaves surrounding the Golden Gate.

The trail follows the former bed of the Northwestern Pacific Railroad, an interurban rail service that ran trains throughout the North Bay counties of Marin and Sonoma. The electric line operated between 1903 and the early 1940s, and the trail was constructed in the late 1970s and early 1980s.

Keep in mind that cycling on the trail, while infinitely satisfying on the stretches in Mill Valley, is not easy when the trail merges with the crowded sidewalks of Sausalito. If you plan to ride or skate, consider stashing your bikes or skates once you reach Gate 6 Road.

The Mill Valley-Sausalito Multiuse Path rolls under the Richardson Bay bridge supporting US 101.

I've set the northern end point for this rail trail at Edna Maguire School, but if you need to tag the whole reach, head north from the school along Lomita Avenue, across Vasco Lane, and proceed on a dirt doubletrack that soon narrows to singletrack in an area that remains moist and muddy through winter and into spring. The Camino Alto Tunnel lies ahead but is impossible to see from trail's end and impossible to reach without a hardy bushwhack. The hope is that one day the tunnel will be opened, connecting with rail trails over the hill in Corte Madera and Larkspur. It's a half mile out and back from the Maguire school to this end point of the trail.

Heading south from the school—the recommended starting point—the paved path slopes gently downhill through a shady and flower-filled corridor bordered by homes to a major intersection at East Blithedale and Camino Alto at 0.7 mile. On the south side of East Blithedale, the trail becomes part of the San Francisco Bay Trail and borders the marsh in Mill Valley's Bayfront Park. At 1 mile pass more parking, for both trail and park, at the end of Sycamore Avenue. Pass a dog run and a trail that leads left (east) and over the bridge to Bayfront Park's ballfields and tot lot.

Recreationalists are treated to wonderful views of Mount Tamalpais as they head north into Mill Valley along the Mill Valley-Sausalito Multiuse Path.

The next 1.5-mile section of trail meanders through the marshes of Bothin Marsh Open Space Preserve, with glorious views of Mount Tamalpais, the wooded hills of Mill Valley and Sausalito, and the shimmering waters of Richardson Bay. This is a great place to bird-watch, frequented by snowy egrets, great blue herons, and other seabirds and songbirds.

At 2.5 miles the trail passes under the Richardson Bridge and emerges next to US 101. The route is wedged between the freeway and the bay for a short stint, eventually breaking away from the highway to border Bridgeway, Sausalito's main artery. Looking toward the waterfront yields views of sailboats and fishing boats bobbing at docks and moorings, and across the bay to the extravagant homes of Tiburon and Belvedere.

At 3.3 miles cross Gate 6 Road. At this point walking is easier and more pleasant than cycling or skating. Shops and restaurants line Bridgeway, which follows the route of the onetime railroad. The rail trail proper ends after 3.5 miles, but if you've come this far, there's no point in missing the action in Sausalito.

Reaching the heart of the town is simple—just continue along Bridgeway for another mile and a half. At Napa Street (4.6 miles), the

The Bay Model Visitor Center

Get an inside look at the waterworks of San Francisco Bay by visiting the San Francisco Bay Model, located adjacent to the Mill Valley–Sausalito rail trail. This working scale-model reconstruction of the bay and its delta allows both scientists and the public to observe the dynamics of tides and other influences on the bay. The model itself, built by the US Army Corps of Engineers in 1956 and expanded and improved in later years, is the centerpiece of the Bay Model Visitor Center, but there are other historical and environmental exhibits at the center as well.

The Bay Model Visitor Center is located at 2001 Bridgeway but is reached via Harbor Road; follow the small Bay Model signs. The model is open from 9 a.m. to 3 p.m. Tues–Sat (closed Sun–Mon). There is no fee. Call (415) 289-3007 for more information or visit www.spn.usace.army.mil/Missions/Recreation/Bay-Model-Visitor-Center.

grassy hummocks of Earl F. Dunphy Park invite both rest and picnics at bayside. Beyond, Sausalito blossoms. On summer weekends the sidewalks are crammed with people speaking a mélange of languages and gazing at displays behind the windows of waterfront shops. Just beyond the central shopping district, views open of San Francisco Bay and its forested islands, and of the glamorous city that glistens on the hills south of the Golden Gate. You can enjoy these views in greater peace by visiting off-season and during the week, but truly, half the fun is watching the people. The end point of this route is Plaza Viña del Mar. Return as you came . . . unless you choose to keep walking along the promenade that traces Bridgeway and the shoreline beyond.

23 LANDS END TRAIL

Riding the cliffs overlooking the narrow entrance to San Francisco Bay, the Lands End Trail offers unbeatable views of the Marin Headlands and the landmark Golden Gate Bridge.

Activities:

Start: Merrie Way trailhead on Point Lobos

Distance: 2 miles one way

Difficulty: Easy. The trail isn't long, but it includes steep stairs and uneven trail surfaces. Mountain biking is limited due to a steep staircase around cliff areas that requires riders to carry their bikes.

Seasons/schedule: Year-round, sunrise to sunset. It's best to avoid Lands End during periods of heavy rainfall—not only can the winds howl as they funnel through the Golden Gate, but erosion is a constant fact of life on these spectacular headlands, and it's exacerbated when trails are used while muddy.

Fees and permits: None

Trail surface and conditions: Mostly well-maintained gravel with sections of pavement

Accessibility: People using wheelchairs have access to sections of the trail at either end point, but the trail is subject to the vagaries of weather, narrows to singletrack in spots, and includes a long staircase.

Canine compatibility: Leashed dogs permitted

Amenities: The parking lot at the Merrie Way trailhead is large but fills quickly on weekends. Restrooms, water, and other necessities (and niceties) are available in the Lands End Lookout Visitor Center, and additional restrooms are in the USS *San Francisco* Memorial parking lot. As for food: You can purchase a delightful bite at the visitor center or venture into any San Francisco neighborhood to dine on amazing, multinational cuisine.

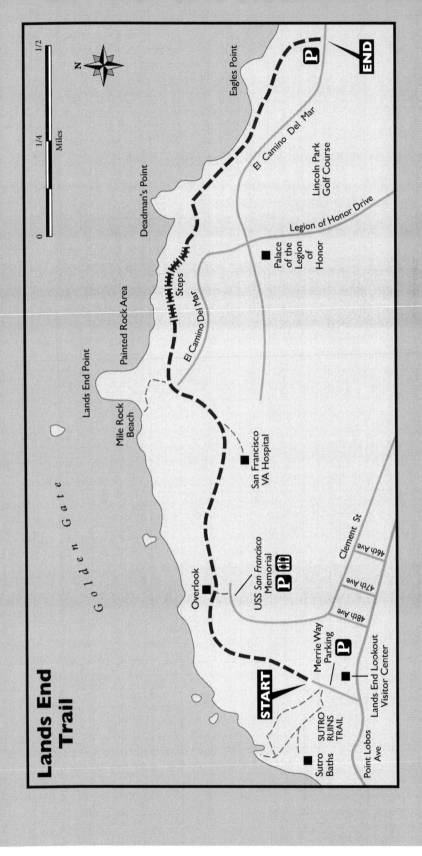

Lands End Trail

N

0   1/4   1/2
Miles

Golden Gate

Lands End Point

Painted Rock Area

Deadman's Point

Eagles Point

Mile Rock Beach

Steps

El Camino Del Mar

El Camino Del Mar

Palace of the Legion of Honor

Legion of Honor Drive

Lincoln Park Golf Course

P

END

San Francisco VA Hospital

Overlook

USS San Francisco Memorial

P

Clement St

46th Ave

47th Ave

48th Ave

START

Merrie Way Parking

P

Lands End Lookout Visitor Center

Point Lobos Ave

Sutro Baths

SUTRO RUINS TRAIL

Trail contact: Golden Gate National Parks; (415) 561-4700; www.nps
.gov/goga. Golden Gate Parks Conservancy, (415) 561-3000; www.parks
conservancy.org/parks/lands-end.

Nearest town: San Francisco

Maps: A downloadable map is available on the Golden Gate Parks Conservancy website at www.parksconservancy.org/parks/lands-end.

Cell service: Good

Transportation: MUNI, 311 (toll-free in San Francisco) or (415) 701-2311;
www.sfmta.com. Golden Gate Transit, 511 (toll-free in the Bay Area) or
(415) 455-2000; www.goldengate.org.

Finding the trailhead: To reach the Point Lobos trailhead from the Golden
Gate Bridge toll plaza on US 101, take the first exit and follow Lincoln Boulevard south and west to El Camino Del Mar. Follow El Camino Del Mar
west to the Palace of the Legion of Honor. At Legion of Honor Drive, turn
left and continue to Clement Street. Go right on Clement Street, which
becomes Seal Rock Drive beyond the San Francisco VA Medical Center,
and continue to the junction with 48th Avenue and El Camino Del Mar.
From here, you can go right to the USS *San Francisco* Memorial parking
area, or go left on El Camino Del Mar for less than 0.1 mile to Point Lobos
Avenue. Turn right onto Point Lobos Avenue, and then right again almost
immediately into the Merrie Way parking lot.

Trailhead GPS: N37 46.809 / W122 30.674

The Main Line

It's not often something man-made enhances the beauty of a naturally
stunning landscape, but San Francisco's elegant Golden Gate Bridge does
just that. It's only been part of the scenery for a handful of generations, but
it's hard to imagine the Golden Gate without its iconic bridge.

Both bridge and landscape are showcased along the Lands End Trail,
which follows the former bed of a steam-powered railroad originally
established by Adolph Sutro, captain of industry and onetime mayor of

The Lands End Trail serves up views of the strait of the Golden Gate and the iconic bridge that spans the mouth of San Francisco Bay.

San Francisco. The railroad was operated by a number of companies from the 1880s to 1925, including the Cliff House and Ferries Railway, but landslides, which plague Lands End, finally forced its closure. It took decades to formalize, but the end of the line had a golden lining: National Park Service ranger Dennis R. Glass notes in his history of railroading at Lands End that "the end of a rail era [marked the beginning of] public access" to what had been an exclusive enclave overlooking the Golden Gate. The newly established Golden Gate National Recreation Area (GGNRA) opened the Lands End Trail in the mid-1970s, and people have flocked to the trail, laid in a strip of wilderness that separates the city from the wind-whipped edge of the continent, ever since. To quote Glass: "It is a site historically and presently for re-creation of the spirit."

The path, which circles crumbling cliffs with views of the narrow passage connecting the Pacific Ocean to San Francisco Bay, is part of the Coastal Trail and is maintained by the GGNRA, an enormous park that spreads north to the spectacular Marin Headlands and south to encompass a string of parklands on the San Francisco Peninsula. Along the way

The Lands End Trail skims rugged shoreline on the south side of the Golden Gate.

you're invited to take in historic sites, overlooks, gardens, and works of art sculpted by human hands and by nature. It's a "come again" trail, an all-time favorite, a gift that keeps on giving.

Begin your walk at the Sutro Baths overlook—or wander down to the ruins of the historic baths themselves—before heading north and east toward the Golden Gate on the wide, obvious railroad grade. Open canopies of cypress trees shade the trail and break the incessant wind that blows off the Pacific; the muffled roar of the ocean is a soothing companion for the entirety of the trail. Ignore narrow spur trails that branch off the main path unless you are inclined to explore: The main trail on the grade is obvious, well traveled, and easy to circle back to.

The path bends around the staircase leading up to the parking area at the USS *San Francisco* Memorial. The overlook here offers lovely vistas across the strait to the Marin Headlands and of the craggy coastline guarding the mouth of the San Francisco Bay on the south side. Views of the Golden Gate Bridge open as the path continues through the thick shade of cypress, and an abundance of wildflowers and other native plants pushes up against the trail's edges, glowing orange and pink beneath the green-bordering-on-black foliage of the evergreens.

As you near the half-mile mark, the trail passes below the edifices of the San Francisco VA Hospital, and spur trails branch left and right. A bit farther along, a paved road drops to meet the rail trail; stay left (seaward) on the dirt route.

The side trail to Mile Rock Beach is at the 0.75-mile mark. If you choose to head down to the overlook and beach, follow the best-maintained trail. It's a steep down-and-up, but the views are amazing.

Back on the Lands End Trail, pass Painted Rocks Cliff (signs warn against climbing here). Go up and right on the long flight of railroad-tie steps; benches offer nice spots to rest and enjoy the views. From the top of the stairs, the trail descends through eucalyptus and spindly bishop pines to yet another trail intersection. Go left, back toward the strait.

Near the cliff's edge again, and around Deadman's Point, views open of the Golden Gate. Bowers of cypress arc over the path, and the exclusive homes of Sea Cliff, with China Beach below, can be seen. It's a bonanza of color on a clear day: the international orange of the bridge, the pastels of the homes, the smoky green-blue of the ocean, the bright blue of the sky, and the bleached sails of boats in the bay.

As you approach trail's end at about 2 miles, the path narrows again and is bounded by thick underbrush. The rail trail leads to the edge of the Lincoln Park Golf Course near the Palace of the Legion of Honor. The wooden overlook at Eagles Point, the turnaround point, offers yet another chance to savor the views before you retrace your steps to the Point Lobos trailhead.

24 BARBARY COAST TRAIL

Aside from the richness of San Francisco's food, shopping, cultural districts, and views, this rail trail offers something few others do: the chance to ride the rails in one of the city's fabled cable cars for a leg of the route.

Activities:

Start: Cable car stop at Hyde and Beach Streets off Fisherman's Wharf

Distance: 3 to 4 miles (give or take, with the cable car shuttle) round-trip

Difficulty: Moderate if you ride the cable car, hard if you don't

Seasons/schedule: Year-round, sunrise to sunset

Fees and permits: A fee is charged to ride the cable car.

Trail surface and conditions: The surface is mixed: concrete sidewalk, brick, asphalt, and boardwalk, and mostly well maintained.

Accessibility: Though technically most of the trail is accessible to people using wheelchairs, negotiating the steep grades on Hyde and Powell Streets is tough for any user, including walkers and cable car operators. The climb over the Stockton grade is also a potential challenge.

Canine compatibility: Leashed dogs permitted on the sidewalks but not on the cable cars

Amenities: Public restroom facilities are scattered along the route, including at the trailheads at Fisherman's Wharf and at Hallidie Plaza at the base of Powell on Market Street. As far as food is concerned, what can I say? Upscale, continental, Chinese, Italian, fast food, seafood . . . if you can't find what you crave somewhere along the line, it probably doesn't exist.

Trail contact: The trail is a project of the San Francisco Museum and Historical Society, which has placed bronze plaques in the sidewalks along the route and conducts guided tours; (415) 537-1105; www.sfhistory.org. Information is also available at https://barbarycoasttrail.org.

Nearest town: San Francisco

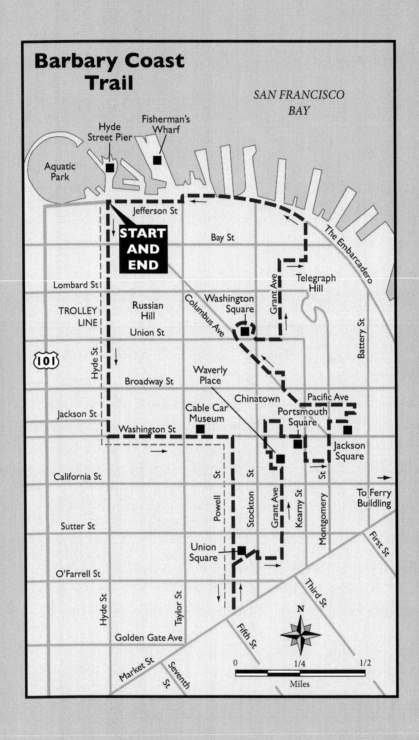

Barbary Coast Trail

SAN FRANCISCO BAY

Hyde Street Pier
Fisherman's Wharf
Aquatic Park
Jefferson St

START AND END

Bay St
The Embarcadero
Lombard St
TROLLEY LINE
Russian Hill
Union St
Telegraph Hill
Washington Square
Grant Ave
Battery St
101
Hyde St
Broadway St
Waverly Place
Chinatown
Pacific Ave
Cable Car Museum
Portsmouth Square
Jackson St
Washington St
Jackson Square
California St
St
St
St
Sutter St
Powell
Stockton
Grant Ave
Kearny St
Montgomery
To Ferry Building
Union Square
First St
O'Farrell St
Hyde St
Taylor St
Third St
N
Golden Gate Ave
Fifth St
Market St
Seventh St

0   1/4   1/2
Miles

Maps: While no downloadable map is available from sponsoring entities, you can purchase a guide to the trail online from www.sfhistory.org. You can also follow the bronze plaques inlaid in the sidewalk along the way.

Cell service: Good

Transportation: MUNI, 311 (toll-free in San Francisco) or (415) 701-2311; www.sfmta.com. Golden Gate Transit, 511 (toll-free in the Bay Area) or (415) 455-2000; www.goldengate.org.

Finding the trailhead: If walking, you can begin this route anywhere along the streets it follows. If you travel the trail as described, you'll begin with a cable car ride from Fisherman's Wharf, at the intersection of Hyde and Beach, where on-street and garage parking are available for a fee. Another option is to begin at 5th and Mission. After parking at one of many parking garages or on the street (all for a fee), you can stroll 1 block north to the Market Street cable car stop, then ride to Fisherman's Wharf and walk the rail trail clockwise.

Trailhead GPS: Cable car stop at Hyde and Beach Streets off Fisherman's Wharf: N37 48.411 / W 122 25.254

The Main Line

The Barbary Coast Trail knits San Francisco's historic highlights together on a long, pleasant walking (and riding) tour. From cable cars to Chinatown to Union Square, from the Financial District to Coit Tower to Fisherman's Wharf, you'll see it all along this route.

The route qualifies as a rail with trail because a portion of it follows the Hyde and Powell Street cable car lines. These tracks, and the open-air cars that ride upon them, are known the world over and provide the perfect start (or end) to an unforgettable tour of the City by the Bay.

The route begins with a cable car ride from the base of Hyde Street at Fisherman's Wharf. The Hyde-Powell cable car route, which dates back to the late nineteenth century, is a National Historical Monument and, according to the San Francisco Museum and Historical Society, was the brainchild of a gentleman who witnessed the ineffectiveness of a team of horses attempting to haul a load up one of the city's steep hills. Hitching a ride, which takes you to the transportation hub downtown at Market and Powell Streets, will most likely involve a long wait in line, but it is well worth both the money and the time. The route can be followed on foot, but given the choice . . .

The cable car takes you up and over Russian Hill, past lovely mansions with awesome views of the bay. Dropping down Washington Street (the descent punctuated by the smell of the cable car's wooden brakes heating up), you'll pass the Cable Car Museum, housed in the old Ferries and Cliff House Railroad building. A final descent through crowded downtown via Powell Street lands you at Market Street, where you'll find a Bay Area Rapid Transit (BART) station, the San Francisco Visitor Center and, a block south via 5th Street, the San Francisco Mint.

From this southernmost point of the trail, locate the bronze marker at the corner of Powell and Market, and head north along Powell, back toward the waterfront. Similar markers—180 of them—are set in the pavement at nearly every street intersection along the route. Complete guides are available for purchase along the route and online; the directions provided here will simply get you from one major attraction to the next.

The walk up Powell Street leads across Ellis and Geary Streets to Union Square, San Francisco's shopping center. The markers lead through the heart of the square to the northeast corner at Post and Stockton. Cross Post and head south on Stockton to quaint Maiden Lane, which is closed to vehicle traffic and offers upscale shopping options. Once the retail heart of the city, Union Square has experienced major disruption following the COVID-19 pandemic, and though it may not be as vibrant as it once was, the square remains a vital cultural fulcrum. Walkers in downtown should also be aware that people experiencing homelessness may be camped on sidewalks.

At the end of Maiden Lane, turn left on Grant and head north across Post, Sutter, and Bush into Chinatown, passing through the historic Dragon's Gate. The transformation is invigorating, as the streets clog with tourists and local residents bustling from shop to shop and restaurant to restaurant. The route leads uphill across Pine to the California Street intersection, where the brick facade of Old Saint Mary's Cathedral marks the northeast corner. Head left on Sacramento to Waverly Place, a narrow alley dubbed the "Street of the Painted Balconies." Emerge onto Jackson and continue to Portsmouth Square, where you'll find restrooms, benches, and

San Francisco's Barbary Coast Trail can either begin or end with a cable car ride.

clusters of local folks hunkered over game boards, along with a monument that commemorates this as the site of the first public school in the city. The square was set to undergo renovation as of fall 2023, so what you see may be different—and better—when you walk there.

Head east from the square along Washington to cross Kearny and descend to Montgomery, at the base of the pyramid-shaped Transamerica Pyramid, famous in the San Francisco skyline. Head right on Montgomery, across Clay, to Commercial Street, a narrow road that was once central to the city's commerce but now is lost in the steel and concrete of a much more modern, albeit transitional in the post-pandemic era, Financial District.

To continue toward Fisherman's Wharf, follow Montgomery north to Jackson. The markers lead you east to Jackson Square, then back north to Pacific and the site of the old Barbary Coast, once home to wild, prosperous, and infamous businesses. Follow Pacific up to Kearny and then turn right along Columbus Avenue into North Beach, home of "beat San Francisco," where authors Jack Kerouac and Allen Ginsberg once hung out. The trail jogs onto Grant, then continues along Columbus, through a complicated intersection at Stockton and Green, and past numerous eateries that feature alfresco seating.

Cross Union to Washington Square, which features broad lawns, a tot lot, restrooms, and the spectacular Saints Peter and Paul Catholic Church on its northern front. Coit Tower, atop Telegraph Hill, rises to the right (east). The main trail climbs to the top of the hill via Greenwich, then descends via Grant, Francisco, and Kearny to the Embarcadero; an alternative route, suitable for people using wheelchairs, follows Stockton and Northpoint to the waterfront.

At the Embarcadero turn left and follow the crowds and the MUNI tracks past the historic piers toward Fisherman's Wharf. The route (now also the Bay Trail) passes Pier 39, the Aquarium of the Bay, the headquarters for the Blue and Gold Fleet (which offers bay cruises and trips to notorious Alcatraz Island), as well as the busy restaurant and shopping district of the wharf itself. Finish the tour back at the cable car base at the bottom of Hyde Street. Ghirardelli Square and Aquatic Park are a block to the west.

25 BLACK DIAMOND MINES REGIONAL PRESERVE RAILROAD BED TRAIL

Mount Diablo dominates the skyline of the East Bay and forms the bedrock upon which the rail trail in Black Diamond Mines Regional Preserve is built. The trail, short and sweet, leads to an abundance of historic sites within the expansive preserve.

Activities:

Start: Black Diamond Mines park entrance station

Distance: 1 mile one way

Difficulty: Easy

Seasons/schedule: Year-round, sunrise to sunset

Fees and permits: An entrance fee is charged.

Trail surface and conditions: Dirt and ballast. The path may be muddy after rains during the winter months.

Accessibility: The trail is not accessible to people using wheelchairs.

Canine compatibility: Dogs must be leashed in developed areas of the preserve and where grazing animals are present, but are allowed off-leash under voice control in open space areas. Keep in mind that dogs off-leash may romp in poison oak and are more likely to have potentially disastrous encounters with wildlife such as rattlesnakes.

Amenities: Restrooms and water are available at the park office, which is near the lower end of the trail. Restrooms are also available near the trail's end. No food is available along the route but can be found in the towns nearby.

Trail contact: East Bay Regional Park District; (888) EB-PARKS or (888) 327-2757; www.ebparks.org/parks/black-diamond. You can reach the park directly by calling (925) 757-2620.

Nearest towns: Pittsburgh, Antioch

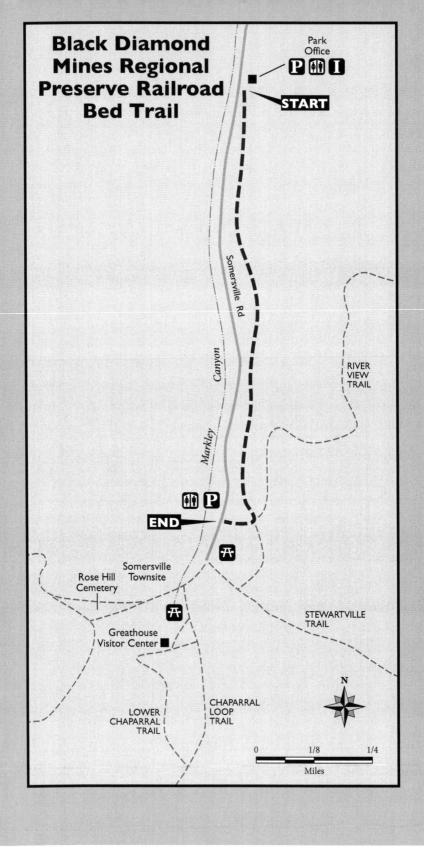

Black Diamond Mines Regional Preserve Railroad Bed Trail

Park Office

START

Somersville Rd

Canyon

Markley

RIVER VIEW TRAIL

END

Somersville Townsite

Rose Hill Cemetery

STEWARTVILLE TRAIL

Greathouse Visitor Center

N

CHAPARRAL LOOP TRAIL

LOWER CHAPARRAL TRAIL

0   1/8   1/4
Miles

Maps: An excellent downloadable map is part of the park brochure available on the East Bay Regional Park District website at www.ebparks.org.

Cell service: Marginal to none

Transportation: No public transportation currently serves the preserve.

Finding the trailhead: From CA 4 in Antioch, take the Somersville Road exit. Go south on Somersville Road for 1.6 miles to where the road enters the Black Diamond Mines Regional Preserve. Go another mile up the canyon to the park entrance station. The lower trailhead for the Railroad Bed Trail is located here, at the south end of the large parking lot on the east side of Somersville Road. Head up the canyon for another mile to reach the upper parking area, where you will also find a good-size parking lot, a corral, and picnic sites. Parking is plentiful at both trailheads.

Trailhead GPS: N37 58.253 / W121 51.721

The Main Line

The foothills of Mount Diablo fold into steep, shadowy canyons shaded by swatches of oak woodland and carpeted in tall grasses and wildflowers. Winter rain feeds these grasses, encouraging them to sprout and blush a vivid green; in summer, drought dries them golden and brittle. This short rail trail traverses the grasslands near the base of the mountain and links to the expansive trail system within Black Diamond Mines Regional Preserve. If it's too short, even as an out-and-back trek, consider the trail a gateway to a greater adventure rich in history and natural beauty.

The railroad that once ran along this grade served what were known as the region's black diamond mines. Millions of tons of these diamonds—better known now as coal—were extracted from these hills over a forty-year period at the end of the nineteenth century. A thriving mining district blossomed around the mines, including five towns, the remains of which lie within the 5,000-acre preserve. The rail line, operated by the Black Diamond Coal & Railroad Company, ran for nearly 6 miles from Pittsburg to Somersville.

The Railroad Bed Trail leads into the heart of Black Diamond Mines Regional Preserve, home to abandoned townsites, abandoned mineshafts, and Rose Hill Cemetery.

After the coal mines were abandoned, entrepreneurs shifted their attention to sand, which was extracted from the region in the 1920s. And when those mines ceased operation, ranchers took to the hills, using the old mining equipment, including railroad ties, to outfit their operations.

Because of its ease, this trail is perfect for children and fledgling mountain bikers. It begins beyond the gate at the south end of the parking lot near the park buildings and entrance station and parallels Somersville Road as it heads up into narrowing Markley Canyon. The stream that runs seasonally from the higher reaches of the park lies west of the road, overhung by pockets of oak trees. The rail trail itself is entirely open to the sun and the rain, bordered only by grasses, thistles, and wildflowers. Bring plenty of water and wear a hat if you plan to hike during the heat of a summer's day.

The canyon grows narrower and the adjacent paved road creeps closer to the trail as you climb toward the Somersville townsite. At about the 0.7-mile mark, the trail traverses a raised bed of gray ballast and sand.

Once past this exposed section of the route, the railbed drops below the elevation of Somersville Road, passing a stately shade tree. It fades from open road to doubletrack as it climbs more steeply to the picnic area and corral at 1 mile.

This is the end of the rail trail proper and the turnaround point, but there is much more to see. Another mile's worth of hiking will allow you to tour the popular Somersville area, which includes the Greathouse Portal and the powder magazine, where explosives used in the mining process were stored.

The trailhead at the upper end point of the rail trail also offers abundant opportunities to take longer treks or mountain bike rides into more remote areas of the park. You can visit the end of the Black Diamond railroad line at Nortonville, stopping at the Rose Hill Cemetery along the way, or head east to the Stewartville townsite. The park brochure, which includes some general interpretive material, is a handy tool for planning other explorations.

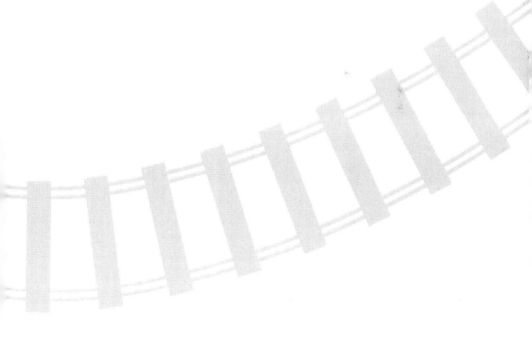

26 OHLONE GREENWAY

This long rail trail is integral to vehicle-free navigation and recreation in three East Bay cities, offering residents and visitors access to community parks and experimental gardens as well as neighborhood schools and businesses. The trail also features intimate contact with the modern Bay Area Rapid Transit railway system.

Activities:

Start: Ohlone Park in Berkeley

Distance: 6 miles one way

Difficulty: Moderate. This relatively long trail is easily broken into segments, which can reduce the difficulty.

Seasons/schedule: Year-round, sunrise to sunset

Fees and permits: None

Trail surface and conditions: Asphalt; mostly well maintained but rough in places

Accessibility: The entire trail is accessible to people using wheelchairs.

Canine compatibility: Leashed dogs permitted

Amenities: No public restrooms are available at either trailhead, and there's only one along the route proper, located at the ball courts near the Berkeley end point. Multiple water fountains are located along the trail. Although there are no restaurants or grocery stores along the path itself, a quick jog onto a neighboring street, especially in Albany and El Cerrito, will land you in shopping districts or malls presenting a parade of culinary outlets.

Trail contacts: The trail passes through three cities. In Berkeley contact the Parks, Recreation & Waterfront Department; (510) 981-6700; https://berkeleyca.gov/your-government/about-us/departments/parks-recreation-waterfront. In Albany contact the Community Development Department; (510) 528-5760; www.albanyca.org. In El Cerrito contact

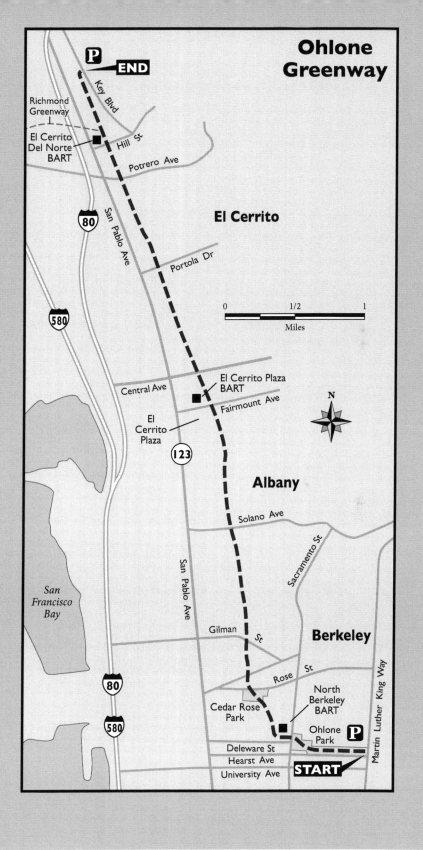

the Recreation Department; (510) 559-7000; www.el-cerrito.org/705/ Ohlone-Greenway-Natural-Area-and-Rain-Ga.

Nearest towns: Berkeley, Albany, El Cerrito

Maps: The most complete map of the entire trail is on the Rails-to-Trails Conservancy's TrailLink app at www.traillink.com/trail-maps/ohlone-greenway.

Cell service: Good

Transportation: Bay Area Rapid Transit (BART) tracks fly directly overhead a long stretch of the trail; (510) 464-6000; www.bart.gov. AC Transit also runs buses in the region: (510) 891-4777; www.actransit.org.

Finding the trailhead: To reach the Ohlone Park end point from I-80 in Berkeley, take the University Avenue exit and head east on University Avenue toward the University of California, Berkeley, campus. Turn left (north) on Milvia Street and go 2 blocks to Hearst Avenue. Ohlone Park is on your left. Park along the street.

To reach the Key Boulevard end point from I-80 in El Cerrito, take the San Pablo Avenue exit (CA 123). Go south on San Pablo Avenue to Conlon Avenue and turn left. Follow Conlon Avenue east for 1 block to its intersection with Key Boulevard and turn right onto Key Boulevard. The trail is located on the right (west) side of Key Boulevard. Again, park along the street.

Trailhead GPS: N37 52.408 / W122 16.401

The Main Line

Although distinctly urban and often utilized as a car-free commuter route for neighborhood folk, the Ohlone Greenway doubles as a recreational trail. Yes, workers and students use the rail trail to walk or ride from their homes to their jobs in city centers or to the University of California, Berkeley, but on any sunny day, you'll also find joggers, cyclists, families out for a stroll, and people walking their dogs on the route.

Except for a short section in Berkeley, the trail runs directly beneath the elevated Bay Area Rapid Transit (BART) tracks. The commuter trains are

The Ohlone Greenway begins in Ohlone Park.

relatively quiet, but their passage is a noisome reminder that the Green-way hosts a rail with trail. That said, the route is nicely landscaped for its entire distance, passing through parks and near community gardens, and is long enough to give those seeking a workout just what they are looking for. As is the case on other long urban trails, travelers may encounter people experiencing homelessness along the route. The trail is described from the Berkeley end point north to the El Cerrito end point, but it is crossed by numerous city streets and can be accessed from any of these points.

The route begins in Ohlone Park, which, like the rail trail, is named for a collective of Native nations that call the Bay Area home. A swath of greenery plunked in the middle of a quiet residential neighborhood, the park offers a tot lot, a dog park, basketball courts, and grassy fields perfectly suited for a pickup game of soccer or Frisbee. The asphalt path heads west toward the bay, weaving back and forth to other meandering paths, until the park ends at the intersection of Delaware and Sacramento Streets at the North Berkeley BART station.

Follow the bike lane that runs along Delaware Street for 2 blocks to its intersection with Acton Street and turn right (north), following the signs for the Ohlone Greenway. Go 2 blocks along Acton Street to its junction with Virginia Street. The Greenway takes off from the northwest corner of the intersection at about the 0.3-mile mark.

The trail weaves across several quiet streets, passing basketball courts that ring with the sounds of people at play, to Cedar Rose Park at 0.5 mile, where a tot lot and rolling lawn invite rest and fun.

At about the 0.8-mile mark, the trail crosses Peralta Avenue and passes two community gardens: the Karl Linn Garden on the right and the Peralta Community Garden on the left, adjacent to the continuation of the trail. The BART tracks rise up to meet the trail, then climb overhead. Pass underneath them at the intersection of Curtis and Gilman Streets at 1 mile. Cross the busy intersection with care and continue on the rail trail into the city of Albany.

At 1.2 miles cross Codornices Creek. The street intersections that follow require concentration, especially the Solano Avenue crossing at the 1.7-mile mark. The trail is nicely landscaped beneath the shade of the tracks and features a parcourse for those who want to add a few crunches or pull-ups to their walking or running routine. Pedestrians can avoid bicycle and skate traffic by stepping onto a winding dirt walkway that parallels the main paved route.

Enter the city of El Cerrito at the 2.4-mile mark and pass the El Cerrito Plaza BART station and the intersection with a link to the Bay Trail at Fairmount Avenue. Although the stretches of trail between roadway intersections become longer and the streets seem less busy, these crossings still demand you use caution.

The landscaping along the trail changes as it passes from city to city. Along the El Cerrito segment, springtime on the trail's verge brings the brilliant orange blooms of poppies and the vivid yellows and greens of clover, as well as riotous calla lilies and other plants that have escaped the confines of gardens. Signs point the way to the local library and other public facilities.

As you near the 4-mile mark, along a section of trail between Schmidt Lane and Potrero Avenue, you'll pass through the unique plant environment designated a Dinosaur Forest. No dinosaurs are present; the name refers to some prehistoric-looking plants that grow in this Urban Forest Demonstration Area, including a wide variety of exotic trees and shrubs marked with interpretive signs.

Reach Hill Street at the 4.6-mile mark and pass the El Cerrito Del Norte BART station. Beyond the station the trail skirts the parking lot of a neighboring apartment building, then climbs to Baxter Creek and its little park, which is nicely accented with small flower beds. The creek was the subject of a preservation effort by a grassroots organization called Friends of Baxter Creek, which promoted an extension of the Ohlone Greenway along the creek to the San Francisco Bay Trail via the Richmond Greenway—now in place and described in the Bonus Track that follows.

The Ohlone Greenway ends beyond Key Boulevard, continuing for about 0.25 mile along Baxter Creek, which has been nicely restored and features a seating area. At about the 6-mile mark, either return as you came or backtrack to the BART station and catch a ride back to Berkeley.

BONUS TRACK: RICHMOND GREENWAY

This urban rail trail provides recreational opportunity for local residents and a ribbon of open space in an otherwise heavily developed cityscape. The route sits on the old Atchison, Topeka, and Santa Fe Railway grade, which runs parallel to Ohio and Chanslor Avenues through an underserved industrial/residential area of Richmond, and then alongside the active Bay Area Rapid Transit rail line. The route connects on its east end with the Ohlone Greenway in El Cerrito, giving users more opportunity to stretch it out on a bike ride, walk, or run, or to get from home to work or school in any of the neighboring cities without using a car.

Like other urban rail trails traversing underserved communities, you may encounter the camps of people experiencing homelessness along the route. You'll also pass through pocket parks with benches and grassy areas, playgrounds, small gardens, dirt biking tracks, ballfields and basketball courts, and public art/graffiti. The complicated landscape reflects the complicated city and metropolitan area that surrounds it.

Activities:

Start: Trailhead on 2nd Street

Distance: 2.5 miles one way

Difficulty: Easy

The Richmond Greenway offers great views eastward into the Berkeley Hills.

Seasons/schedule: Year-round, sunrise to sunset

Fees and permits: None

Trail surface and conditions: Asphalt. The trail offers access to pocket parks that may be occupied by people experiencing homelessness.

Accessibility: The entire route is accessible to people using wheelchairs.

Canine compatibility: Leashed dogs permitted

Amenities: Restrooms are available in pocket parks along the route. Food and water are available elsewhere in Richmond and El Cerrito.

Trail contact: City of Richmond Public Works/Parks Department; (510) 231-3004; www.ci.richmond.ca.us/1118/Richmond-Greenway-Project

Nearest towns: Richmond, El Cerrito

Maps: The best map is available on the Rails-to-Trails Conservancy's Trail-Link website at www.traillink.com/trail/richmond-greenway.

Cell service: Good

Transportation: Bay Area Rapid Transit (BART), (510) 464-6000; www.bart .gov. AC Transit, (510) 891-4777; www.actransit.org.

Finding the trailhead: The greenway can be accessed from the neighborhood roads it intersects, with parking available streetside. A small parking lot is available near its west end, at the 2nd Street junction. From I-580 in Richmond, take the Canal Boulevard exit. Head north on Canal Boulevard for 0.3 mile to the West Ohio Avenue/Garrard Boulevard (Richmond Parkway) intersection. Turn right (east) on West Ohio; go 0.5 mile to 2nd Street and turn left (north). A small parking area is at the trailhead on the right (east) side of 2nd Street just north of the intersection with West Ohio Avenue. The trail also extends west from this junction, linking to the Richmond Parkway. The western end point is at the El Cerrito Del Norte BART station.

Trailhead GPS: N37 55.882 / W122 22.038

27 IRON HORSE REGIONAL TRAIL

Oak-shaded greenbelts, quiet neighborhoods, modern business districts, quaint shopping areas, long stretches that work the muscles, sunshine, rolling hills—the lengthy Iron Horse Trail, a California classic, tallies it all and adds up to a wonderful recreational experience.

Activities:

Start: Trailhead at Monument Lane and Mohr Lane in Concord

Distance: 25.5 miles one way to the Dublin/Pleasanton BART Station; 32 miles one way end-to-end

Difficulty: Strenuous if taken as a whole, but when broken into smaller chunks, the rail trail is easy to moderate.

Seasons/schedule: Year-round, sunrise to sunset

Fees and permits: None

Trail surface and conditions: Asphalt and concrete with a parallel dirt walkway on some segments; the route is well used and well maintained.

Accessibility: The entire trail is accessible to people using wheelchairs.

Canine compatibility: Leashed dogs permitted

Amenities: Public restrooms are scattered along the trail, at the BART station and Walden Park in Walnut Creek, at Hap McGee Park in Danville, and at the San Ramon Community Center and Park in San Ramon. You can pick up a bite to eat at innumerable places along the northern reaches of the trail. Grocery stores, fast-food joints, snazzy restaurants, and coffeehouses are available at the trail's midpoint in the Danville area. South of Danville the trail passes through more residential areas; it is not until you reach the mall at Alcosta Boulevard that you again encounter convenient eats.

Trail contact: East Bay Regional Park District; (888) EB-PARKS or (888) 327-2757; www.ebparks.org/trails/interpark/iron-horse

Nearest towns: Concord, Pleasant Hill, Walnut Creek, Alamo, Danville, San Ramon, Dublin, Pleasanton

Maps: A downloadable, printable map is available on the East Bay Regional Parks site at www.ebparks.org/trails/interpark/iron-horse.

Cell service: Mostly good

Transportation: Bay Area Rapid Transit (BART), (510) 464-6000; www.bart .gov. AC Transit, (510) 891-4777; www.actransit.org

Finding the trailhead: The trail parallels I-680 through the towns and cities of Concord, Pleasant Hill, Walnut Creek, Alamo, Danville, San Ramon, Dublin, and Pleasanton. It can be accessed at numerous points along its route.

Limited street parking is available on Mohr Lane at the trailhead located east of I-680 on Monument Boulevard (the start of this route description). You can also pick up the trail at the Walnut Creek BART station on Treat Boulevard; this too is east of I-680, with parking located north of the station on Coggins Drive. The northernmost trailhead as of summer 2023 was at Marsh Drive near CA 4 in Concord.

The park-and-ride parking lot on the east side of the interstate at Rudgear Road in Danville offers good parking and trail access. Cross to the west side of the freeway and go about 25 yards north along the frontage road to the trailhead. You can also pick up the trail in downtown Danville, near the Danville Depot on West Prospect Avenue at Diablo Road.

Parking is available at the San Ramon Community Center and Park. From I-680, take Bollinger Canyon Road east toward Alcosta Boulevard. The park is on the north side of the road.

The southernmost access for this route is at the Dublin/Pleasanton BART station, just off I-580.

Trailhead GPS: Monument Boulevard trailhead: N37 56.871 / W122 03.096

The Main Line

From Silicon Valley–esque business districts to trailside lemonade stands, you'll see it all along the lengthy and popular Iron Horse Regional Trail.

At its northern end, the Iron Horse rail trail is urban and metropolitan, passing through business districts with high-rise buildings and busy four-lane roads. At its center, in Alamo and Danville (arguably the prettiest

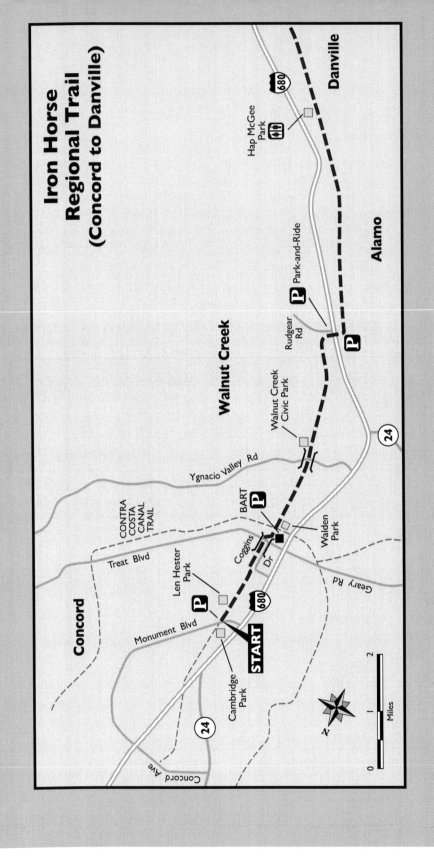

Iron Horse Regional Trail (Concord to Danville)

Danville

680

Hap McGee Park

Alamo

Park-and-Ride

Rudgear Rd

Walnut Creek

Walnut Creek Civic Park

Ygnacio Valley Rd

CONTRA COSTA CANAL TRAIL

Treat Blvd

Len Hester Park

BART

Coggins Dr

Walden Park

Geary Rd

Monument Blvd

Concord

Cambridge Park

START

680

24

24

Concord Ave

N

Miles

0   1   2

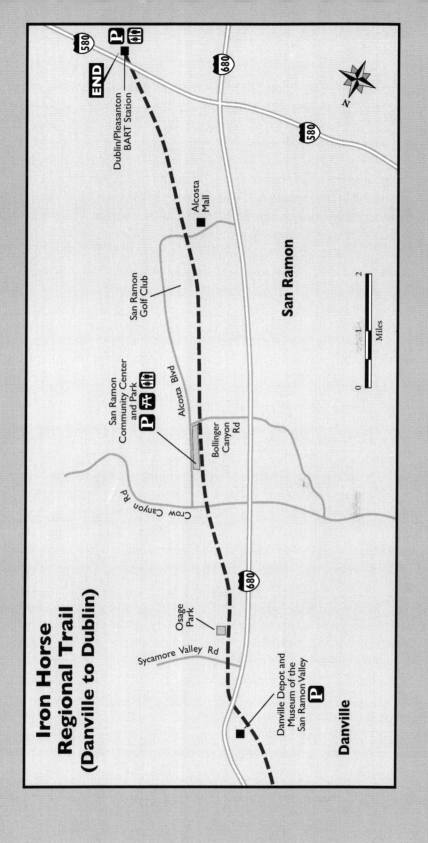

section of the trail), the path passes through wealthy suburbia on a swath of oak-shaded pavement bordered by lush grasses, wildflowers, and well-kept homes. Downtown Danville is quaint, outfitted with upscale supermarkets and coffee shops.

South of Danville, both the neighborhoods and the trail are more exposed. Gone are the shady oaks, replaced by a wide treeless greenbelt upon which the grasses are vividly green in winter and spring, and dry to a crackling yellow in summer and fall. Wooden fences delineate the boundary between the trail and the neighborhoods on either side of it.

Beyond Crow Canyon Road, the trail passes through industrial complexes boxed neatly in glass and masonry, with large parking lots abutting the trail. Continuing south, the trail passes through the San Ramon Golf Club, where trail users are protected from wayward golf balls by a bower of mesh-like fencing. The setting is gritty and urban at trail's end in Dublin.

The rail trail follows the right-of-way of the Southern Pacific Railroad, which established a branch line in the San Ramon Valley in 1890 to serve the farming and ranching communities that had sprung up in the fertile, then-sparsely populated area. The railroad served the valley and its burgeoning towns for about seventy years, until people's preference to travel by car rendered the rail line obsolete. The tracks were abandoned in 1975 and by the early 1980s, cities in the valley had begun to acquire the right-of-way and set it aside for a trail. By the end of the 1980s, sections of the trail had been constructed, paved, and dedicated, and the Iron Horse rail trail began its own ascendancy. The East Bay Regional Park District has expanded the rail-trail corridor from what's described here north to CA 4 (Marsh Drive) in Concord and south and east to Livermore; the entire route is a bit more than 32 long miles one way.

The existing trail can be done in its entirety by fit cyclists or fit cyclists using pedal-assisted electric bikes, or in segments either on wheels or on foot. I found the section from Rudgear Road to Danville to be the prettiest—and probably the most enjoyable for hikers and runners—with the segment in San Ramon the most conducive to exercise-oriented cycling, running, and skating. Every part of the trail offers wonderful recreational opportunities to neighborhood residents.

The trail is described beginning in the north at Monument Boulevard in Concord and running southward to the Dublin/Pleasanton BART

A cyclist climbs a bridge on the Iron Horse Trail.

station. The streetlight at Mohr Lane offers safe passage across Monument Boulevard, where you pick up the southbound trail. The path runs through well-kept subdivisions, crossing intersections with tree-lined neighborhood streets via crosswalks, railroad bridges, and underpasses, to Coggins Drive. A scenic bridge spans busy Treat Boulevard at 2.7 miles, arcing over the eight-lane roadway and landing at the BART station on the south side of the thoroughfare.

The intersection with the Contra Costa Canal Trail is at 3 miles. Continue straight (south) through the greenbelt (or goldbelt once the grasses dry in summer); at 3.1 miles you can venture right (west) into Walden Park, which features a tot lot, picnic tables, water, and restrooms.

The rail trail proceeds south to the Ygnacio Valley Road bridge in Walnut Creek at about 4.2 miles; this is followed by a more traditional trestle bridge. A couple of street crossings come in quick succession at about the 5-mile mark; the first at Mount Diablo Boulevard, the second leading to the west side of Newell Avenue. Beyond Newell the trail is squeezed between apartment buildings and businesses and an ivy-draped wall that serves as a barrier to South Broadway, which runs parallel.

At about 6.5 miles arrive at the intersection of Rudgear Road and I-680. The park-and-ride lot is on the southeast corner of the intersection. Pass under the interstate and cross the frontage road (Danville Boulevard); the trail continues about 25 yards north of the stoplight on the frontage road. A small Iron Horse Trail parking lot is available here.

The setting of the rail trail now gives the impression of being almost rural, passing through an oak woodland greenway spread with grasses and wildflowers and bordered by large homes with tasteful fences and ornamental shrubbery. Cross a number of small neighborhood roads before the trail's intersection with Stone Valley Road at 9 miles, where the scenery becomes more urban. Cross a bridge at Hemme Avenue. At about 10 miles, follow Camille Avenue left (east) to Hap Magee Ranch Park, where you will find water and restrooms.

Cross another small bridge before Hartford Road, then travel south for a mile to West Prospect Avenue, where the Danville Depot and the Museum of the San Ramon Valley border the path; visit www.museumsrv.org for more information on these attractions.

Now in downtown Danville, the trail circles the west side of a shopping center and traces Railroad Avenue. Cross Prospect Avenue and San

Ramon Valley Boulevard before passing under the interstate at about the 12.5-mile mark.

By the time the rail trail crosses Sycamore Valley Road at 13.2 miles, it has taken on a decidedly suburban aspect, passing through a broad greenbelt that resonates with noise from the nearby freeway. From this point to Alcosta Boulevard, the route can be hot and dry—especially in summer—with no water available save that found at the San Ramon Community Center, which is at about the 17.5-mile mark at the Bollinger Canyon Road crossing. Between Sycamore Valley Road and Bollinger Canyon Road, you'll cross Fostoria Road, where a large "golf ball" and power station adorn the east side of the path. Cross Crow Canyon Road as well, which is bordered by industrial buildings. At 18 miles pass a park with a tot lot at Montevideo Road.

The power poles that have been shadowing the trail since Crow Canyon Road end at Pine Valley Road. At about 19.5 miles you will reach the San Ramon Golf Club, passing under the arch of fencing that protects trail users from stray golf balls.

At about the 23-mile mark, cross Alcosta Boulevard. The trail skirts a shopping mall, crosses a bridge, and drops into a greenbelt bordered by a canal on the west side. Look for egrets, herons, ducks, and other waterfowl in the waterway as you pass.

At about 24 miles the Iron Horse crosses Amador Valley Boulevard, then follows the canal for another 0.2 mile to a bridge. On the far side of the span, the rail trail intersects the Alamo Creek Trail. Go left, then quickly right to remain on the Iron Horse Trail; an old trestle reminds you of the origins of the path.

Cross Dougherty Drive at 24.5 miles, and the route enters a decidedly more industrial setting. Another bridge and the Dublin Boulevard crossing signal the approaching turnaround point at the Dublin/Pleasanton BART station, in the shadow of I-580 at 25.5 miles. Unless you've arranged a pickup or want to ride the train back to Walnut Creek, return as you came.

Plans call for the Iron Horse Regional Trail to eventually extend 55 miles, from Suisun Bay in the north to Livermore. Stay tuned.

28 LAFAYETTE-MORAGA REGIONAL TRAIL

Rolling, grassy hills trimmed with spreading oaks form the back-drop for this scenic rail trail. The route links exclusive residential communities with St. Mary's College, the community park at Moraga Commons, and more rustic trails in parks in the neighboring watershed.

Activities:

Start: Olympic Boulevard trailhead in Lafayette

Distance: 7.6 miles one way

Difficulty: Moderate due to length

Seasons/schedule: Year-round, sunrise to sunset

Fees and permits: None

Trail surface and conditions: Asphalt and concrete

Accessibility: The entire trail is accessible to people using wheelchairs. The Valle Vista Staging Area parking lot is unpaved.

Canine compatibility: Leashed dogs permitted

Amenities: No restrooms are available at the Olympic Boulevard Staging Area, but restrooms are available at the Moraga Commons and at the Valle Vista Staging Area. Few opportunities to grab a bite to eat or fill your water bottle are available along the trail in Lafayette, but once you enter Moraga, you will find grocery stores and restaurants near the path.

Trail contact: East Bay Regional Park District; (888) EB-PARKS or (888) 327-2757; www.ebparks.org/trails/interpark/lafayette-moraga

Nearest towns: Lafayette, Moraga

Maps: A downloadable, printable map is available on the East Bay Regional Parks site at www.ebparks.org/trails/interpark/lafayette-moraga.

Cell service: Mostly good

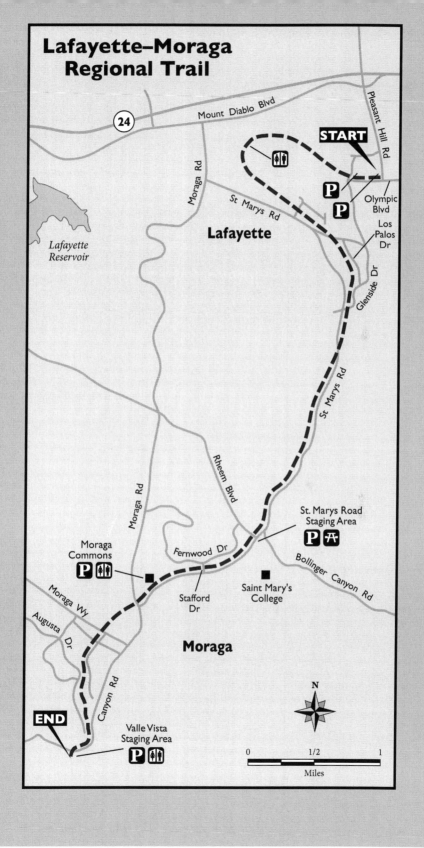

Lafayette–Moraga Regional Trail

24

Mount Diablo Blvd

Pleasant Hill Rd

START

P

P

Olympic Blvd

Moraga Rd

St Marys Rd

Lafayette

Los Palos Dr

Lafayette Reservoir

Glenside Dr

St Marys Rd

Rheem Blvd

St. Marys Road Staging Area

P

Moraga Rd

Fernwood Dr

Moraga Commons

P

Bollinger Canyon Rd

Stafford Dr

Saint Mary's College

Moraga Wy

Augusta Dr

Moraga

Canyon Rd

N

END

Valle Vista Staging Area

P

0   1/2   1

Miles

Transportation: The County Connection, (925) 676-7500; https://county connection.com

Finding the trailhead: To reach the northern end point in Lafayette, take the Pleasant Hill Road exit from CA 24. Go right (south) on Pleasant Hill Road for 0.9 mile to Olympic Boulevard. Go right (west) on Olympic Boulevard for about 0.1 mile to the parking area, which is on the right side of the road. Ample parking is available.

To reach the Valle Vista Staging Area from CA 24, take the Pleasant Hill exit, go south onto Pleasant Hill Road, then turn right (west) on Mount Diablo Boulevard. Follow Mount Diablo Boulevard to Moraga Road and turn left (south). Go south on Moraga Road to St. Marys Road, and turn left (east). Follow St. Marys Road, which traces the route of the rail trail, to Canyon Road. Canyon Road continues south to the Valle Vista Staging Area parking lot.

Trailhead GPS: N37 53.165 / W122 05.654

The Main Line

The Lafayette-Moraga Regional Trail has many facets: the neat and quiet neighborhoods of Lafayette, the pastoral setting of Saint Mary's College, playful Moraga Commons, the relative wildness of the Valle Vista Staging Area. The route is more local than the nearby Iron Horse Regional Trail, but its combined charms make it abundantly appealing.

The rail trail lies on the former bed of the Sacramento Northern Railroad; a scattering of railroad crossing signs hints at its past. But where electric trolleys enabled people to get from one destination to the next without breaking a sweat, now hikers, cyclists, and skaters propel themselves through the sun-splashed hills.

The trail is described from north to south, but direction makes no difference, as the trail is an up-and-down affair, with the high point at the "pass" near Saint Mary's College. Beginning at the Olympic Boulevard trailhead, go west on the paved path, which meanders among the old trees of an orchard for 0.2 mile to the second parking lot at the intersection of Reliez Station Road and Olympic Boulevard. Cross Reliez Station

Road to continue. The rail trail runs within a narrow greenbelt that passes between residences.

At about 0.5 mile the trail crosses Hawthorn Drive. Pass a railroad sign, then cross Foye Drive at about the 1-mile mark. Beyond, the path weaves through the Moraga Pumping Plant complex, crosses a bridge, then proceeds through more neighborhoods. A brief section of the trail is on Brookdale Court, a residential street, but resumption of the rail trail proper is just ahead.

By the 2-mile mark, intersections with neighborhood streets are spaced a bit farther apart. Pass the Las Trampas Pool complex at about 2.5 miles and continue south.

At about 3 miles cross busy St. Marys Road. Parking is available midway along the trail at South Lucille Lane; Lafayette Community Park is to the east, across Las Trampas Creek.

Once across St. Marys Road, the trail passes into more scenic terrain, rolling below the folds of the oak-covered hills. At about 3.5 miles a waterfall drips from the rocks on the right (west) side of the trail during the rainy season.

The route climbs to cross Rheem Boulevard at about 4 miles. To the left (east) is the Saint Mary's College campus, its buildings sparkling white among the greens and golds of the surrounding hills. Parking for trail users is available here and the rail trail itself, which begins its descent at this point, is accompanied by a parcourse.

The trail wanders down to Moraga Commons at 5.5 miles, where you'll find restrooms, water, ample parking, lawns for picnicking, a disc golf course, a skate park, and a playground for the wee ones. The trail skirts the park, then crosses Moraga Road.

On the other side of Moraga Road, the trail surface changes from asphalt to concrete. The trail also becomes markedly less scenic—in fact, it's merely a glorified sidewalk—as it passes Moraga Ranch and a shopping center. Continue southwest along School Street to Country Club Drive, and go right (west) along Country Club Drive to the rail trail, which heads left (southwest) before the bridge spanning Moraga Creek.

The route snakes between homes and the creek to an S-curve behind apartment buildings, then climbs beside Canyon Road to hilltop views at about the 7-mile mark. From this high point, the trail drops down and south to the Valle Vista Staging Area, with restrooms and loads of parking.

The staging area also serves as the trailhead for the Rocky Ridge Trail and other trails in the watershed managed by the East Bay Municipal Utility District (EBMUD).

Unless you have arranged for a shuttle, this is the turnaround point. Return as you came.

BONUS TRACK: MONTCLAIR RAILROAD TRAIL IN SHEPHERD CANYON

The Shepherd Canyon Trail, also known as the Montclair Railroad Trail, traces Shepherd Canyon Road and Shepherd Canyon Creek up into the hills above metropolitan Oakland. The route winds through a well-heeled residential area in the Montclair neighborhood and then passes into a lovely swath of open space shaded by oak woodland that encompasses Shepherd Canyon Park. The trail and its linear park provide local residents and visitors with a scenic escape and cyclists access to the string of East Bay Regional Park properties that span the ridgeline.

Built on a grade established by the Sacramento Northern Railroad, part of an extensive interurban passenger and freight railway system link-ing San Francisco to the capital city and points beyond, the right-of-way was eventually abandoned after revenues were sucked dry by the Great Depression and passengers by the allure of the automobile.

The path also carries historic importance as the flashpoint of local community activism. The ascendancy of the automobile brought with it more than a lack of passenger interest in rail travel—it also prompted a highway-building boom. One of those highways was set to run through the canyon and include the unused rail corridor, but local residents mounted a vociferous and ultimately successful campaign that shut the highway plan down. When the freeway fizzled, the East Bay Regional Park District and the city of Oakland developed an operating agreement that allowed transformation of the railroad right-of-way into a trail. Read more about the rail trail's history at www.montclairrrtrail.org.

The route begins down and west of the Shepherd Canyon Park trail-head, above a shopping center in Montclair Village. It crosses Snake Road, then continues upcanyon alongside Shepherd Canyon Road. The trail merges streetside at Escher Drive and continues to its end at Saroni Drive.

The bike path that extends along Saroni Drive climbs to Skyline Boulevard and provides access to the regional parks on the ridge.

Activities:

Start: Shepherd Canyon Park

Distance: 1.5 miles one way

Difficulty: Easy

Seasons/schedule: Year-round, sunrise to sunset

Fees and permits: None

Trail surface and conditions: Asphalt; the trail is well maintained.

Accessibility: The entire trail is accessible to people using wheelchairs.

Canine compatibility: Leashed dogs permitted

Amenities: No amenities are available along the trail, but you can find water, restrooms, food, and whatever else you might need in Montclair and neighboring towns.

Trail contact: City of Oakland Parks, Recreation, and Youth Development Department; (510) 238-7275; parksandrec@oaklandca.gov. You can also visit www.shepherdcanyon.org or www.montclairrrtrail.org to learn more.

Nearest town: Oakland

Maps: The best map of the route is on the Rails-to-Trails Conservancy's TrailLink app at www.traillink.com/trail-maps/shepherd-canyon-trail -(montclair-railroad-trail).

Cell service: Good

Transportation: Bay Area Rapid Transit (BART), (510) 464-6000; www.bart .gov. AC Transit, (510) 891-4777; www.actransit.org

Finding the trailhead: To reach the Shepherd Canyon Park access point, which lies near the midpoint of the trail, from CA 13 in Oakland, take the

Park Boulevard exit. Head east (uphill) on Park Boulevard to Mountain Boulevard and go left, paralleling the freeway. At the first stoplight, go right on Snake Road. Follow Snake Road to where it splits and go right on Shepherd Canyon Road. Follow Shepherd Canyon Road to the light at the fire station. Shepherd Canyon Park, with parking, is northeast of the fire station on the right (south) side of Shepherd Canyon Road.

The southwestern end point for the trail is on Medau Place near Mountain Avenue in Montclair. The northeastern end point is at Saroni Drive off Shepherd Canyon Road.

Trailhead GPS: N37 49.532 / W122 12.143

29 PENITENCIA CREEK TRAIL

Tucked in the hills east of San Jose, this rail trail passes through beautiful country that once attracted visitors not only for the spectacular natural setting, but also for the mineral waters that bubbled to the surface near a creek shaded by alders and oaks.

Activities: 🦆 🏛️ 🛼 🎡 🚲 🏃 🎿 🦌

Start: Alum Rock Park Visitor Center

Distance: 2.4 miles one way; 1.8 miles of the Penitencia Creek Trail is on the abandoned railroad corridor

Difficulty: Easy

Seasons/schedule: Year-round, 8 a.m. to a half hour after sunset. The paved section of the trail is passable year-round, but the dirt sections may be difficult or impassable when winter rains turn the surface to mud.

Fees and permits: An entrance fee is charged.

Trail surface and conditions: The section from Penitencia Canyon to Quail Hollow Picnic Area is dirt singletrack. The surface is paved from Quail Hollow to the dirt road 100 yards west of the railroad bridge, then a broad dirt track to the border of the developed section of the park near the visitor center. The route is paved past the visitor center and Youth Science Institute, then narrows to a dirt track for the last mile, ending at the confluence of Penitencia and Aguague Creeks.

Accessibility: The paved portion of the trail is accessible to people using wheelchairs.

Canine compatibility: No dogs allowed; the park is a protected wildlife sanctuary.

Amenities: Restrooms are available at the Eagle Rock and Quail Hollow picnic areas in the western part of the park, at the visitor center, and at the Live Oak Picnic Area in the eastern reaches of the park. Water is also available in the park, but bring a picnic lunch. Groceries and all the other goodies you might require are available in San Jose.

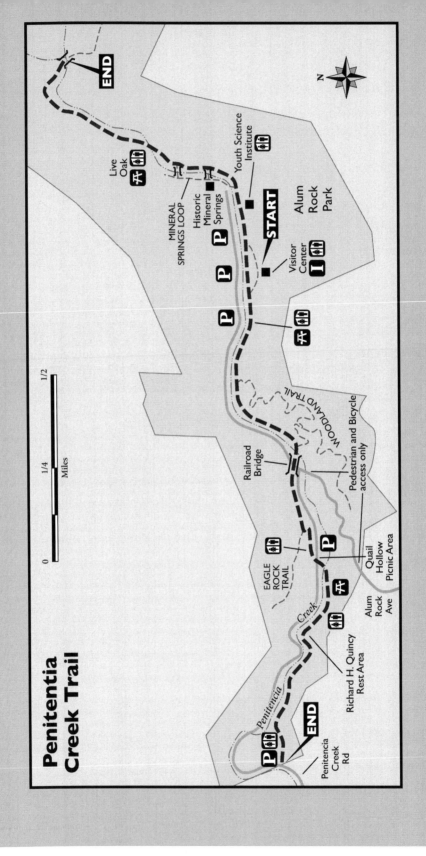

Penitentia Creek Trail

END

Live Oak

Youth Science Institute

MINERAL SPRINGS LOOP

Historic Mineral Springs

P P

P

START

P

Alum Rock Park

Visitor Center

I

Railroad Bridge

WOODLAND TRAIL

Pedestrian and Bicycle access only

Quail Hollow Picnic Area

EAGLE ROCK TRAIL

P

Alum Rock Ave

Penitencia Creek

Richard H. Quincy Rest Area

Penitencia

END

P

Penitencia Creek Rd

N

0   1/4   1/2

Miles

Trail contact: Alum Rock Park, 15350 Penitencia Creek Rd., San Jose; (408) 259-5477; www.sanjoseca.gov/prns

Nearest town: San Jose

Maps: Trail maps are available online on the Alum Rock Park website, www .sanjoseca.gov/Home/Components/FacilityDirectory/FacilityDirectory/ 2088/; georeferenced maps are available for use on a cellphone through Avenza Map

Cell service: Good

Transportation: Valley Transportation Authority, (408) 321-2300; www .vta.org

Finding the trailhead: From I-680 in San Jose, take the McKee Road exit. Go west on McKee Road for 0.2 mile to Capital Avenue. Turn left onto Capital Avenue and go 1.1 miles to Penitencia Creek Road. Turn right (west) on Penitencia Creek Road and go 1.9 miles to the park's entrance station.

To reach the east end of the rail trail, follow the main park road east for 0.6 mile from the entrance station to the large parking lot near the visitor center.

Trailhead GPS: Park entrance: N37 23.827 / W 121 49.537

The Main Line

Alum Rock Park, nestled in a steep canyon in the hills east of sprawling San Jose, has been a retreat for the city-weary for more than a century. Mineral springs—some infused with soda, others smelling of sulfur—as well as a tea garden, restaurant, and dance pavilion, were among the park's lures in the early part of the twentieth century. These days you can't soak in the mineral waters, but you can enjoy the scenery and history of the park from the rail trail that rolls through it.

Alum Rock was a popular resort from 1890 to the early 1930s, and for two bits you could get there via the steam trains of the San Jose and Alum Rock Railroad. The story goes, the journey up to the resort wasn't too bad,

Grottos capture mineral spring water in Alum Rock Park.

but apparently the open cars behind the "steam dummies," or engines, frequently jumped the tracks on the ride back down into town.

At the turn of the twentieth century, railroad owner Hugh Center converted his Alum Rock steam line to an electric narrow-gauge line, and the railway continued to prosper until the Great Depression, when it gradually fell into disuse. The hard times culminated with the dismantlement of the San Jose and Alum Rock Railroad in 1934. The rails and other equipment were salvaged, and remnants of the line that couldn't be salvaged can be seen along the Penitencia Creek Trail, which follows its namesake waterway through much of the park.

The flat track takes visitors past concrete abutments that once supported the tracks, and across an old trestle near Alum Rock. A rich riparian forest of buckeye, maple, walnut, and alder lines the shores of the creek, with the steep walls of the Penitencia Creek canyon rising to grassy heights to the north and south.

The best place to begin the rail trail is at the visitor center. The Penitencia Creek Trail is the paved path wedged between the creek and the lawns fronting the center. Head west on the trail, past the log cabin, where the trail's surface changes from pavement to dirt.

The track continues west along the creek, passing intersections with the Woodland Trail at 0.2 mile and 0.5 mile. At both, stay right (west) on the old railroad bed. At about 0.8 mile you reach the concrete trestle that arcs around Alum Rock to an intersection with the Eagle Rock Trail (the trestle was closed for repairs as of fall 2023). At this point leave the railbed for about 0.2 mile, navigating a quick switchback down to Penitencia Creek Road, and follow this west to the Quail Hollow Picnic Area at 1 mile.

At Quail Hollow cross the creek on a ramshackle bridge, then head west to pick up the trail at the western edge of the picnic area. The route narrows to singletrack as it winds down the south side of Penitencia Creek, passing a couple of concrete abutments and a section of trail supported by a lovely stone retaining wall.

At about 1.8 miles the trail leaves creek-side and enters an open, rustic picnic area. A steep dirt-and-railroad-tie staircase leads down to the parking area on Penitencia Creek Road. Return along the same route to the visitor center.

Exploring Alum Rock Park

Although the section of the Penitencia Creek Trail that heads east from the visitor center to the confluence of Penitencia and Aguague Creeks is not entirely on the railroad grade, it makes a fascinating addition to the route.

From the visitor center, follow the trail east past the greens, the Ramada, and the Youth Science Institute to the mineral springs, grottoes, and picnic area. Pools, fonts, and alcoves shelter the different mineral springs, and an interpretive display describes some of the park's history. About a half mile from the visitor center, the trail crosses to the north side of the creek, the pavement ends, and the route narrows to singletrack. Follow the gently climbing route for another half mile, under the heavy shade of the oaks, buckeyes, and maples, to the overlook and bridge at the confluence of Penitencia and Aguague Creeks.

From the creek crossing, you can return as you came, or you can hitch up onto the South Rim trail and take the high road back into the heart of the park. Other hiking and mountain biking options are also available; download the park map and explore.

A bridge spans the confluence of Penitencia and Aguague Creeks in Alum Rock Park.

BONUS TRACK: BOL PARK BIKE PATH

The Bol Park Bike Path is short but sweet, running alongside Matadero Creek through a peaceful neighborhood in Palo Alto, down the Peninsula from the city of San Francisco. The short path is primarily used by local families seeking a brief romp on a bike or on foot, or by students making their way to the local high school. The path gets bonus points for its playground and natural setting, but it lacks parking and formal trailheads at its end points.

The history of the rail corridor upon which the bike path is built isn't easy to find—a newspaper account describes the persistent efforts of a local community activist who successfully petitioned Southern Pacific for the mile-long strip after it was abandoned in the 1970s. The same activist, many years later, rallied his neighbors to help plant trees and other landscaping alongside the route.

Bol Park's history as a "donkey pasture" is more prominent. Donkeys have cropped the grasses in the small pocket of parkland since the days when Cornelis Bol, a physicist who conducted research at nearby Stanford University, owned the land, and new generations of donkeys have carried on the tradition of entertaining passersby on the rail trail.

The path's southern end point is adjacent to Gunn High School on Miranda Avenue.

Activities:

Start: Bol Park in Palo Alto

Distance: 1.5 miles one way

Difficulty: Easy

Seasons/schedule: Year-round, sunrise to sunset

Fees and permits: None

Trail surface and conditions: Well-maintained asphalt

Accessibility: The entire trail is accessible to people using wheelchairs.

Canine compatibility: Leashed dogs permitted

Amenities: No restrooms, food, or water is available along the trail, but you can find these and more throughout Palo Alto.

Trail contact: City of Palo Alto; (650) 329-2136; www.cityofpaloalto.org

Nearest town: Palo Alto

Maps: The best map is on the Rails-to-Trails Conservancy's TrailLink website at www.traillink.com/trail-maps/bol-park-path.

Cell service: Good

Transportation: Valley Transportation Authority, (408) 321-2300; www.vta .org

Finding the trailhead: To reach the Hanover Street end point and Bol Park trailhead from I-280, take the Page Mill Road exit. Go north on Page Mill Road for about 1.5 miles to Porter Drive. Turn right (southeast) on Porter Drive, which becomes Hanover Street. The northernmost end point is wedged between parking lots of two businesses on the right (southeast) side of Hanover Street, but no parking is available here.

To reach Bol Park, continue down Page Mill Road to El Camino Real. Turn right on El Camino Real and follow it to Matadero Avenue. Turn right onto Matadero Avenue and proceed to Laguna Avenue. Go left on Laguna Avenue a short distance to the park.

Trailhead GPS: N37 24.747 / W122 08.404

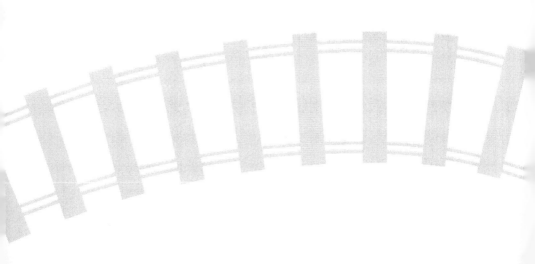

DOWN THE COAST

30 HALF MOON BAY COASTSIDE TRAIL

The Half Moon Bay Coastside Trail offers everything you'd expect from a seaside rail trail, including outstanding views across the bay to the Pacific, spectacular bird-watching, and the invigorating mix of calm and turbulence that only a walk along windswept bluffs can generate.

Activities:

Start: Half Moon Bay State Beach Visitor Center

Distance: 7.5 miles one way total; about 3 miles one way from the Half Moon Bay State Beach Visitor Center to the Redondo Beach parking area

Difficulty: Moderate due only to length

Seasons/schedule: Year-round, sunrise to sunset

Fees and permits: A fee is charged for day use at Half Moon Bay State Beach

Trail surface and conditions: Asphalt within the park boundaries; unpaved singletrack at its southern end

Accessibility: The paved portions of the trail are accessible to people using wheelchairs.

Canine compatibility: Leashed dogs permitted on the Coastside Trail and in campgrounds, but no dogs are allowed on beaches.

Amenities: Restrooms, water, and information are available at the Half Moon Bay State Beach Visitor Center. Other amenities, including restaurants and grocery stores, are available in Half Moon Bay.

Trail contact: Half Moon Bay State Beach; (650) 726-8819; www.parks .ca.gov (search for park by name)

Nearest town: Half Moon Bay

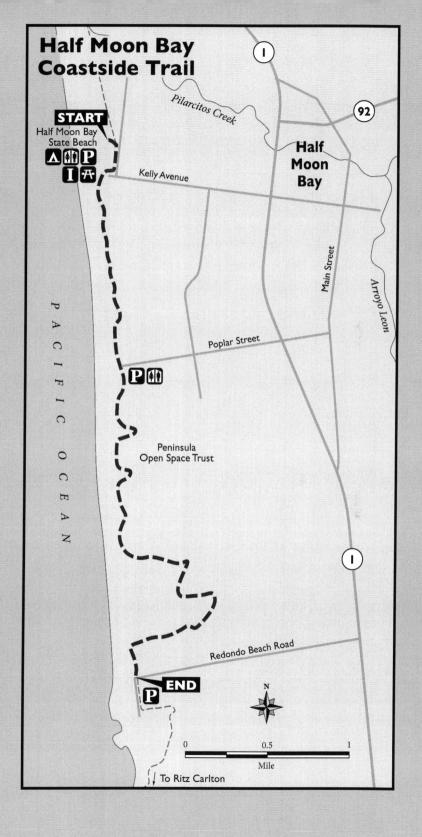

Half Moon Bay Coastside Trail

① 92 Half Moon Bay

Pilarcitos Creek

START
Half Moon Bay State Beach

Kelly Avenue

Main Street

Arroyo Leon

Poplar Street

P A C I F I C   O C E A N

Peninsula Open Space Trust

①

Redondo Beach Road

P **END**

N

0   0.5   1
Mile

To Ritz Carlton

Maps: A map is available in the downloadable brochure for Half Moon Bay State Beach at www.parks.ca.gov. The map on the Rails-to-Trails Conservancy TrailLink website is also a good resource; www.traillink.com/trail-maps/half-moon-bay-coastside-trail.

Cell service: Good to marginal

Transportation: No public transportation serves the trail.

Finding the trailhead: From the junction of CA 1 and CA 92 in Half Moon Bay, go south on CA 1 to Kelly Avenue. Turn right onto Kelly Avenue and follow it to its end at the Half Moon Bay State Beach entrance station. Park in the large day-use lot.

Trailhead GPS: N37 28.013 / W122 26.713

The Main Line

Half Moon Bay clings to its modest beach town vibe in spite of its proximity to both San Francisco and Silicon Valley, and has been able to maintain a solid reputation as a surfing mecca in spite of, and because of, the amazing waves generated by the submerged topography off Pillar Point, site of the legendary Mavericks surf competition.

The town has another regional draw: the Half Moon Bay Coastside Trail, which rides the abandoned right-of-way of the short-lived Ocean Shore Railroad. The Ocean Shore line offered passengers a spectacular ride down the coast from San Francisco to Pacifica in the north, and was planned to link to Santa Cruz in the south. The full length of the line was never hitched, according to historians, in part due to the 1906 San Francisco Earthquake, which demolished a stretch of the newly established railway (among many other things).

The railway also had the unfortunate luck of having to compete with automobile travel. Cars were, in those early years of the twentieth century, beginning to capture the attention, and pocketbooks, of tourists from the city seeking respite on the beach. The line did have its upsides, however: It carried a number of folks to seaside vacations, helped transport the fresh

The Half Moon Bay Coastside Trail swings across the Seymour Bridge about a mile south of the Half Moon Bay State Beach Visitor Center.

produce of the coastal region to the hungry urban centers inland, and laid the foundation for a spectacular rail trail.

This route begins at the easily accessible midpoint of the trail in Half Moon Bay State Beach. From the parking lot, head south on the paved trail, which is bounded by the sea on the west and by windswept grassland and pastureland on the east. Side trails from neighborhood streets join the path at intervals, and others offer access to beach overlooks from the bluff top and access to the strand itself. Benches line the trail as well.

The route is straightforward, following the bluff top and occasionally swinging around cuts in the cliffs. The Poplar Beach access and parking lot, with restrooms and picnic facilities, is at the 1-mile mark. Continue south on the paved trail to where the path swings inland to cross the Seymour Bridge at 1.25 miles, briefly tucking into the shade provided by windswept Monterey pines. Beyond the bridge the trail surface, for a brief stretch, is well-maintained dirt and decomposed granite in a little interpretive wildlife sanctuary.

The Half Moon Bay Coastside Trail traverses the blufftops above Poplar Beach.

Cross another footbridge at 1.5 miles, emerge onto open bluff top again, and confront a maze of trails. In fall 2023 there were no trail signs indicating the Coastside Trail specifically, but if you trend right, toward the bay, at the junctions and keep heading south, you won't get lost. At the 2.4-mile mark, another ravine sweeps inland and takes the Coastside Trail with it, swinging about 0.3 mile eastward before arcing back seaward.

The Redondo Beach parking lot, and the turnaround, is at about the 3-mile mark (depending on the paths followed). You can continue south from there to the end point at the Ritz-Carlton—and its golf links—at about 3.5 miles. Either way, return as you came.

Alternatively, you can head north from the parking lot in Half Moon Bay State Park toward Pillar Point and the site of Mavericks, again enjoying spectacular views, bird-watching, access to the beaches, and thrilling surfer watching if the swell is good. The rail trail proper ends at Miramar, on Magellan Avenue, about 5.5 miles north of the visitor center parking lot.

BONUS TRACK: LOS GATOS CREEK TRAIL

The Los Gatos Creek Trail is a regional gem, spanning more than 10 miles from the foothills of the Santa Cruz Mountains into the flatlands of Campbell and San Jose. A portion of the route, following Los Gatos Creek from near the historic Forbes Mill Annex in downtown Los Gatos to the spillway at Lexington Reservoir, is built on the abandoned corridor of the South Pacific Coast Railroad, which offered passenger service from Alameda (through Los Gatos) to Santa Cruz on the narrow-gauge line.

The railway was the brainchild of James G. Fair, who made his fortune in mining and retired to the San Francisco Bay area for his health. The railroad company was established in 1876, and the line through to Santa Cruz, built primarily by Chinese labor, was complete four years later, enabling passengers who'd previously traveled to the seaside city via stagecoach to travel more comfortably.

While this lovely trail at the base of the Santa Cruz Mountains links Los Gatos to points farther east, only the trail segment from Los Gatos proper to near the Lexington Reservoir follows the former railroad right-of-way proper. From the trailhead, the route drops onto the railbed and heads essentially south and upstream, with Los Gatos Creek flowing on the left and traffic on CA 17 flowing on the right.

By the half-mile mark, the rail trail and the highway have diverged, and the setting for the trail has settled into shade. The Flume Trail parallels on the far side of the creek. The track edges up against the highway again as it nears the Lexington Reservoir. At the 1.2-mile mark, the trail climbs steeply off the railroad's easy grade and away from the creek, where views open across the canyon onto the reservoir's earthen dam. You can continue across the spillway and up onto the dam to check out the views before retracing your steps back to the trailhead.

Activities:

Start: Trailhead on East Main Street at Maple Place

Distance: 1.6 miles one way on the rail trail proper

The rail-trail section of the Los Gatos Creek Trail ends with views of the Lexington Reservoir's earthen dam.

Forbes Mill Annex

It's worth taking a left on the Los Gatos Creek Trail to visit the Forbes Mill Annex, a picturesque historic structure that once served by a spur of the South Pacific Coast Railroad and is now a State Historical Landmark. The annex was once attached to the original mill, four stories tall and built in the 1850s to grind flour. The main mill was demolished in the early 1920s, but the two-story annex has withstood the test of time. Over the years it has not only been used as a marginally successful flour mill—the National Park Service notes the founder, James Alexander Forbes, "knew nothing about flour milling, over extended himself and was forced into bankruptcy"—but also as a power plant, a brewery, a substation and storehouse for the Pacific Gas & Electric Company, a youth center and, finally, as a museum.

Difficulty: Moderate. There are two steep sections: one that takes you down onto the railroad grade and another that leads up to the pedestrian bridge across the spillway at Lexington Dam.

Seasons/schedule: Year-round, sunrise to sunset

Fees and permits: None

Trail surface and conditions: Dirt. The trail is popular and well maintained but may be muddy during and after winter and spring rainstorms.

Accessibility: The trail is not accessible to people using wheelchairs.

Canine compatibility: Leashed dogs permitted

Amenities: The trail begins in charming downtown Los Gatos, where you will find a selection of restaurants. There is no water available along the trail, so be sure to bring what you'll need. Water fountains are at the Main Street trailhead and on the trail below Main Street. There are no public restrooms along the route.

Trail contacts: Town of Los Gatos Parks and Public Works Department; (408) 399-5770; www.losgatosca.gov/48/Parks-and-Public-Works. Santa Clara County Parks; (408) 355-2200; www.sccgov.org.

Nearest towns: Los Gatos, Campbell, San Jose

Maps: A good, downloadable map to the entire trail, including the rail trail, are on the Los Gatos parks department website (www.losgatosca.gov/907/Los-Gatos-Creek-Trail) and on the Santa Clara County Parks website (https://parks.sccgov.org/santa-clara-county-parks/los-gatos-creek-county-park).

Cell service: Good

Transportation: Santa Clara Valley Transportation Authority, (408) 321-2300; www.vta.org

Finding the trailhead: From CA 17, take the Los Gatos/Saratoga/CA 9 exit. Go south on CA 9 to where it ends on Los Gatos Boulevard. Turn right (southwest) on Los Gatos Boulevard, which becomes East Main Street. The trailhead is 0.8 mile south of CA 9 at the intersection of East Main and Maple Place. Parking is available along the street and on the bridge along Main Street.

Trailhead GPS: N37 13.271 / W121 58.894

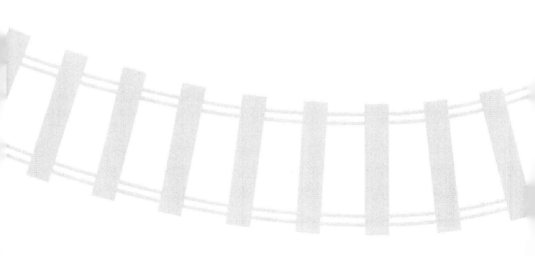

31 LOMA PRIETA GRADE TRAIL

The trees within the Forest of Nisene Marks are so thick, and the environment appears so pristine, that it's hard to fathom the rail trail upon which you tread was once part of an extensive logging operation in the Aptos Creek Canyon.

Activities:

Start: Porter Family Picnic Area trailhead

Distance: 9 miles round-trip

Difficulty: Hard. The rail trail is relatively steep, and completing the entire loop will take most of a day.

Seasons/schedule: Year-round, sunrise to sunset. The trail is best tackled when dry, between the months of May and Oct.

Fees and permits: An entrance fee is charged.

Trail surface and conditions: Dirt

Accessibility: The trail is not accessible to people using wheelchairs.

Canine compatibility: Leashed dogs are allowed below the Porter Picnic Area.

Amenities: No food or water is available along the trail; pack in what you will need. You'll find restaurants in Aptos and lots of eateries in nearby Santa Cruz. The nearest restrooms are located at the Porter Family Picnic Area, which is 0.2 mile south of the trailhead.

Trail contact: The Forest of Nisene Marks State Park; (831) 763-7064; www .parks.ca.gov (search for park by name)

Nearest town: Aptos

Maps: A map is available online at www.parks.ca.gov in the downloadable brochure.

Cell service: None

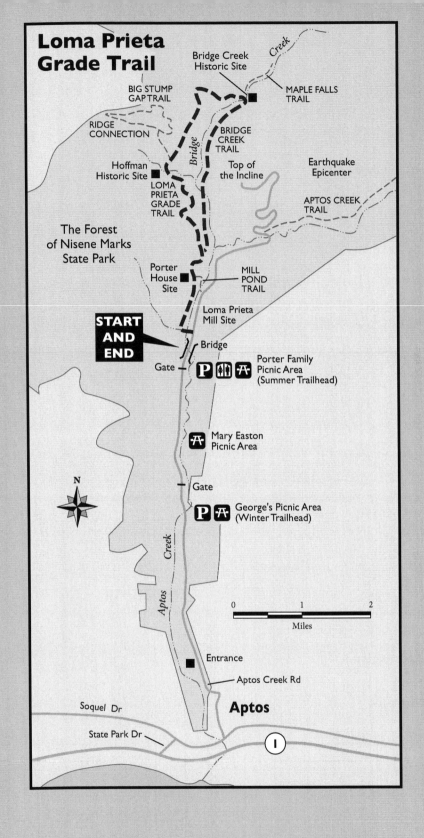

Loma Prieta Grade Trail

Creek

Bridge Creek
Historic Site

MAPLE FALLS
TRAIL

BIG STUMP
GAP TRAIL

RIDGE
CONNECTION

BRIDGE
CREEK
TRAIL

Bridge

Hoffman
Historic Site

Top of
the Incline

Earthquake
Epicenter

LOMA
PRIETA
GRADE
TRAIL

APTOS CREEK
TRAIL

The Forest
of Nisene Marks
State Park

Porter
House
Site

MILL
POND
TRAIL

Loma Prieta
Mill Site

**START
AND
END**

Bridge

Gate

Porter Family
Picnic Area
(Summer Trailhead)

Mary Easton
Picnic Area

N

Gate

George's Picnic Area
(Winter Trailhead)

Creek

Aptos

Entrance

0   1   2
Miles

Aptos Creek Rd

Soquel Dr

Aptos

State Park Dr

I

Transportation: There is no public transportation available within the park.

Finding the trailhead: To reach the Forest of Nisene Marks State Park from CA 1 (the Pacific Coast Highway) in Aptos, take the State Park Drive exit. Go north on State Park Drive for 0.1 mile to Soquel Drive and turn right (east). Go 0.5 mile on Soquel Drive to Aptos Creek Road and turn left (north). Follow Aptos Creek Road for about 0.7 mile to the Forest of Nisene Marks entrance station. The pavement ends at this point. Follow the park road another 1.2 miles to George's Picnic Area, which is the trailhead during the winter season. Parking is at the picnic area and along the park road. In the summer you can proceed another 1.1 miles to the Porter Family Picnic Area, where you will find parking as well. The park is popular so arrive early or, if no parking is available, plan your exploration for another day.

Trailhead GPS: N37 00.045 / W121 54.341

The Main Line

In the Forest of Nisene Marks, nature proves it can renew itself, which is especially reassuring given the wildfires that have ravaged other popular parks in the Santa Cruz Mountains. The original redwoods and Douglas firs that grew here, thriving on moisture from the Pacific Ocean, were extensively logged in the early 1900s, but you'd never know it now. The evergreens, along with oaks, madrones, and bay laurels, have grown back with a vengeance, creating a jungle that envelops park trails in a benevolent green light—one that even illuminates the trail on the grade of the railroad used to haul the ancestor trees down and out of the canyon.

That's not to say the landscape doesn't bear the scars of the operations run by the Loma Prieta Lumber Company. Along the former Loma Prieta Railway grade, you can spy old railroad ties half-buried in the loamy soils and stacked trailside. Other signs of human activity in the Aptos Creek Canyon, like the site of the Porter House and the remnants of the Loma Prieta Mill Site, huddle in clearings amid the trees.

The railroad operated in the steep canyon beginning in 1910 and was abandoned in the early 1920s. A farming family from Salinas purchased

The Loma Prieta Grade Trail burrows through the dense woodlands in the Forest of Nisene Marks.

the property in the 1950s and later donated the area to the California State Parks system in honor of their matriarch, Nisene Marks. Under the family's ownership, and later under the stewardship of the park, the forest has become a prime example of rejuvenation.

As if all the logging and railroading history and the natural beauty weren't enough, the park is also site of the epicenter of a major earthquake that rocked the San Francisco Bay Area in 1989. One of the other trails in the park takes you past this interesting artifact of more modern history.

The Loma Prieta Grade Trail is a lollipop loop starting and ending about 0.4 mile beyond the gate that blocks the roadway to motor vehicles at the Porter Family Picnic Area. No bikes are allowed on the trail, and a bike rack is provided for those who pedal to the trailhead.

The grade takes off past the gate on the left side of the main park road, with Aptos Creek running loud and clear to the right. The forest chatters in the almost ever-present ocean breeze, stirring the treetops, rattling limbs, and sending cones and small branches tumbling to the ground. The path is soft and duff-covered, muffling footfalls, and the shade is so thick it's almost dark beneath the canopy, even at noon on a bright, sunny day.

Within a quarter mile the trail narrows to a footpath etched in the mountainside, dropping through a drainage and crossing a small bridge. Climb back onto the railroad grade, passing a pile of moss-covered railroad ties stashed beside the trail, and continue gently upward on the grade.

Pass the clearing surrounding the Porter House site, with its interpretive sign and bench, at about the 1.5-mile mark. A side trail leads east to the Aptos Creek Fire Road, which serves as the main route through the park. The rail trail then loops through another drainage, using yet another small bridge, to the trail fork at the intersection with the Bridge Creek Trail at 1.8 miles.

You can do the loop in either direction. If you travel to the left (northwest), you will climb first to the Hoffman Historic Site at 3.7 miles. Named for the man who was camp superintendent and nicknamed Camp Comfort, this logging camp operated between 1918 and 1921. The railroad grade was used to haul huge redwoods out of Big Tree Gulch.

Beyond the camp the trail continues to the intersection with Big Stump Gap Trail, which leads to the ridge in the western reaches of the park. Remain on the rail trail, which continues northward and reaches its apex. At this point the route leaves the railroad grade and makes a sharp right-hand (eastward) turn.

Drop to the Bridge Creek Historic Site at the 6-mile mark. Not much remains of this logging camp, which was washed downstream by El Niño–strengthened storms that battered California in 1982. A side trail leads left (north) off the loop at this point and follows Bridge Creek to Maple Falls.

The next leg of the loop follows the Bridge Creek Trail down along the namesake waterway; you won't rejoin the railroad grade until near the end of the loop. From the Bridge Creek Historic Site, turn right and head downstream, crossing to the other side of Bridge Creek about 1.5 miles below the historic camp. Pick up the Loma Prieta Railway grade again just above the Porter House site, and retrace your steps back to the trailhead.

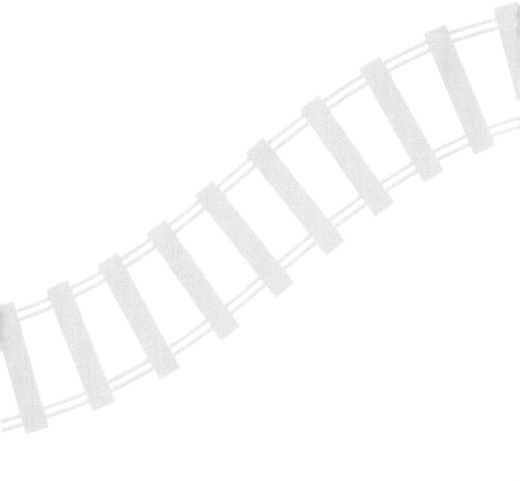

32 MONTEREY BAY COASTAL RECREATION TRAIL

This section of a much-longer rail trail immerses you in the culture of one of California's most celebrated seaside towns. If you are lucky, otters will be frolicking in the kelp off the coast of Pacific Grove and seabirds will take wing over the estuary in Seaside. There's no doubt sparkling sailboats will be moored in Monterey Bay near Fisherman's Wharf. It's a lovely outing that can be extended into a daylong adventure by continuing to Castroville.

Activities:

Start: Lover's Point

Distance: 5 miles one way from Pacific Grove to Seaside; 18 miles one way to reach Castroville

Difficulty: Moderate to hard, depending on how far you go

Seasons/schedule: Year-round, sunrise to sunset. Although temperatures are usually moderate, Monterey Bay is subject to the marine influence, and the fog can be dense and cold when it is in. Be prepared for swift changes in temperature.

Fees and permits: None

Trail surface and conditions: Asphalt and concrete, with a dirt walking path alongside the paved trail in Pacific Grove

Accessibility: The entire trail is accessible to people using wheelchairs.

Canine compatibility: Leashed dogs permitted

Amenities: You'll find everything you need along the trail as it passes through the urbanized areas. An abundance of restaurants can be reached from the trail in Monterey's Cannery Row and Fisherman's Wharf areas. Restrooms can be found in parks, beaches, and private business establishments along the route.

Trail contact: City of Monterey Parks and Recreation Department; (831) 646-3866; https://monterey.org/city_hall/parks___recreation/beaches,_parks ___playgrounds/monterey_bay_coastal_rec_trail/index.php

Nearest towns: Pacific Grove, Monterey, Seaside

Maps: The best map is downloadable from the Rails-to-Trails Conservancy's TrailLink site at www.traillink.com/trail-maps/monterey-bay-coastal -recreation-trail.

Cell service: Good in town(s); patchy along more rural stretches

Transportation: Monterey-Salinas Transit, (888) 678-2871; https://mst.org

Finding the trailhead: To reach the parking lot at Lovers Point in Pacific Grove, follow CA 1 to the CA 68 exit. After about 2.2 scenic miles, the highway veers left onto the famed 17-Mile Drive; stay right (straight) on Forest Avenue. Follow Forest Avenue about 2 miles to Lighthouse Avenue. Turn left onto Lighthouse Avenue, go 2 blocks to 17th Street, and turn right. Follow 17th Street for about 0.3 mile to the Lovers Point parking lot, which is on the right (north) side of the road about 100 yards before the Lovers Point Inn.

To reach the Pacific Grove/Lovers Point trailhead from downtown Monterey, head toward the ocean to Del Monte Avenue. From the intersection of Del Monte Avenue and Washington Street, south of Cannery Row and the Monterey Bay Aquarium, follow Del Monte Avenue through the tunnel to the first road fork. Ignore the signs for Cannery Row and the aquarium, staying northbound on Lighthouse Avenue. Once you enter Pacific Grove, stay left on Central Avenue to 17th Street. Turn right on 17th and go down toward the bay for about 0.2 mile to the trailhead.

To reach the Seaside trailhead from CA 1, take the Seaside/Del Rey Oaks exit. Go east on CA 218 (Camino Del Rey), drive about 50 yards, and turn right onto Roberts Avenue and then into the Roberts Lake Park parking lot, which faces the small estuary. The bike path that begins here leads to the rail trail, which is located on the far (east) side of the estuary.

Parking lots are available at both end points, but these are popular places, so arrive early to ensure you can find a spot.

Trailhead GPS: Lovers Point trailhead: N36 37.481 / W121 55.016; Roberts Lake trailhead: N36 36.508 / W121 51.512

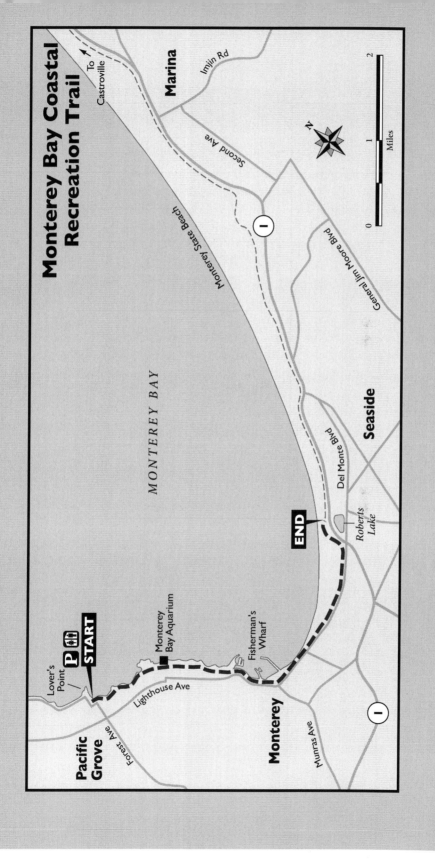

The Main Line

||||||||||||||||||||||||||||||||||||||||||||||||||||||||||||||||||||||||||||||||||||||||||||||||||||||||||||||||||||||||||||||||||||||||||||||||||||||||

Some might gaze with longing upon the gingerbread dollhouses that overlook the craggy shoreline of Pacific Grove. There's no denying it: The folks who live in these historic homes reside in an area of unsurpassed scenic and cultural beauty. The sea otters have it pretty darn good, too. From the sun-splashed kelp beds on which they lounge, the views are just as spectacular, and because they work from home, they get to enjoy those vistas day in and day out—and they don't have to deal with traffic.

Folks traveling the Monterey Bay Coastal Recreation Trail get a glimpse into how the sea otters live—and sea lions and seabirds—as well as the chance to sample many other amenities offered by the popular resort town of Monterey. The rail trail, part of the much longer California Coastal Trail, wanders through historic Cannery Row, past the eateries and museums of Fisherman's Wharf, along the beaches at San Carlos Park and Monterey Bay Park, and through a colonnade of eucalyptus to a seabird-speckled estuary in Seaside.

The rail trail follows the former bed of a Southern Pacific line that began in Spanish Bay and ran north to San Francisco. During the heyday of the area's fisheries in the 1930s and 1940s, the line served the canneries, taking goods to the markets in the north and bringing supplies back south to Monterey. It also served as a passenger line, with a turntable located at Lovers Point in Pacific Grove.

You can begin anywhere along the route, but the trail is described starting at Lovers Point and ending at Seaside. At the outset, spectacular rocky shoreline borders the path on the waterside; on the southeast the charming Victorians of Pacific Grove overlook the bay. Heading toward Monterey on rail trail, bicyclists and skaters are restricted to the paved track while hikers and walkers may stroll along the dirt pathway that parallels the pavement. At 0.3 mile pass a mural describing the history of the area; to the west the lumpy crags poking out of the bay host cormorants, seagulls, and pelicans, and clumps of kelp serve as beds for the frolicsome otters. A small park, with manicured grass and benches shaded by cypress, lies at the half-mile point.

A cyclist pedals past the marina that borders a section of the Monterey Bay Coastal Recreation Trail.

At 0.8 mile historic homes give way to historic warehouses, and the trail passes the Hopkins Marine Station on the west. Cross Eardley Avenue at 1 mile and enter Cannery Row proper. The trail is now concrete, and walkers, cyclists, and skaters share the same path. A series of street crossings follows. Pass the Monterey Bay Aquarium, the cannery buildings, and a strip of historic, culinary, and shopping delights as you proceed through town.

The route continues to San Carlos Beach and Fisherman's Shoreline Park at 1.5 miles. A sloping lawn shaded by cypress drops to a blue bay dotted with sparkling fishing and sailing vessels. At 2 miles the trail deposits you on Fisherman's Wharf in the square that fronts the Custom House Museum.

Beyond the wharf, the route splits, with hikers able to continue on a waterside track and users on wheels shunted east around a parking lot. The bike path crosses Washington Street and parallels Del Monte Avenue to Del Monte Beach and Monterey Bay Park at 2.5 miles. Now asphalt again, the rail trail veers waterside into the park, then continues between the small dunes sheltering the beach on the bay side and sprawling lawns in the park.

Beyond the park the path becomes more utilitarian, serving local residents who need to travel car-free from point A to point B. It passes between

Peek into the Deep

Luminous jellyfish that look like psychedelic egg drops. Leopard sharks and sunfish flying from inky darkness to blue light in a tank that holds a million gallons of seawater. Otters playing in kelp beds two stories high. Anchovies spinning a silvery, swirling web. The Monterey Bay Aquarium is home to these incredible creatures and more, offering glimpses into a mysterious undersea world and displaying animals and plants that thrive in a realm we can glimpse behind glass.

This amazing aquarium, which provides a forum for study of the wildlife protected within the Monterey Bay National Marine Sanctuary, is located 1 block south of the Monterey Bay Coastal Recreation Trail in Monterey's Cannery Row. From the trail, you can enjoy the flat, glittering expanse of Monterey Bay and the wildlife that abides on or near its surface. Within the aquarium, you can observe the environment below the bay's surface—from the magic of tide pools to the mysterious depths of the Monterey Canyon.

Contact the aquarium at (831) 648-4800 for more information, or visit www.mbayaq.org for schedules and tickets.

warehouses and businesses into a strip of eucalyptus that serves as a barrier between trail and the adjacent roadway (Del Monte Avenue). You'll pass the site of the Portola-Crespi Monument, commemorating Spanish colonization of California by explorer Don Gaspar de Portolá and Franciscan Father Juan Crespí, and trailhead/seaside parking access as you continue.

The trail rolls beneath overpasses as it enters the city of Seaside at 4.1 miles, near the intersection of Del Monte Avenue and Roberts Avenue. The emergent railroad tracks pass through a small bower of cypress; the paved trail runs alongside them for another 0.2 mile to Camino Del Rey. The rail corridor continues ahead, running between shopping centers and the busy thoroughfare, continuing to Marina and on toward Castroville. Unless you have arranged a shuttle, return as you came.

SIERRA NEVADA

33 MOUNTAIN QUARRY RAILROAD TRAIL

The boundless wealth of California's Gold Country is on full display along this rail trail—not wealth ripped from the ground with pick and pan, mind you, but a visual bonanza of wildness cradled in the canyon of the storied American River.

Activities:

Start: The confluence of the North Fork and Middle Fork of the American River

Distance: 2 miles of this 4-mile out-and-back section of the Western States/Pioneer Express Recreation Trail are on railroad grade. The entire Western States Trail is 100 miles long, and about 35 miles of the route are on abandoned railbed.

Difficulty: Moderate

Seasons/schedule: Year-round, sunrise to sunset

Fees and permits: None

Trail surface and conditions: Dirt and gravel. The trail is extremely popular and well maintained, but it's rough and quite narrow in places. You may encounter snow in the winter and early spring.

Accessibility: The route is not accessible to people using wheelchairs.

Canine compatibility: Leashed dogs permitted

Amenities: Portable restrooms are available at confluence trailheads, which are clustered around the Old Foresthill Road Bridge. No other amenities are available. Be sure to bring plenty of water, especially in summer, when the canyon bottom bakes in the sun. If you must drink from the river, filter the water first.

Trail contact: Auburn State Recreation Area; (530) 885-4527; www.parks .ca.gov (search for park by name). Auburn State Recreation Area Canyon Keepers is another good source of information about the trail; www.canyon keepers.org.

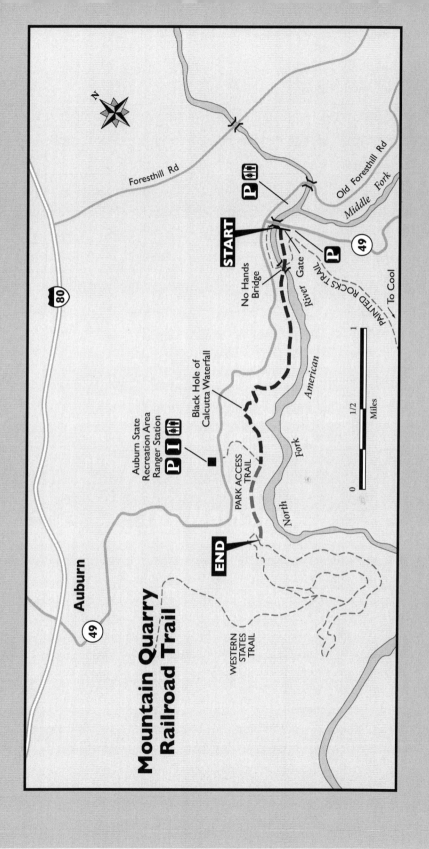

Nearest town: Auburn

Maps: Auburn State Recreation Area is massive, but a confluence trail map is available within the park brochure at www.parks.ca.gov.

Cell service: Nope

Transportation: The Auburn Transit shuttle runs from various locations in the city of Auburn to the confluence between 9 a.m. and 5 p.m. on weekends from Apr 1 to Oct 1; www.auburn.ca.gov/585/Confluence-RouteCheck.

Finding the trailhead: From I-80 in Auburn, take the CA 49/Placerville/ Grass Valley exit. Go south toward Placerville on CA 49, following the signs through the quaint downtown area. Just out of town, CA 49 dives into the American River Canyon. Drive 2.3 miles down the canyon and veer right (south) over the bridge. It's a total of 3.3 miles from Auburn to the confluence, where roadside parking—which fills quickly, especially on weekends—is available. The trailhead is at the gate (#150) immediately on the southeast side of the bridge. Be cautious accessing the trailhead from roadside parking or parking areas for adjacent trailheads, as pedestrian walkways along the shoulders of the roadways are nonexistent.

Trailhead GPS: N38 54.894 / W121 02.404

The Main Line

These days, the American River nourishes fertile Central Valley farmland, is harnessed for water and power by the cities and towns it flows through, and provides world-class recreational opportunities for hikers, cyclists, equestrians, long-distance runners, and paddle-sport enthusiasts. In the past the focus of human activity on the river and its three forks was the extraction of gold, which spawned the rush that birthed the state of California in the mid-nineteenth century.

This route, also known as the Black Hole of Calcutta Waterfall Trail, follows a length of abandoned railbed once owned by the Mountain Quarry Railroad, which transported limestone from quarries on the Middle Fork American River to Auburn, where it hitched up with the Southern Pacific

The No Hands Bridge, a remnant of the heyday of the Mountain Quarry Railroad, is a scenic start to this popular rail trail.

line that continued to Sacramento. A number of artifacts from the rail-roading days lie along the track, but the most stunning is the No Hands Bridge, which got its name, according to local guides, because for many years it had no railings. Once the longest bridge of its kind in the world (according to the guides), the span survived the collapse of the Hell Hole Dam in 1964.

Another threat to the trail—and to the future of the entire Auburn State Recreation Area—emerged in the 1960s, when plans to build the Auburn Dam were announced. Thus far, because of vehement opposition from recreationalists and environmentalists, the dam hasn't materialized, and the canyons set to be submerged in a reservoir instead have become a tourist destination. The railroad grade is part of an extensive trail system within the Auburn State Recreation Area, mined these days for the pleasure of hikers, mountain bikers, anglers, paddlers, and other outdoor enthusiasts.

The rail trail begins on the south side of the bridge spanning two forks of the American River at the busy confluence. Head west and downriver, passing the junction at 0.2 mile with the Painted Rocks Trail, which climbs to the hamlet of Cool. Stay right and cross the No Hands Bridge; the trail beyond the bridge is broad and easy, offering dynamic views of the river and canyon. Gravel paths break off to the riverside but the way forward is obvious, the railroad grade traversing the south-facing hillside above the waterway. In summer this hillside is hot and dry and covered with sparse scrub, in sharp contrast to the dense evergreen forest thriving on the moister north-facing slope of the canyon.

Round a bend marked by the first of several concrete buttresses, the foundations of short trestles that spanned ravines along the river, at the 0.8-mile mark. The trail narrows to singletrack and loops through the gully. Pass the second foundation on the other side; the date 1921 is inscribed in the concrete. The path widens briefly and then plunges through another drainage at 1 mile, where the trestle foundation is dated 1915.

At 1.1 miles dip through a third drainage sporting trestle foundations—the site of the Black Hole of Calcutta, a lovely ephemeral waterfall shrouded in thick foliage (including poison oak). Enjoy the brief shade, then climb away from the waterfall, passing yet another trestle foundation, to a trail marker and past a path that climbs right toward the recreation area's ranger station. The trail continues westward, now about 100 feet above the river flowing green and deep in its bed.

Skirt Eagle Rock, a towering black-streaked formation at the 1.7-mile mark, enjoying views of the river unimpeded by brush or trees. Pass a mile marker at 2.1 miles. At this point the rail trail proper ends on the concrete foundation to the left. The Western States Trail arcs sharply right, leaving the railroad grade behind for a time as it continues its long roll through the foothills. This is the turnaround. Unless you want to make the climb up to Auburn, retrace your steps.

34 TRUCKEE RIVER BIKE TRAIL

Boisterous. If a single word could describe the Truckee River Trail in summer, that would be it. The trail hums with activity during the height of the season, as colorful rafts packed with paddlers spill down the Truckee River, and hikers, cyclists, and skaters trace a parallel course on the rail trail that also originates on the shores of Lake Tahoe.

Activities:

Start: 64-Acres Park near the junction of CA 89 and CA 28 in Tahoe City

Distance: 10 miles out and back

Difficulty: Moderate due only to length

Seasons/schedule: Year-round, sunrise to sunset

Fees and permits: None

Trail surface and conditions: Weather-worn, sometimes bumpy asphalt

Accessibility: The entire trail is accessible to people using wheelchairs, but snow may preclude wheelchair use during the winter months.

Amenities: Portable restrooms are available at the trailhead, River Ranch, and at points along the trail. A number of restaurants and grocery outlets are available in Tahoe City, and River Ranch, near the trail's western end point, also offers the opportunity for riverside dining.

Trail contact: Tahoe City Public Utility District, Parks and Recreation Department; (530) 583-3440, ext. 10; www.tcpud.org

Canine compatibility: Leashed dogs permitted

Nearest town: Tahoe City

Maps to consult: The Tahoe City PUD site offers a good downloadable map to the Truckee River Trail and other paved paths on Lake Tahoe's West Shore; www.tcpud.org/sites/default/files/documents/bike_trail_map.pdf.

Cell service: Good near town, marginal in the canyon, good again as you near River Ranch

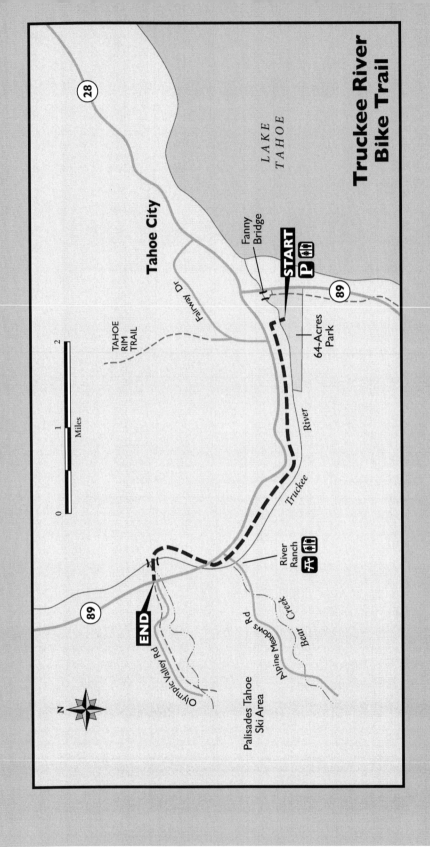

Truckee River Bike Trail

Tahoe City

LAKE TAHOE

28

89

89

START

END

Fanny Bridge

64-Acres Park

Truckee River

River Ranch

TAHOE RIM TRAIL

Fairway Dr

Olympic Valley Rd

Alpine Meadows Rd

Bear Creek

Palisades Tahoe Ski Area

N

0   1   2
Miles

Transportation: Tahoe Truckee Area Regional Transit (TART), (530) 550-1212; https://tahoetruckeetransit.com

Finding the trailhead: From the signalized intersection of CA 89 and CA 28 in Tahoe City, go 0.2 mile south on CA 89 to a signed right turn into the large trailhead parking area at 64-Acres Park. You can also reach the trailhead lot from the roundabout just down CA 89 from the intersection. The parking lot may seem huge but is sure to be packed during the summer season. Visit another time if the lot's overflowing, and be courteous by not parking in private lots, driveways, and along roadways.

Trailhead GPS: N39 9.877 / W120 8.840

The Main Line

The Truckee River has carved easy passage through the mountain rim that separates Lake Tahoe from the historic town downriver that shares the river's name. The waterway, though it can move swiftly when swollen with snowmelt, is remarkably gentle between the lake and Truckee, meandering along the floor of a heavily wooded canyon. Its recreation-friendly demeanor has made the river the destination of an army of rafters, anglers, and sightseers in the summertime, and it harbors a rail trail of unparalleled popularity with walkers and cyclists.

On any summer weekend, both trail and river are packed. The rafts—vivid orange, sunburst yellow, and electric blue—are stuffed with people whooping and singing as they bounce downstream. On the trail, folks are dressed with equal brilliance. It is the ultimate family adventure, with strollers, training wheels, and dogs on leashes as much in evidence as the Lycra and intensity of more serious athletes.

If you feel the urge to forsake the trail temporarily for the translucent waters of the Truckee, by all means, jump in. The water is cold, clear, and reflects the mottled browns of the sand and river cobbles that pave its bed, fading to a cool blue in deeper swimming holes.

The relative flatness of the river valley no doubt made it inviting to the D. L. Bliss family, founders of the Lake Tahoe Railway and Transportation Company and onetime major landowners along the Lake Tahoe shoreline.

A young outdoors person enjoys a stroll down the Truckee River Trail.

A narrow-gauge line first connected Truckee and Tahoe City in the early 1890s and was used to transport timber from the Tahoe basin to mills in Truckee; the lumber was then shipped by rail out of the Sierra Nevada to the burgeoning cities of Sacramento and San Francisco. The original Lake Tahoe Railway line was leased to Southern Pacific in 1925 and converted to standard gauge. Passengers and freight were transported via the line through the 1930s and into the early years of World War II. The line was abandoned in 1943; by then cars were traveling what was known as Truckee Turnpike.

The trailhead is on the lake side of the river. From the parking lot, cross the arcing bridge to get to the trail proper and go left, following both the river and CA 89 downstream into the canyon. The trail dips under the roundabout and swings past businesses accessed from the highway, but within the first mile you've left most signs of civilization (other than the busy roadway) behind. The Truckee initially is hidden behind a dense cover of riparian vegetation, but soon comes into view as the rail trail passes a scattering of private homes.

Cyclists pedal downstream alongside the Truckee River outside Tahoe City.

Having left Tahoe City behind, the trail rolls along uninterrupted for a long stretch. For the most part the route is open to the sun and river views, only occasionally broken by brief shady stretches overhung by evergreens and crowded with willows and lush riparian undergrowth. Portable restrooms are placed at intervals, and short side trails lead to beaches where you can rest or swim.

Civilization encroaches on recreation again at about the 3.5-mile mark. Climb a short hill and pass through the staging area for rafting companies picking up joyful clients who've enjoyed a scenic float downriver. This is just the beginning of a busy and often crowded stretch of trail, so proceed with courtesy and caution. River Ranch and Bells Landing lie just downstream; from the trail you can observe the bustle of bodies and rafts, a bonanza of color and activity, at the landing. Patrons of River Ranch watch from the deck of this riverside resort at the intersection of CA 89 and Alpine Meadows Road.

To continue on the rail trail, cross Alpine Meadows Road. The route changes demeanor immediately, as though the gate that marks the beginning of this portion of the path is more than a barrier to cars. Although still paved, the trail is wilder and seems more secluded: There are no rafts

Rafters can be seen from the Truckee River Trail.

on the river and the highway noise fades as the trail drops below grade. It's a lovely stretch, complete with restrooms and paved ramps that offer access to the Truckee. Pass the 4-mile marker as you approach the highway bridge that spans the river; the trail slides under and then continues downstream to its own river crossing on a bridge that tucks it up against the side of CA 89.

At the 5-mile mark, the rail trail deposits travelers at the entryway to the Olympic Valley ski resort, at the intersection of CA 89 and Olympic Valley Road. This is the turnaround point. Gather your strength for the return journey by channeling athletic prowess from the Olympic flame and rings at the ski area entrance ... unless you have arranged a car ride back to the trailhead at the lake, of course.

Historic Railroad Tunnels on Donner Summit

Technically, I suppose the path through the historic railroad tunnels on Donner Summit is a rail trail, but it's more an immersion in darkness, graffiti, and thrill-seeking. There's no formal trailhead, there's no formal trail manager, and there's no formal maintenance, other than by artists who create the murals and paintings that decorate the tunnel walls.

That said, this series of tunnels, or snowsheds, built by Chinese labor, once protected the transcontinental tracks that linked the wealth of the newly minted state of California to the rest of the nation. By the time the railway was in use, the vagaries of winter in the Sierra Nevada had become notorious. Accumulations of snow in wet winters were both deadly, as in the case of the ill-fated Donner Party, and inconvenient, shutting down highways, isolating mountain towns, and causing the roofs of mountain cabins to collapse.

The tunnel hike is about 5 miles out and back, with the railroad grade extending beyond the last tunnel. Accessing the tunnels is a cross-country affair, though trail users have sketched out the route with cairns and rock-lined paths across the granite. Because no formal land manager maintains the route, I won't provide details, but the trek is popular and I'd be remiss not to acknowledge its existence. You'll want to venture into the tunnels in late summer or fall, when the snow has melted and runoff from the mountainside has subsided. Bring a flashlight or headlamp to cope with the darkness and an insulating layer to cope with the coolness. Breaks in the tunnels offer chances to step into the light and enjoy views of Donner Lake and the Tahoe rim beyond.

With luck and persistent advocacy, perhaps one day the tunnels will be "official." Stay tuned.

35 SUGAR PINE RAILWAY—STRAWBERRY BRANCH

This segment of rail trail follows the historic Sugar Pine Railway, which winds through the forested gorge of the South Fork Stanislaus River and explores the remnants of logging operations dating back to the early and mid-1900s.

Activities:

Start: Fraser Flat trailhead outside Twain Harte

Distance: 3 miles one way

Difficulty: Moderate

Seasons/schedule: Year-round, sunrise to sunset. Hiking and mountain biking are best in summer and fall; you may cross-country ski on the trail during winter when the snow sticks.

Fees and permits: None

Trail surface and conditions: Gravel and dirt

Accessibility: The trail is not accessible to people using wheelchairs.

Canine compatibility: Leashed dogs permitted

Amenities: No restrooms are available at either trailhead or along the trail. The nearest facilities are in the Fraser Flat Campground. You can find eateries and grocery stores in nearby Twain Harte. Bring food and water, and you can picnic along the route.

Trail contact: Stanislaus National Forest, Summit–Mi-Wok Ranger District; (209) 965-3434; www.fs.usda.gov/recarea/stanislaus/recreation

Nearest towns: Strawberry, Twain Harte

Maps: Downloadable trail maps don't offer much detail but are available from the Rails-to-Trails Conservancy's TrailLink app at www.traillink .com/trail-maps/sugar-pine-railway-trail/ and from the Tuolumne County

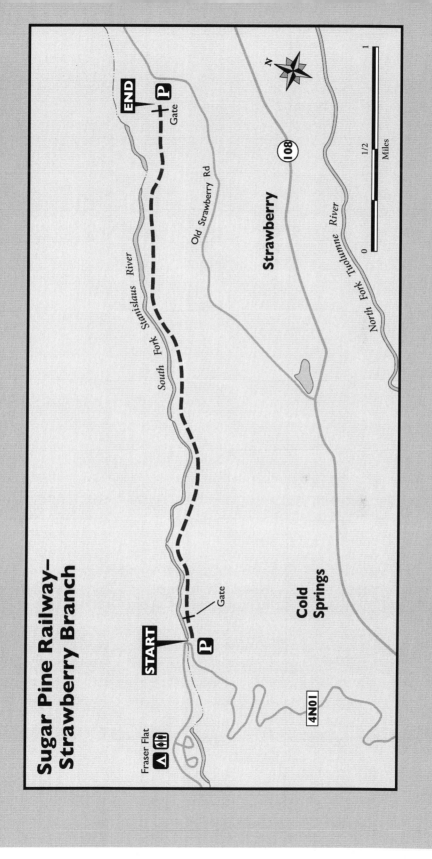

Sugar Pine Railway–
Strawberry Branch

START

Fraser Flat

P

Gate

South Fork Stanislaus River

Old Strawberry Rd

END

P

Gate

Strawberry

108

North Fork Tuolumne River

N

Cold Springs

4N01

0   1/2   1
Miles

Transportation Council at www.tuolumnecountytransportationcouncil
.org/single-post/2016/08/10/strawberry-to-fraser.

Cell service: None

Transportation: None

Finding the trailhead: Access to the trail varies depending on the time of
year. In summer you can reach the Fraser Flat trailhead by heading east
from Twain Harte on scenic CA 108 to Stanislaus Forest Road 4N01/Fraser
Flat Road, which is well signed. Turn left (north) onto winding FR 4N01 and
go about 2.5 miles to the bridge over the South Fork Stanislaus River. The
trailhead is on the right (east) side of the road before you cross the river.

The eastern trailhead serves as the only access to the trail in the winter
months. To reach this end point, continue on CA 108 to Old Strawberry
Road, which is about 2 miles east of the turnoff to Fraser Flat. Turn left
(north) on Old Strawberry Road and go about 2 miles to the trailhead,
which is on the left (west) side of the road.

Trailhead GPS: Fraser Flat trailhead: N38 10.318 / W120 03.763

The Main Line

|||||||||||||||||||||||||||||||||||||||||||||||||||||||||||||||||||||||||||||||||||||||||||||||||||||||||||||||||||||||||||||||||||||||||||

The Stanislaus River gains momentum in the canyon traced by this section of the Sugar Pine Railway, tumbling with the vigor of an adolescent
through a narrow passage cut from smoky granite. Evergreen trees—
timber ready to harvest to those who built the railroad—grow thickly on
either side of the river, enveloping the route in shade and insulating it
from signs of civilization clustered in villages along CA 108.

The Strawberry Branch is just a short sampling of the extensive web
of main lines and spurs that once wound through this neck of the woods.
The Sugar Pine Railway alone included about 70 miles of main line and
approximately 400 miles of spurs, branches, and sidings. The rails were
laid down in the rugged foothills just after the turn of the twentieth century and were used to transport harvested old-growth trees to sawmills
for processing. The railroad ceased operation in 1965. The abandoned

A family enjoys a bike ride/hike along the Strawberry Branch of the Sugar Pine Railway trail.

grades—including the grade of the Strawberry Branch rail trail—are very mild, belying the steepness of the terrain that surrounds them.

The rail trail is lined with interpretive posts keyed to an informational packet that is available from the Mi-Wok Ranger Station in Mi-Wuk Village (if open) or the Summit Ranger Station in Pinecrest.

The trail makes for fine hiking and the mountain biking, especially for the beginner, is sublime. The route is described climbing northeast from the bridge spanning the Stanislaus near the Fraser Flat Campground to Old Strawberry Road, but it can be traveled in either direction. For an out-and-back journey, however, the Fraser Flat trailhead is the best starting point because it is all downhill on the return trip.

Begin on the south side of the bridge; the route is barricaded to prohibit use by motorized vehicles. Interpretive posts are passed quickly within a third of a mile, calling attention first to the old logging camp at Fraser (now the Fraser Flat Campground); then to Camp Lowell, a logging camp used for a single season in the early twentieth century; and finally to the rigors of building a railroad in the foothills. The path is a gentle roller coaster, dipping through shallow gullies as it climbs through thick stands of conifers. You can catch glimpses of the South Fork Stanislaus in the canyon to the left through brief openings between the trunks of the trees.

At about the 1.1-mile mark, the gorge deepens, and the remains of a flume appear on the opposite side of the canyon. Called the Philadelphia Ditch, the flume was used by gold miners a century ago. Less than a quarter of a mile beyond, pass a diversion dam used for power generation.

Pass through the cattle gate at about the 1.5-mile mark, then continue up through the lovely woodland to where the forest opens a bit and filtered sunlight illuminates the glistening river. The grade splits here; remain on the main (and obvious) path that continues northeast to the Old Strawberry Road trailhead. The trail veers away from the riverside at about the 2.5-mile mark and crosses through yet another of the gullies that lend the grade its rolling profile.

Post 8 marks the remnants of research projects conducted within the US Forest Service's Stanislaus-Tuolumne Experimental Forest, which served as a laboratory for foresters and other scientists from 1927 to 1969. The research station is located across the South Fork Stanislaus and now houses forest service employees. The post is at the edge of a small meadow, which the trail crosses before returning to the woods.

At the trail intersection at 2.8 miles, the railroad grade heads off to the left, but to reach the Strawberry Branch end point, go right on the narrow footpath that leads up steeply to the Old Strawberry Road trailhead. Unless you have arranged a shuttle, this is the turnaround point; return as you came.

36 WEST SIDE RAIL TRAIL: HULL CREEK TO CLAVEY RIVER

The foothills of the Sierra Nevada are expansive and remain sparsely touched by humanity, putting the wild in the wildland-urban interface. This section of the West Side Rails winds through this isolation on a track that once rang with the squeal of wheels on metal and now rings with the wind and birdcall.

Activities:

Start: Hull Creek trailhead

Distance: 8 miles one way

Difficulty: Hard

Seasons/schedule: Year-round, sunrise to sunset. Hiking and mountain biking are best in summer and fall; you may cross-country ski on the trail during winter if the snow sticks.

Fees and permits: None

Trail surface and conditions: Dirt

Accessibility: The trail is not accessible to people using wheelchairs.

Canine compatibility: Leashed dogs permitted

Amenities: No restrooms are available at the trailhead or along the trail. Practice leave-no-trace principles by burying waste at least 8 inches underground and packing out toilet paper. You'll also not find food or water along the trail, so bring all you'll need. There are restaurants and grocery stores in Twain Harte and other villages along CA 108.

Trail contact: Stanislaus National Forest, Summit–Mi-Wok Ranger District; (209) 965-3434; www.fs.usda.gov/recarea/stanislaus/recreation

Nearest town: Long Barn

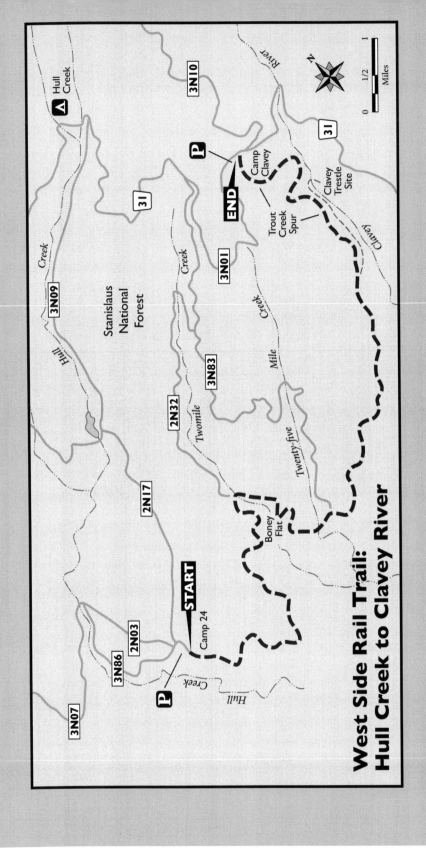

West Side Rail Trail:
Hull Creek to Clavey River

Maps: Best to check in with rangers at the Summit or Mi-Wok Ranger Stations for a map and directions for this lonely trail. A map is also available on the Rails-to-Trails Conservancy's TrailLink app at www.traillink.com/trail-maps/westside-rails-to-trails-(hull-creek-to-clavey-river).

Cell service: None

Transportation: None

Finding the trailhead: An absolutely gorgeous drive leads to the remote trailheads for this route. To reach the Hull Creek end point from CA 108 in Long Barn, turn east off the highway at the Merrell Springs turnoff, where there are signs for Hull Creek and Clavey River. Turn right (south) onto Long Barn Road and go 0.1 mile to FR 3N01 (a.k.a. Stanislaus CR 31 and North Fork Road). Follow FR 3N01/CR 31 across the North Fork Tuolumne River at 2 miles, then continue for about 6.3 miles to FR 3N07, which sports a sign for the West Side Rail Tour. Turn right onto FR 3N07. This well-graded dirt road leads for about 3 miles (a total of 9.3 miles from CA 108) to an intersection; stay on FR 3N07. At the second road fork 0.1 mile farther, at the William R. Rolland Memorial Plantation, go left (east) on FR 3N86. Parking for the West Side Rail Tour is 2 miles ahead. The trail formally begins above the crossing of Hull Creek, where you will find limited parking, but continue for another mile to a parking pullout where several forest roads (3N86 and 2N17, plus the rail trail) converge at the site of Camp 24, which was home to a thriving logging operation until 1960.

To reach the Clavey River trailhead, continue past the turnoff at FR 3N07, traveling a total of 15.5 miles on North Fork Road (FR 3N01/CR 31) to its intersection with FR 3N86 at Camp Clavey. This is the terminus of the rail trail. Parking is available in pullouts along the dirt road.

Trailhead GPS: Hull Creek crossing: N38 03.005 / W120 05.769 (Caution: Do not use this waypoint to navigate to the trailhead; wayfinding via GPS is notoriously unreliable in the Sierra Nevada.)

The Main Line

|||||||||||||||||||||||||||||||||||||||||||||||||||||||||||||||||||||||||||||||||||||||||||||||||||||||||||||||||||||||||||||||||||||||||||||||||||||||||||||||||||||||||||||||||||||||||||

The dense woods of the Stanislaus National Forest embrace this section of the former West Side Lumber Company railway—now a rough-and-tumble rail trail—in an evergreen setting that harkens back to the height of the area's lumbering days.

The Stanislaus National Forest revived this segment of the West Side line, which was abandoned in the 1960s, as a recreational trail and has compiled a brochure detailing the route via a good (and necessary) map and interpretation keyed to signposts along the trail. Quite a bit of the route can be traveled in a passenger car, still more in a four-wheel-drive vehicle, but the precious solitude of the rail trail is best experienced on foot. Mountain biking is also popular but can be challenging, requiring portages over washouts and downed trees. The route sees use by off-highway vehicles, especially on weekends, so be prepared to share the route; the rail trail doubles as FR 3N86.

The rail trail follows a leg of one of the four railroads that provided access to the abundant timber in the region. Like its neighbors, including the Sugar Pine Railway, the West Side Railroad Company laid down a remarkable amount of track, including a main line that reached nearly 70 miles from the town of Tuolumne south to the Hetch Hetchy Valley in Yosemite National Park, known as the Hetch Hetchy & Yosemite Valley Railway.

The West Side rails were narrow-gauge lines, which were easier to carve into steep mountainsides but resulted in less stability for the trains on the tracks. The width of the grade these days, however, is perfect for hikers, cyclists, or equestrians who wish to travel side by side, discussing the railroad history that unfolds along with spectacular views of the high country.

Interpretation begins just above FR 3N86's intersection with Hull Creek, where signpost 1 marks one of the railroad's sidings. But the best parking is at signpost 2, at about the 1-mile mark, which was the site of Camp 24, once a bustling hub and now little more than a wide spot in the road.

A mountain biker rides the West Side Rails near the Clavey River.

The route continues across open, scrub-covered hillsides, passing post 3 at the site of an old oil tank. Leave open ground for the rest of the journey as the railbed dives into the forest, with views opening only occasionally southward as you traverse the mountainside.

Pass posts 4 and 5 at about 2.5 miles, which direct your attention to various types of railroad paraphernalia and to the meadow at Boney Flat. Just beyond, two large stakes stand on either side of the trail, forming a rustic portal. If you are still in a passenger car, this marks the end of the line for you; if you're in a four-wheel-drive vehicle, you've got another mile and a half or so to travel before you'll have to bail out.

The route cuts a broad switchback around Boney Flat. Negotiate an easy detour around a missing bridge at the Twomile Creek crossing, which is at about 3 miles. The trail also intersects FR 2N32. At this point the track is no longer passable to motor vehicles. Arc south on the gently inclining rail trail, which dips into another drainage that is washed out and clogged with fallen logs.

At post 6 you reach the halfway point of the rail trail. The post marks the site of Camp 25 and Twenty-Five Mile Creek. The rail trail curves back to the east beyond the creek and winds through the woods to its intersection with Forest Road 3N83, which branches off first to the right, and then to the left at signpost 7 (at the 5.5-mile mark). A cedar tree bearing the scars of chains used by steam donkeys—large machines that pulled logs from where they were cut to where they could be loaded onto railroad cars—is the focal point of this interpretive waypoint.

The trail gently meanders northeast beyond the junction with FR 3N83, winding through a pleasant forest that opens to allow fleeting views down into the Clavey River drainage. Cross the occasional creek, usually dry by late summer, and pass a few interpretive signposts: Post 8 points out the difficulty these seasonal streams posed to railroad builders, post 9 marks the location of yet another logging camp, and post 10 brings your attention to the telephone line that served the loggers and railroad workers, sections of which now lie on the ground along the route.

At about the 6.5-mile mark, reach post 11, which marks the start of the Trout Creek Spur. The spur will lead you to trail's end at Camp Clavey—again, an old logging camp. But it's worth your while to branch off to the right (northeast), dropping from Buffalo Landing, once the site of feverish logging activity, toward the Clavey River, where you can view the remains of the Clavey River trestle. The wooden trestle, which stood more than 75 feet above the river, has burned, but its foundations are still visible.

To finish the hike, climb up to Camp Clavey via the Trout Creek Spur, which ascends more steeply than the rest of the grade before topping out among the evergreens that encroach upon the clearings at Camp Clavey. The end of the rail trail (and of FR 3N86) is at its intersection with FR 3N01 at about the 8-mile mark.

Unless you have arranged a shuttle, the quickest return is along the same route. But a web of Forest Service roads winds through the woods, offering wonderful opportunities for exploration for those with a good map, a compass, and the wits to use them both.

BONUS TRACK: WEST SIDE RAIL TRAIL: TUOLUMNE CITY TO NORTH FORK TUOLUMNE RIVER

This trail follows another of the many railroad grades plowed through the foothills of the Sierra Nevada by the West Side Flume and Lumber Company. The grade, carved in the mountainsides by Chinese and Native American laborers at the turn of the twentieth century, traces the steep canyon of the North Fork Tuolumne River, passing leftover rails and ties, to the River Ranch Campground. Part of the Hetch Hetchy and Yosemite Valley Railway, the line transported timber harvested from the dense woodlands to the sawmill in Carters, now Tuolumne City.

These days, rather than timber, travelers on the rail trail harvest views and solitude. The trek is known for its wildflower displays in season, for its proximity to the rollicking Tuolumne River, and for its spectacular mountain vistas. From the trailhead, the grade heads gently up the south-facing wall of the canyon that cradles the North Fork Tuolumne River. The route is exposed and lovely, offering wonderful views of the canyon and foothills as it climbs. The route nears its end on Cottonwood Road; from there it is a short hop down to River Ranch Road, where you can pick up your shuttle or head back the way you came.

Activities:

Start: Trailhead at Mira Monte and Buchanan Roads outside Tuolumne City

Distance: 5.5 miles one way

Difficulty: Hard due to the trail's length and rough surface

Seasons/schedule: Year-round, sunrise to sunset

Fees and permits: None

Trail surface and conditions: Dirt and original ballast. Hiking and mountain biking are best in late spring, summer, and fall; you may cross-country ski during winter if the snow sticks.

Accessibility: This rough path is not accessible to people using wheelchairs.

Canine compatibility: Leashed dogs permitted

Amenities: There are no restrooms along the trail. Practice leave-no-trace principles by burying waste at least 8 inches underground and packing out toilet paper. Restrooms are available at River Ranch Campground at the Cottonwood Road end point. No food is available along this rail trail, but restaurants and grocery stores are available in Twain Harte and other towns along CA 108. No water is available along the trail either, so be sure to pack plenty.

Trail contact: Stanislaus National Forest, Summit–Mi-Wok Ranger District; (209) 965-3434; www.fs.usda.gov/recarea/stanislaus/recreation

Nearest town: Tuolumne City

Maps: A rough downloadable map and brochure are available at www .fs.usda.gov/Internet/FSE_DOCUMENTS/fseprd706904.pdf.

Cell service: None

Transportation: Tuolumne County Transit, (209) 532-0404; www.tuolumnecountytransit.com

Finding the trailhead: From the Mi-Wok Ranger Station in Mi-Wuk Village, follow CA 108 west for 2.9 miles to Tuolumne Road. Go left (east) on Tuolumne Road and follow it for 6.7 miles to Carter Street (a.k.a. Stanislaus FR 1N04/FR 14) in Tuolumne City. Go left on Carter Street to Buchanan Road and turn right. Follow Buchanan Road to the trailhead, which is located at the intersection of Mira Monte Road and Buchanan Road. Parking is available at the trailhead.

Trailhead GPS: N37 58.387 / W120 13.625

37 MERCED RIVER TRAIL

As rough-and-tumble as the river it follows, as enchanting as the canyon that cradles it, the Merced River Trail is one of the most challenging and beautiful of California's rail trails.

Activities:

Start: Briceburg

Distance: 16 miles round-trip; there is no bridge at the Bagby end point. Most travelers begin at Briceburg and travel downstream to the confluence with the North Fork of the Merced River, then return as they came.

Difficulty: Hard but worth it

Seasons/schedule: Year-round, sunrise to sunset

Fees and permits: None

Trail surface and conditions: Original ballast and dirt; railway-wide to begin, then narrowing to singletrack. The track gets rougher and harder to navigate on a bike the farther you go. Hiking is best in the summer and autumn months. You can cross-country ski on the trail during the winter if the snow sticks. The trail is least hospitable when wet and should be avoided if flooded.

Accessibility: The trail is not accessible to people using wheelchairs.

Canine compatibility: Leashed dogs are permitted, and leashes are highly recommended as this is rattlesnake country.

Amenities: Restrooms are available at Briceburg, in the campgrounds along the gravel access road, and at the campground in Bagby. No food or water are available along the trail. Pack in and pack out everything you need or use, including toilet paper. All amenities are available in the nearby town of Mariposa, at the lodges located east of Briceburg along CA 140, and in Yosemite National Park.

Trail contact: Bureau of Land Management, Merced River RMA; (209) 379-9414; www.blm.gov/visit/merced-river

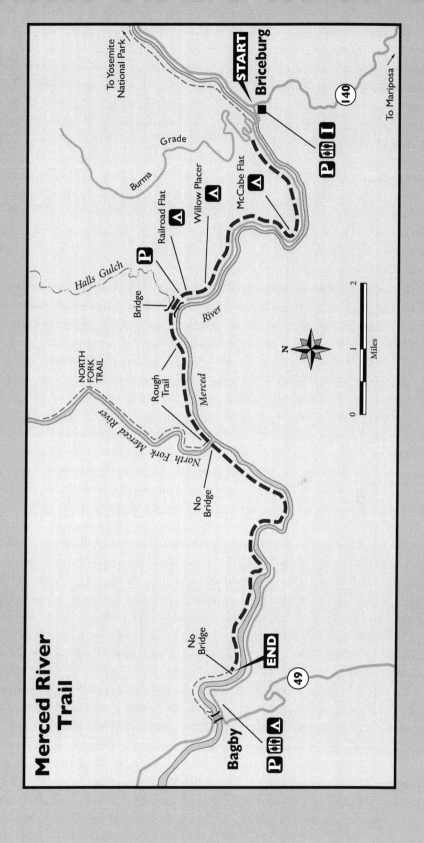

Merced River Trail

Nearest town: Mariposa

Maps: A downloadable map is available at www.blm.gov/sites/blm.gov/files/docs/2021-06/MercedRiverRecArea8x14_map_508c.pdf or by visiting the BLM website for Merced River Trail.

Cell service: None

Transportation: While there is no direct public transportation to either trail end point, Yosemite Area Regional Transportation System (YARTS) provides service along the CA 140 corridor; (877) 559-2787; https://yarts .com.

Finding the trailhead: To reach the Briceburg end point, head east on CA 140 from Mariposa for almost 12 miles to the Briceburg Visitor Center. Parking is available at the picnic area wedged between the Briceburg building and the Merced River.

Trailhead GPS: N37 36.271 / W119 58.077

The Main Line

This one is far from tame.

Most of the rail trails in this guide are relatively easy paved routes that earn their difficulty by virtue of their length. Not the Merced River Trail. This comes as close to a wilderness experience as you will find on any rail trail in Northern California—even the longest ones, like the Bizz Johnson or the Great Shasta, and even those don't present the same challenge as the Merced River Trail.

Lest I scare you off, rest assured this rail trail is well worth the effort. Wandering through some of the most spectacular country in the mountains of California, the route follows the Wild and Scenic Merced River, which originates in Yosemite National Park's high country and passes through this steep-walled gorge before spilling into a wider river valley shaded with spreading oaks and cloaked in wildflowers in spring. The Merced is immensely popular with whitewater rafters, so look for these adventurers when the river runs high.

The Merced River Trail winds through a steep-walled gorge.

While the grade makes for a superlative long hike, especially during wildflower season in March and April, it's an extremely technical (and marginally enjoyable) mountain bike ride. You must ford the North Fork Merced River at the trail's midpoint, which can be a challenge, dangerous, or impossible when flows are high. Because there's no bridge at the Bagby end point, the journey is a round-trip affair totaling 16 miles; given that distance, most hikers venture only as far as the North Fork confluence and return as they came. In late season (or drought season), when water levels in Lake McClure are low, trekkers might be able to follow the old railroad grade out of the canyon to the bridge on CA 49 at Bagby, but when the water is up, the last 2 miles of the route are flooded. Contact the trail manager or check at the Briceburg Visitor Center to learn more about the status of the trail at the time of your visit.

The rail trail follows the right-of-way of the Yosemite Valley Railroad. Trains ran through the Merced River Valley to El Portal, just west of Yosemite National Park, from 1906 to 1945, serving the logging, mining, and tourist industries in the scenic canyon. The railroad began to fall into disuse once CA 140 was completed in 1926. Both Briceburg at the east end of the trail and Bagby at the west end, where the Merced flows into Lake McClure, were once way stations along the railroad.

In the summer season you can either begin at the Briceburg Visitor Center, where you will find ample parking, or you can drive 4.5 miles down the good gravel road to the trailhead at Railroad Flat Campground, where you will find more limited parking. If you are cycling, the road from Briceburg to Railroad Flat is an enjoyable warm-up. It too follows the old railroad grade and offers wonderful views of the river.

The trail proper begins at the west end of the Railroad Flat Campground, beyond the gate. The trail reaches a bench at about the quarter-mile point, at the bridge that spans Halls Creek. A private home is perched on the north slope of the river canyon beyond the creek crossing, and another little bridge spans a seasonal stream just below the house. The trail narrows to singletrack amid a jumble of rocky debris deposited by floods. Stay straight (west) on the riverside track at the switchback that leads up toward the residence. At the 0.6-mile mark, the footpath winds through the narrowing gorge, with steep cliffs overhanging the route on the north. Unless you are an exceptionally skilled mountain biker, you'll be walking your bike through this section. The walk is absolutely

The Bountiful Merced River Valley

The area surrounding the Merced River Trail positively blossoms with opportunities to enjoy the outdoors. Hiking, mountain biking, and horseback riding are just a few of the possibilities. More than 70 miles of the river have been designated "Wild and Scenic," and all along its upper sections you will find high-caliber whitewater rafting and fishing. The rustic campgrounds west of Briceburg, which are managed by the Bureau of Land Management (BLM), cradle delightful sites that front the river. And Yosemite National Park, undoubtedly one of the most spectacular places on earth—and the birthplace of the Merced—lies less than 20 miles upstream.

There is also abundant history to be explored in the canyon, including the portion of the old Yosemite Valley Railroad that continues along the north side of the Merced from Briceburg to El Portal. The Briceburg Visitor Center itself is a historic site, having served as a store, a post office, and a regular stop for the railroad (among other incarnations) before it was sold to the BLM in the late 1980s. The quaint stone structure was restored to pristine condition and has since served as a public information center and gateway to the wonders of the Merced River Valley.

wonderful because the slower pace—and the diminished fear of crashing and burning—will permit you to truly enjoy the lovely canyon.

The bike portage/singletrack hike, accented by the occasional blooming dogwood tree in season, continues for about 1 mile. Then the canyon opens a bit and you can look across to the rusted flume that traces the canyon's southern wall.

The rail trail, now bordered by grasses, continues its gentle descent through the broadening canyon to the confluence of the North Fork Merced River at about the 3-mile mark. There is no bridge here; you must ford the brisk river, which can be knee-deep even in late season, and may be impassable when water levels and flows are high. The trail leads to the most obvious ford. The concrete remains of the trestle that spanned the confluence are at the mouth of the North Fork; upstream (north) of the trestle and ford are the remains of a rustic stone structure. This makes a fine picnic and turnaround point for those seeking a pleasant day hike.

Once across the North Fork, you can use one of two routes to climb back onto the railroad grade. The right (northern) route leads directly to the path; the left (southern) leads about 50 yards to an inviting clearing in which you will find the sun-splashed pilings for the defunct trestle, then climbs to the rail trail.

The route west of the North Fork is broad, pebbly, and bordered by grasses that grow blonder as the summer progresses. A narrow creek, which may be dry in late season, spills down from the north to cross the trail at about the 5-mile mark.

Farther downstream, the path pulls northwest, away from the Merced, and is shaded by a sparse canopy of thin pines. Brush and shade encroach on the route before it spills back into the more open river basin, where the Merced, when summer drains its fury, threads through channels it has carved in its cobbled bed. The canyon now wears the mantle of the lower foothills, including shady oak and buckeye trees and thickening grasses peppered with wildflowers. These tufts of grass squeeze the trail, confining it to a narrow swath on the broader grade.

The rail trail ends at the ruins of the trestle that once spanned the stream spilling from Solomon Canyon into the Merced. To the west the river thickens into an arm of Lake McClure. This is the turnaround point; retrace the route from here.

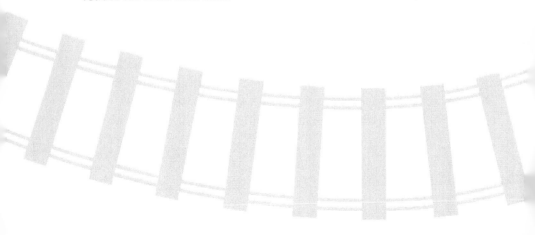

ABOUT THE AUTHOR

Tracy Salcedo has written more than two dozen FalconGuides to destinations in Colorado and California, including *Hiking Lassen Volcanic National Park*, winner of the National Outdoor Book Award for Outdoor Adventure Guidebook, *Hiking Waterfalls Northern California*, *Hiking Through History San Francisco*, and her best-selling *Best Easy Day Hikes Lake Tahoe*, among others. She is also the author of *Historic Yosemite National Park*, *Historic Denali National Park and Preserve*, *Death in Mount Rainier National Park*, and *Search and Rescue Alaska*. When she's not writing books, Salcedo writes stories about natural history, community activism, travel, and other topics for local newspapers and magazines. She lives and works in California's Wine Country. Learn more by visiting her website at laughingwaterink.com.

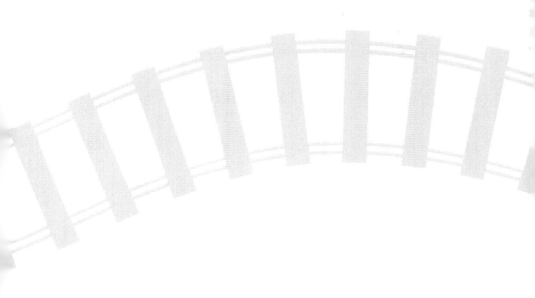